How the Words of Jesus Became Gospel

How the Sources of Q, Signs, Passion, and Thomas Compare to the New Testament

by Joseph Lumpkin

How the Words of Jesus Became Gospel
How the Sources of Q, Signs, Passion,
and Thomas Compare to the New Testament

Fifth Estate Publishing, Blountsville, AL 35031

Printed on acid-free paper

Library of Congress Control No:

ISBN: 9781936533787

Fifth Estate, 2019

Table of Contents

Introduction

Jesus was a man of few words, simple words, and a deeply challenging message. However, through the years his words and message have been clouded with additions and redactions. How can we possibly know the words he spoke? What were his original teachings? Where did his message stop and the many changes begin? Hidden in the gospels themselves are the source materials containing the original message preached by Jesus.

Before the gospels were written, there were proto-gospels, notes, lists and collections used to construct the gospels we have today. Some gospels were used and built upon to form other, expanded gospels. **The "Q" Document** was used as a memory tool and literary scaffolding by Matthew and Luke in the writing of their gospels. Although many scholars believe Mark had access to the oldest parts of Q, others believe he did not. Since Mark predates Matthew and Luke they believe Mark was used as a template for Matthew and Luke. This would mean that Matthew started with Mark and added the Q sayings missing from Mark, along with Matthew's own stories, which is why Matthew seems to be simply an expansion of Mark's gospel. Of all the theories, the most accepted is the two source hypothesis, which maintains that Mark did not use Q but Matthew and Luke used both Q and Mark as their source materials.

The existence of a document containing a catalog of sayings was just a theory until the discovery of the **Gospel of Thomas.** Thomas is not Q, but is similar to Q in that it is an early repository of sayings of Jesus. Thomas and Q appear to be documents composed by people who followed Jesus and recorded his words. The Gospel of Thomas is a collection of 114 saying attributed directly to Jesus and proved the existence of a source material, which scholars believed explained why the wording of the synoptic gospels of Matthew, Mark, and Luke were so similar.

Mark also used a document called the **Passion Narrative** to establish a chronology and form the story of the crucifixion of Jesus. Since Matthew and Luke used Mark as a second source, the passion narrative occurs in their gospels also.

The gospel of John used a different source, called the **Signs Gospel**, which explains why it is so different to Mark, Matthew, and Luke. We will examine the writings behind the gospels. If the Christian faith is built upon the four gospels of Matthew, Mark, Luke, and John, then the underpinning documents, called "Q Gospel", Signs Gospel", and "Passion Narrative" are the foundation upon which these four gospels were based. They are the gospels behind the gospels and predate everything in the New Testament. They are the foundation stones of the faith upon which the four pillars of the gospels are built.

The Sayings Gospel or The Lost Gospel of Q

The Two-source hypothesis (or 2SH) is an explanation for the synoptic problem, which is the pattern of similarities and differences between the three Gospels of Matthew, Mark, and Luke. It posits that the Gospel of Matthew and the Gospel of Luke were based on the Gospel of Mark and a hypothetical sayings collection originating from the Christian Oral Tradition called Q. For the Two-source theory to work Q had to actually be a written document by the time it was used. The designation or name "Q" derives from the German word "Quelle," which means "Source."

Imagine, if you will, the child's game of "telephone" or "gossip" where the first person in a line of ten people tells the person in front of him or her a story and the person who has just heard the story tells it in turn to the next person, and so on until it gets to the tenth person, who tells the story aloud and compares it to the original story. The changes to the story are amazing and the two versions are barely noticeable as the same tale. This is how the gospels would have been dissimilar if Q had remained an oral tradition. Instead, Matthew and Luke are much more similar than not, proving both drew from at least one written source along the way.

Another view leading to the belief of a single written source can be seen every day in eyewitness events and reports. If two people, in this case Matthew and Luke, were to witness a single event and write about it, the wording of the stories and the details would vary greatly. Their vantage point, vocabulary, personalities, preferences, educations, writing styles, and other factors would allow the stories to diverge greatly. However, if they drew from the same single written source, relying on it as a base on their story, the two gospels would be very close. That is what we see demonstrated in the synoptic gospels. What variations do occur can be traced back to translation differences if Q had been written in Aramaic and Matthew and Luke written in Greek. The reason we expect Q to be in a written form is seen in the similarity of wording between Matthew and Luke with slight differences tracked back to Greek synonyms of Aramaic words.

The Gospel of Mark is usually dated between 60 and 100 A.D. Given the time that passed from the writing of the gospels, historical data proving or disproving the authenticity and authorship of the gospels are lacking, but we do have the following very obscure witness.

In the first half of the second century, Papias, a bishop of Hierapolis, wrote a five volume treatise called An Exposition of the Lord's Oracles. This book was in part a collection of oral folklore about early Christianity. Papias would ask people of age what they remembered about the formative years of the church. Eusebius commented on the writings of Papias, and on Papias himself, calling him a man of low intelligence and correcting ideas Papias had, which Eusebias claimed came from misinterpreting information from his interviews. Although this work is now lost, isolated fragments have been preserved in quotations and references by Irenaeus (c. 185), Eusebius (c. 300), and others. The following fragments relate to Papias's testimony on the authorship of the gospels:

14And in his own writing he [Papias] also hands down other accounts of the aforementioned Aristion of the words of the Lord and the traditions of the presbyter John, to which we refer those truly interested. Of necessity, we will now add to his reports set forth above a tradition about Mark who wrote the gospel, which he set forth as follows:

15And the presbyter would say this: Mark, who had indeed been Peter's interpreter, accurately wrote as much as he remembered, yet not in order, about that which was either said or did by the Lord. For he neither heard the Lord nor followed him, but later, as I said, Peter, who would make the teachings anecdotally but not exactly an arrangement of the Lord's reports, so that Mark did not fail by writing certain things as he recalled. For he had one purpose, not to omit what he heard or falsify them.

16Now this is reported by Papias about Mark, but about Matthew this was said, Now Matthew compiled the reports in a Hebrew manner of speech, but each interpreted them as he could.

17He himself used testimonies from the first epistle of John and similarly from that of Peter, and had also set forth another story about a woman who was accused of many sins before the Lord, which the Gospel according to the Hebrews contains. And let these things of necessity be brought to our attention in reference to what has been set forth.

So, Mark wrote down what Peter said about the life of Jesus, but it was not recorded in order, that is to say, chronologically at first.

Mark was probably written between 70 and 74 A.D. since he is writing to an audience that witnessed the destruction of the temple and takes that act as a sign of the coming apocalypse.

Modern scholars have advanced numerous elaborations and variations on the basic hypothesis of the source materials used to construct Mark, and even completely alternative hypotheses. Nevertheless, the Two-source hypothesis is supported by most biblical critics from all continents and most denominations.

Since the Q document has been lost, we can reconstruct it by using the "double tradition" material, that which is present in both

Matthew and Luke but not Mark. However, Q may also contain material that is preserved only by Matthew or only by Luke as well as material that is paralleled in Mark (called Mark/Q overlaps). The Mark overlap has led some to speculate that Mark had access to Q also, or at least parts of it.

Although the temptation story and the healing of the centurion's son are usually ascribed to Q, the majority of the Q material consists of sayings. For this reason, Q is sometimes called the Synoptic Sayings Source or the Sayings Gospel. Some scholars have observed that the Gospel of Thomas and the Q material, as contrasted with the four canonical gospels, are similar in their emphasis on the sayings of Jesus instead of the passion of Jesus.

Arguments in favor of the Two Source hypothesis state that Q can be discerned once Matthew's personal addition of collected and related materials are discounted.

C. M. Tuckett believes that variations between Matthew and Luke are due to variant translations of an Aramaic Q. It is doubtful if more than a very few cases of variation between Matthew and Luke can be explained in this way. Many of the alleged translation variants turn out to be simply cases of synonyms, and the differences between Matthew and Luke can often be explained just as well are due to the fact that two evangelists are telling the story in their own individual ways, one leaving out a story and substituting another. However, when the same source is used verbiage is so similar that it must have come from a common source.

Udo Schnelle comments in his book, *The History and Theology of the New Testament Writings*, The Sayings Source presumably originated in (north) *Palestine*, since its theological perspective is directed primarily to Israel. The proclamations of judgment at the beginning and end of the document are directed against Israel . The bearers of the Q tradition understand themselves to be faithful to the Law.

In the book *Ancient Christian Gospels*, Helmut Koesterm points out that the coming judgment explicitly in Q is written with the view to two Galilean towns, Chorazin and Bethsaida: even Tyre and Sidon will be better off in the coming judgment. These are the only names of places which occur in Q, besides a mention of John the Baptist's story in Jordan. It is, therefore, tempting to assume that the redaction of Q took place somewhere in Galilee and that the document as a whole reflects the experience of a Galilean community of followers of Jesus.

Even the sayings used for the original composition of Q were known and used elsewhere at an early date. They were known to Paul and were used in Corinth by his opponents. They existed in eastern Syria and were bases for the composition of the *Gospel of Thomas*. They were quoted by *1 Clement* in Rome at the end of the 1st century. The document itself, in its final redacted form, was used for the composition of Matthew and Luke, which both originated in the Greek-speaking church outside of Palestine. Thus, it is possible the Gospel of Thomas is a non-redacted and earlier form, which shows a fuller and more accurate representation of the sayings of Jesus. This is important to note. Helmut Koesterm and many other scholars mention redactions to Q.

(New Oxford American Dictionary)

redaction | ri'dak sh ən |

noun

the process of editing text for publication.

• a version of a text, such as a new edition or an abridged version.

Q, that is the "original" Q, was being changed, added to, edited, abridged, and was morphing, along with the evolution of the beliefs and doctrines of the faith itself. In other words, the original Q, and thus the portal through which to see the original words and deeds of Jesus, was being swept away. As the faith was being altered, so was Q. The Gospel of Thomas was being added to also, but not nearly with the speed and distortion of Q.

Udo Schnelle attempts to date Q by observing, "The Sayings Source was composed before the destruction of the temple, since the sayings against Jerusalem and the temple in Luke 13.34-35Q do not presuppose any military events. ...The positive references to Gentiles in Q (cf. Luke 10.13-15Q; Luke 11.29-31Q; Matt. 8.5-13 Q; Matt. 5.47 Q; Matt. 22.1-10 Q) indicate that the Gentile mission had begun, which is probably to be located in the period between 40 and 50 AD."

Burton Mack states, "Mark wrote his story of Jesus some time after the war and shortly after Q had been revised with the Q additions. If we date Q around 75 C.E. to give some time for the additions obviously prompted by the war, Mark can be dated between 75 and 80 C.E. . . . For Mark, Q was extremely useful, for it had already positioned Jesus at the hinge of an epic-apocalyptic history, and it contained themes and narrative material that could easily be turned into a more eventful depiction of Jesus' public appearance. Q provided Mark with a large number of themes essential to his narrative. "

Mack continues: "Q also provided material that could easily be turned to advantage as building blocks in a coherent narrative account. The John-Jesus material was a great opener. The figure of the Holy Spirit was ready-made to connect the Q material in John and Jesus with the miracle stories Mark would use. Q's characterization of Jesus as the all-knowing one could be used to enhance his authority as a self-referential speaker in the pronouncement stories Mark already had from his own community. The notion of Jesus as the son of God could be used to create mystique, divide the house on the question of Jesus' true identity, and develop narrative anticipation, the device many scholars call Mark's "messianic secret." The apocalyptic predictions at the end of Q could then become instructions to the disciples at that point in the story where Jesus turns to go to Jerusalem. And, as scholars know, there are a myriad of interesting points at which the so-called overlaps between Mark and Q show Mark's use of Q material for his own narrative designs."

It is likely the trouble encountered in the dating of Q is due in part from various redactions and additions within Q. One theory presents three stages of development of the document. Although the elements would have occurred over a relatively short period of time, say 30 years, they can be seen in the following breakdown.

"Q1" - Describing Jesus as a Philosopher - Teacher

Prior to the writing of Q1, the Gospel message was passed verbally among individuals and groups. About 50 AD, or about twenty years after the death of Jesus, this oral tradition was written down. Thus, Q1 may be the truest report of Jesus' sayings. We will refer to it as Q1. The topics covered by Q1 are:

- who will belong to the "Kingdom of God"
- treating others (the Ethic of Reciprocity; a.k.a. Golden Rule)
- do not judge others
- working for the Kingdom
- asking for God's help
- do not fear speaking out
- don't worry about food, clothing, possessions

- the Kingdom will soon arrive
- the cost of being a follower
- the cost of rejecting the message

In a 2005 article, B.A. Robinson states, "What is remarkable about Q1 is that the original Christians appeared to be centered totally on concerns about their relationships with God and with other people, and their preparation for the imminent arrival of Kingdom of God on earth. Totally absent from their spiritual life are almost all of the factors that we associate with Christianity today. There is absolutely no mention of (in alphabetic order): adultery, angels, apostles, baptism, church, clergy, confirmation, crucifixion, demons, disciples, divorce, Eucharist, great commission to convert the world, healing, heaven, hell, incarnation, infancy stories, John the Baptist, Last Supper, life after death, Mary and Joseph and the rest of Jesus' family, magi, miracles, Jewish laws concerning behavior, marriage, Messiah, restrictions on sexual behavior, resurrection, roles of men and women, Sabbath, salvation, Satan, second coming, signs of the end of the age, sin, speaking in tongues, temple, tomb, transfiguration, trial of Jesus, trinity, or the virgin birth.

Jesus is described as a believer in God, but there are no indications that he was considered more than a gifted human being. His role was not as a Messiah or Lord but philosopher-teacher. The Gospel contains strong statements which are anti-family and which oppose Jewish religious rules. Rewards and punishments are described as occurring in this life, not after death. The "Kingdom of God" is

described as a type of utopian society on earth which his followers were creating, not some future location in heaven after death. God is presented as a loving father with an intimate concern for the welfare of believers. The Holy Spirit is mentioned, but appears as a gift given by God, not as a separate person of the Trinity. There is no reference to Jesus' death having any redeeming function; in fact, there is no mention of the crucifixion or resurrection at all."
Jesus was preaching a social message.

Some authors identify the contents of Q by numbering the sayings QS1 to QS64. Using this identification system, the Q1 material can be found at the following locations in the Gospel of Luke:

Q Location	Luke Location	Comments
QS7	6:20a	Start of the Beatitudes
QS8	6:20b-23	
QS9	6:27-35	
QS10	6:36-38	
QS11	6:39-40	
QS12	6:41-42	
QS13	6:43-45	
QS14	6:46-49	
QS19	9:57-62	"Foxes have holes; bury the dead"
QS20	10:1-11	Sending the 70 disciples
QS26	11:1-4	Lord's prayer
QS27	11:9-13	"Seek and ye shall find"
QS35	12:2-3	Speaking publicly

QS36   12:4-7   Fearing retaliation

QS38   12:13-21 Inheritance; parable of the rich fool

QS39   12:22-31 Worrying about the future

QS40   12:33-34 Give your possessions away

QS46   13:18-21 Mustard seed, leaven

QS50   14:11 & 18:14 Humility

QS51   14:16-24 The great supper

QS52   14:26-27 and 17:33   Anti-family sayings; saving life

QS53   14:34-35 Savorless salt

"Q2" - Describing Jesus as an Apocalyptic Prophet:

After the material of Q1 had been established as the doctrine of the newly formed Christian community other materials were added. Prophetic and apocalyptic elements were creeping in. Teaching was turning from a social gospel to a more apocalyptic vision. The new sayings were written in response to the serious civil unrest and upheavals in Palestine associated with the Roman-Jewish war. Another motivation was the rejection that they had experienced by their families and by the Jewish people generally. The new sayings were written circa 60 to 70 AD. These introduce us to John the Baptist and his disciples. The additions were meant to be passed off as the words of Jesus and John, even though the sayings were conceived by others three to four decades after Jesus' death. The sayings introduced in this period could be considered pseudepigrapha, which are writings using a famous person's name,

in this case Jesus and John, to add validity to the words of an
unknown author.

"Q3" - Retreat from the World

Additional sayings appear to have been added during the mid 70's
AD. This was at a time that the Jews were driven from Palestine and
The Roman-Jewish war had concluded. This places Q3 in the
timeframe just after the book of Mark was written. This is why
Mark did not contain Q3. As before, the sayings were falsely
attributed to Jesus. Matthew and Luke would write their gospels
using this version of Q, taking in all segments of Q1-Q3 and also
incorporating the Gospel of Mark into their writings. The author of
the Gospel of Thomas seems to have used the same material as that
of Q1 and Q2 in his writing, but not the Q3 additions. Thomas was
likely written before the evolution of the Q3 phase.

The common material in Q and Mark (cf. Mark 1.2; 1.7-8; 1.12-13;
3.22-26, 27-29; 4.21, 22, 24, 25; 4.30-32; 6.7-13; 8.11, 12; 8.34-35; 8.38;
9.37, 40, 42, 50; 10.10-11; 10.31; 11.22-23; 12.37b-40; 13.9, 11, 33-37)
has repeatedly led to the hypothesis of a literary dependence of
Mark on Q. But if Mark had known Q, his criteria for selecting the
material he used, and especially the sayings he omitted, cannot be
explained. The reasons given remain hypothetical. There are
arguments for Mark as a supplement to the sayings source, and Q
as supplement to Mark. Since Mark excludes parts of the Q material,

one possibility is that Mark had access to the pre-redacted Q, and what we see included in Mark is the purer and earlier form of Q.

Helmut Koester states (op. cit., p. 150):

"The original version of Q must have included wisdom sayings as well as eschatological sayings. It cannot be argued that Q originally presented Jesus as a teacher of wisdom without an eschatological message. The close relationship of the *Gospel of Thomas* to Q cannot be accidental. Since the typical Son of Man sayings and announcements of judgments which are characteristic of the redaction of Q are never paralleled in the *Gospel of Thomas*, it is evident that its author had no knowledge of the final version of Q, nor of the secondary apocalyptic interpretation that the redactor of Q superimposed upon earlier eschatological sayings. The *Gospel of Thomas* is either dependent upon Q's earlier version or upon clusters of sayings employed in its composition.

For the followers of Jesus whose tradition is represented in the original composition of Q, the turning point of the ages is the proclamation of Jesus. He proclaims his teachings and announces the Kingdom is near. Judgment is coming. These sayings not only define the moment, they are also the rule of life for the community of the new age insofar as Jesus continues to speak in sayings of wisdom and in rules for the community. Jesus was viewed as the embodiment of heavenly Wisdom but his departure does not constitute a change in the urgency of the message. It increases it. Jesus' death would not be seen as a crisis of his proclamation. The disciples have as their task to carry on his proclamation. Any emphasis upon Jesus' suffering, death, and resurrection would be meaningless in this context, except to point out how evil the world had become, which to the Jews was quite obvious. "

Thus Q cannot be seen as a teaching supplement to Pauline theology at all. Q's theology and soteriology are fundamentally different from the doctrines Paul would later teach.

Helmut Koester states (op. cit., p. 165): "On the other hand, the Synoptic Sayings Source is an important piece of evidence for the continuation of a theology of followers of Jesus that had no relationship to the kerygma (message/preaching) of the cross and resurrection. It is evident now that this was not an isolated phenomenon. The opponents of Paul in 1 Corinthians 1-4, the *Gospel of Thomas*, the *Dialogue of the Savior*, and the opponents of the Gospel of John in the Johannine community all shared this understanding of the significance of Jesus' coming."

What does all this mean? In the beginning of the ministry of Jesus a small group of people took notes. They wrote down his sayings and deeds. One of these compilations became the Gospel of Thomas. The other became known as Q. This document, called Q, would go on to be used as one of sources of information for Matthew and Luke, but not before it had undergone many changes. Mark was also used as a foundation for Matthew and Luke. Mark may have had access to a version of Q, but if so it would have been an earlier version, before the additions and redactions. Knowing that Q was used as a gospel to the gospels, it seems fitting that we look at what was written before Matthew and Luke wrote their stories.

Following will be two versions of Q. The first is from a 1910 article, which uses Matthew and Luke to deduce the contents of Q. The second version is a more modern take on Q using the Gospel of Luke.

The Text of the Gospel Source "Q"

The Reconstructed Text of Q from the Sacred Texts Journals Christian Articles of THE OPEN COURT,

A MONTHLY MAGAZINE

Volume XXIV

CHICAGO, published by THE OPEN COURT PUBLISHING COMPANY 1910

[Professor Wellhausen has discovered that both Matthew and Luke have used in addition to the Gospel of Mark another source (Quelle) which he designates by the initial Q, a name which has been generally adopted by theologians. The reconstruction here presented is according to Harnack.

The numbers which appear at the beginning of each fragment are the designations by which they are now referred to in theological literature. They follow upon the whole the order of Luke.

1.1

(Matt. iii. 5, 7-12; Luke iii. 3, 7-9, 16-17.)

(When from all the region around Jordan, John saw many [or: the multitudes] coming to baptism, he said unto them): O generation of vipers, who hath warned you to flee from the wrath to come? Bring forth therefore fruits meet for repentance; and think not [begin not] to say within yourselves: We have Abraham to our father, for I say unto you that God is able of these stones to raise up children unto Abraham. And now the axe is laid unto the root of the trees; therefore every tree which bringeth not forth good fruit is hewn down and cast into the fire. I baptize you with water unto repentance; but he that cometh after me is mightier than I, whose shoes I am not worthy to bear; he shall baptize you with (the [Holy] Ghost and) with fire; whose fan is in his hand, and he will thoroughly purge his floor, and gather his wheat unto the garner, but he will burn up the chaff with unquenchable fire.

(The baptism of Jesus, together with the descent of the Spirit and the voice from heaven.)

2.

(Matt. iv. 1-11; Luke iv. 1-13.)

Jesus was led up of the Spirit into the wilderness to be tempted of the devil, and when he had fasted forty days and forty nigh he was afterward an hungered, and the tempter said to him: If thou be the Son of God, command that these stones become bread, and he answered: It is written, Man shall not live by bread alone. Then he taketh him up to Jerusalem and setteth him on the pinnacle of the temple, and saith to him: If thou be the Son of God, cast thyself down; for it is written, He shall give his angels charge concerning thee, and in their hands they shall bear thee up lest at any time thou dash thy foot against a stone. Jesus said to him: Again it is written, Thou shalt not tempt the Lord thy God. Again he taketh him up unto an exceeding high mountain and sheweth him all the kingdoms of the world and the glory of them; and said unto him: All these things will I give thee, if thou wilt worship me. And Jesus saith unto him: It is written, The Lord thy God shalt thou worship and him only shalt thou serve. And the devil leaveth him.

3.

(Matt. v. 1-4, 6, 11, 12; Luke vi. 17, 20-23.)

(. . . multitudes . . . he taught his disciples, saying . . .)

Blessed are the poor in spirit, for theirs is the kingdom of God;

Blessed are they that mourn, for they shall be comforted;

Blessed are they that hunger, for they shall be filled;

Blessed are ye, when men shall revile you and persecute you and shall say all manner of evil against you falsely. Rejoice and be exceeding glad, for great is your reward in heaven; for so persecuted they the prophets which were before you.

4.

(Matt. v. 39-40; Luke vi. 29.)

Whosoever shall smite thee on the (thy right) cheek turn to him the other also; and if any man will sue thee at the law and take away thy coat, let him have thy cloak also.

5.

(Matt. v. 42; Luke vi. 30.)

Give to him that asketh thee, and from him that would borrow of thee turn not thou away.

6.

(Matt. v. 44-48; Luke vi. 27, 28, 35b, 32, 33, 36.)

I say unto you: Love your enemies and pray for them which persecute you, that ye may be the sons of your Father, for he maketh the sun to rise on the evil and on the good (and sendeth rain on the just and on the unjust). For if ye love them which love you, what reward have ye? Do not even the publicans the same? And if ye salute your brethren only, what do ye more than others? Do not even the Gentiles the same? Be ye therefore merciful as your Father is merciful.

7.

(Matt. vii. 12; Luke vi. 31.)

All things whatsoever ye would that men should do to you, do ye even so to them.

8.

(Matt. vii. 1-5; Luke vi. 37, 38, 41, 42.)

Judge not, that ye be not judged; for with what judgment ye judge, ye shall be judged; and with what measure ye mete, it shall be measured to you again. And why beholdest thou the mote that is in thy brother's eye, but considerest not the beam that is in thine own eye? Or how wilt thou say to thy brother: Let me cast out the mote out of thine eye; and behold, a beam is in thine own eye? Thou hypocrite, first cast out the beam out of thine own eye, and then shalt thou see clearly to cast out the mote out of thy brother's eye.

11.

(Matt. vii. 16-18; xii. 33; Luke vi. 43-44.)

The tree is known by the fruit. Do men gather grapes of thorns, or figs of thistles? Even so every good tree bringeth forth good fruit, but a corrupt tree bringeth forth evil fruit. A good tree cannot bring forth evil fruit, neither can a corrupt tree bring forth good fruit.

12.

(Matt. vii. 21, 24-27; Luke vi. 46-49.)

(Not everyone that saith unto me: Lord, Lord! shall enter into the kingdom of God, but he that doeth the will of the Father.) Therefore whosoever heareth these sayings of mine and doeth them, I will shew you whom he is like. He is like (or in place of the last; twelve words: He shall be likened) unto a man which built his house upon a rock. And the rain descended, and the floods came, and the winds blew and beat upon that house, and it fell not; for it was founded upon a rock. And every one that heareth these sayings of mine and doeth them not, shall be likened unto a man which built his house upon the sand. And the rain descended and the floods came, and the winds blew and beat upon that house, and it fell, and great was the fall of it.

9.

(Matt. xv. 14; Luke vi. 39.)

If the blind lead the blind, both shall fall into the ditch.

27.

(Matt. vi. 9, 11-13; Luke xi. 2-4.)

(Father, give us this day our daily bread, and forgive us our debts, as we forgive our debtors, and lead us not into temptation.)

28.

(Matt. vii. 7-11; Luke xi. 9-13.)

Ask, and it shall be given you; seek, and ye shall find; knock, and it shall be opened unto you. For every one that asketh receiveth; and he that seeketh findeth; and to him that knocketh it shall be opened. Or what man is there of you, whom if his son ask bread, will he give him a stone? Or if he ask for fish, will he give him a serpent? If ye then, being evil, know how to give good things (gifts) to your children, how much more will the Father from heaven give good things to them that ask him.

31.

(Matt. v. 15; Luke xi. 33.)

Men do not light a candle and place it under a bushel, but on candlestick; and it giveth light unto all that are in the house.

32.

(Matt. vi. 22, 23; Luke xii. 34-35.)

The light of the body is the (thine) eye; if therefore thine eye be single (generous, unclouded), thy whole body shall be full of light; but if thine eye be evil (selfish, of poor sight), thy whole body shall be full of darkness. If therefore the light that is in thee be darkened, how great is that darkness [scil. in the whole]!

35.

(Matt. vi. 25-33; Luke xii. 22-31.)

Therefore I say unto you: Take no thought for your life, what ye shall eat; nor yet for your body, what ye shall put on. Is not the life more than meat and the body more than raiment? Behold the ravens (or: the fowls of the air); for they sow not, neither do they reap nor gather into barns; yet God feedeth them. Are ye not much better than they? Which of you by taking thought can add one cubit unto his stature? and why take ye thought for raiment? Consider the lilies, how they grow? They toil not, neither do they spin; and yet I say unto you (that) even Solomon în all his glory was not arrayed like one of these. Wherefore if God so clothe the grass of the field which to-day is, and to-morrow is cast into the oven shall he not much more clothe you, O ye of little faith? Therefore take no thought saying: What shall we eat? or What shall we drink? or Wherewithall shall we be clothed? For after all these things do the nations (of the world) seek; for your Father knoweth that ye have need of all these things. But seek ye his kingdom, and all these things shall be added unto you.

36.

(Matt. vi. 19-21; Luke xii. 33-34.)

Lay not up for yourselves treasures upon earth, where moth and rust doth corrupt, and where thieves break through and steal: but lay up for yourselves treasures in heaven, where neither moth nor rust doth corrupt, and where theives do not break through nor steal; for where thy (your) treasure is, there will thy (your) heart be also.

39.

(Matt. v. 25-26; Luke xii. 58-59.)

Agree with thine adversary quickly, whiles thou art in the way with him; lest at any time the adversary deliver thee to the judge and the judge to the officer and thou be cast into prison. (Verily) I say unto thee, thou shalt by no means come out thence, till thou hast paid the uttermost farthing.

41.

(Matt. vii. 13-14; Luke xiii. 24.)

Enter ye in at the strait gate; for wide (is the gate) and broad is the way that leadeth to destruction, and many there be which go in thereat. Because strait is the gate and narrow is the way which leadeth unto life, and few there be that find it.

47.

(Matt. v. 13; Luke xiv. 34-35.)

Ye are the salt (of the earth); but if the salt have lost its savour, wherewith shall it be salted? It is thenceforth good for nothing but to be cast out and to be trodden under foot of men.

49.

(Matt. vi. 24; Luke xvi. 13.)

No man can serve two masters; for either he will hate the one and love the other, or else he will hold to the one and despise the other. Ye cannot serve God and mammon.

51.

(Matt. v. 18; Luke xvi. 17.)

(Verily I say unto you): Till heaven and earth pass, one jot or one tittle shall in no wise pass from the law.

52.

(Matt. v. 32; Luke xvi. 18.)

(I say unto you: Whosoever shall put away his wife causeth her to commit adultery, and whosoever shall marry her that is divorced committeth adultery.

13.

(Matt. vii. 28; viii. 5-10, 13; Luke vii. 1-10.)

He entered into Capernaum, and there came unto him a centurion beseeching him and saying: Lord, my servant lieth at home sick of the palsy, grievously tormented. He saith unto him: I will come and heal him. The centurion answered and said: Lord, I am not worthy that thou shouldest come under my roof; but speak the word only and my servant shall be healed. For I am a man under authority, having soldiers under me, and I say to this man, Go, and he goeth; and to another, Come, and he cometh; and to my slave: Do this, and he doeth it. When Jesus heard it he marvelled and said to them that followed, (Verily) I say unto you, Not even in Israel have I found such faith. (And Jesus said to the centurion: [Go thy way;] as thou hast believed, be it done unto thee. And the servant was healed in the selfsame hour.)

17.

(Matt. viii. 19-22; Luke ix. 57-60.)

(Someone said to him): I will follow thee whithersoever thou goest; and Jesus saith unto him: The foxes have holes, and the birds of the air have nests; but the Son of man hath not where to lay his head. Another said to him: Suffer me first to go and bury my father; but he saith unto him: Follow me, and let the dead bury their dead.

18.

(Matt. ix. 37-38; Luke x. 2.)

He saith unto them (or: to his disciples): The harvest truly is plenteous, but the labourers are few; pray ye therefore the Lord of the harvest that he will send forth labourers into his harvest.

16.

(Matt. x. 7; Luke ix. 2; x. 9-11.)

As ye go, preach, saying that the kingdom of God is at hand.

20.

(Matt. x. 12-13; Luke x. 4-6.)

(Carry neither purse, nor scrip, nor shoes, and salute no man by the way) And when ye come into a house, salute it; and if the house be worthy, let your peace come upon it; but if it be not worthy, let your peace return to you.

21.

(Matt. x. 10b; Luke x. 7.)

(And in the same house remain, eating and drinking such things as they give); for the labourer is worthy of his hire.

22.

(Matt. x. 15; Luke x. 8-12.)

(. . . Into whatsoever city ye enter and they receive you, eat such things as are set before you and say unto them: The kingdom of God is at hand. But into whatsoever city ye enter and they receive you not, go your ways out into the streets of the same and say: Even the very dust of your city which cleaveth to our feet do we wipe off against you). (Verily) I say unto you: It shall be more tolerable for the land of Sodom and Gomorrha (or in place of the last six words: Sodom) in that day (or: in the day of judgment) than for that city.

19:

(Matt. v. 16a; Luke x. 3.)

Behold I send you forth as sheep in the midst of wolves.

34a.

(Matt. x. 26-33; Luke xii. 2-9.)

There is nothing covered that shall not be revealed, and hid that shall not be known. What I tell you in darkness that speak ye in light; and what ye hear in the ear that preach ye upon the house-tops. And fear not them which kill the body but are not able to kill the soul; but rather fear him which is able to destroy both soul and body in hell. Are not two (five) sparrows sold for a farthing (two farthings)? And one of them shall not fall on the ground without God. But the very hairs of your head are all numbered. Fear ye not (therefore), ye are of (much) more value than (many) sparrows. Whosoever therefore shall confess me before men, him will the Son of man (or: I) confess also before the angels of God; but whosoever shall deny me before men, him will I also deny before the angels of God.

34b.

(Matt. xii. 32; Luke xii. 10.)

. . . And whosoever speaketh a word against the Son of man, it shall be forgiven him; but whosoever speaketh (a word) against the Holy Ghost, it shall not be forgiven him.

38.

(Matt. x. 34-36; Luke xii. 51, 53.)

Think ye that I came to send peace on earth? I came not to send peace, but a sword. For I came to set a man at variance against his father, and the daughter against her mother, and the daughter-in-law against her mother-in-law. (And a man's foes shall be they of his own household.)

45.

(Matt. x. 37; Luke xiv. 26.)

(He that loveth father and mother more than me, is not worthy of me; and he that loveth son or daughter more than me, is not worthy of me.)

46.

(Matt. x. 38; Luke xiv. 27.)

He that taketh not his cross and followeth after me is not worthy of me.

57.

(Matt. x. 39; Luke xvii. 33.)

He that findeth his soul shall lose it, and he that loseth his soul shall find it.

10.

(Matt. x. 24-25; Luke vi. 40.)

The disciple is not above his master, nor the servant above his lord. It is enough for the disciple that he be as his master, and the servant as his lord.

24.

(Matt. x. 40; Luke x. 16)

(He that receiveth you receiveth me, and he that receiveth me receiveth him that sent me.)

14.

(Matt. xi. 2-11; Luke vii. 18-28.)

Now when John had heard in the prison the works of Christ, he sent his disciples and said unto him: Art thou he that should come, or do we look for another? And he answered and said unto them: Go and shew John again those things which ye do hear and see, the blind receive their sight, and the lame walk, the lepers are cleansed, and the deaf hear, the dead are raised up, and the poor have the gospel preached to them; and blessed is he whosoever shall not be offended in me. And as they departed, he began to say unto the multitudes concerning John: What went ye out into the wilderness to see? A reed shaken with the wind? But what went ye out for to see? A man clothed in soft raiment? Behold they that wear soft clothing are in kings' houses! But what went ye out for to see? A prophet? Yea, I say unto you, and more than a prophet! For this is he of whom it is written: Behold I send my messenger before thy face, which shall prepare thy way before thee. (Verily) I say unto you among them that are born of women there hath not risen a greater than John (the Baptist); notwithstanding he that is least in the kingdom of God is greater than he. . . .

50.

(Matt. xi. 12-13; Luke xvi. 16.)

The prophets and the law were until John; since that time the kingdom of God suffereth violence, and the violent take it by force (or: From the days of John until now the kingdom of God, etc.: for all the prophets and the law prophesied until John) . . .

15.

(Matt. xi. 16-10; Luke vii. 31-35;)

Whereunto shall I liken this generation (and to what is it like)? It is like unto children sitting in the markets and calling unto their fellows, saying: We have piped unto you, and ye have not danced; we have mourned unto you, and ye have not lamented. For John came neither eating nor drinking, and they say: He hath a devil! The Son of man came eating and drinking, and they say, Behold a man gluttonous and a winebibber, a friend of publicans and sinners! But wisdom is justified of her children.

23.

(Matt. xi. 21-23; Luke x. 13-15.)

Woe unto thee, Chorazin! woe unto thee, Bethsaida! For if the mighty works which were done in you had been done in Tyre and Sidon, they would have repented long ago in sackcloth and ashes. But (I say unto you) it shall be more tolerable for Tyre and Sidon (at the day of judgment, or: at the judgment) than for you. And thou Capernaum shalt thou have been exalted to heaven? To hell shalt thou be cast down.

25.

(Matt. xi. 25-27; Luke x. 21-22.)

At that time he said: I thank thee, O Father, Lord of heaven and earth, because thou hast hid these things from the wise and prudent, and hast revealed them unto babes; even so [I thank thee] Father, for so it seemed good in thy sight. All things are delivered unto me of my Father, and no man knoweth (the Son but the Father, neither knoweth any man) the Father save the Son, and he to whomsoever the Son will reveal him.

26.

(Matt. xiii. 16-17; Luke x. 23b-24.)

Blessed are your eyes, for they see, and (your) ears, for they hear; (for verily) I say unto you that many prophets (and kings) have desired to see those things which ye see and have not seen them, and to hear those things which ye hear and have not heard them.

29.

(Matt. xii. 22-23, 25, 27-28, 30, 43-45; Luke xi. 14, 17, 19, 20, 23-26.)

(He healed) a dumb man possessed with a devil, (insomuch that) the dumb spake and the multitudes (all) were amazed . . . every kingdom divided against itself is brought to desolation . . . and if I by Beelzebub cast out devils, by whom do yout children cast them out? therefore they shall be your judges. But if I cast out devils by the Spirit of God, then the kingdom of God is come unto you . . . He that is not with me is against me, and he that gathereth not with me scattereth abroad . . . When the unclean spirit is gone out of a man he walketh through dry places seeking rest and findeth none. (Then) he saith, I will return into my house from whence I came out; and when he is come he findeth it empty (and) swept and garnished. Then goeth he and taketh with himself seven other spirits more wicked than himself, and they enter in and dwell there, and the last state of that man is worse than the first.

30.

(Matt. xii. 38-39, 41-42; Luke xi. 16, 29-32.)

We would see a sign from thee. But he said: An evil and adulterous generation seeketh after a sign, and there shall no sign be given to it but the sign of Jonah. For as Jonah was a sign unto the Ninevites, so shall also the Son of man be to this generation. The men of Nineveh shall rise in judgment with this generation, and shall condemn it, because they repented at the preaching of Jonah, and behold a greater than Jonah is here. The queen of the south shall rise up in the judgment with this generation and shall condemn it, for she came from the uttermost parts of the earth to hear the wisdom of Solomon, and behold a greater than Solomon is here.

40.

(Matt. xiii. 31-33; Luke xiii. 18-21.)

(Unto what is the kingdom of God like? and to what shall I liken it? It is like to a grain of mustard seed which a man took and sowed in his field, and it grew and becameth a tree, and the birds of the air lodged in the branches thereof.)

(And again he said): To what shall I liken the kingdom of God? It is like unto leaven which a woman took and hid in three measures of meal till the whole was leavened.

44.

(Matt. xxiii. 12; Luke xiv. 11.)

Whosoever exalteth himself shall be abased, and he that humbleth himself shall be exalted.

42.

(Matt. viii. 11-12; Luke xiii. 28-29.)

I say unto you: They shall come from the east and from the west, and shall sit down with Abraham and Isaac and Jacob in the kingdom of God; but the children of the kingdom shall be cast out; there shall be weeping and gnashing of teeth.

48.

(Matt. xviii. 12-13; Luke xv. 4-7.)

How think ye? If a man have an hundred sheep, and one of them be gone astray, doth he not leave the ninety and nine upon the mountains, and go and seek that which has gone astray? And if so be that he find it, (verily) I say unto you he rejoiceth more of it than of the ninety and nine which went not astray.

53.

(Matt. xviii. 7; Luke xvii. 1.)

It must needs be that offenses come; but woe to that man by the offense cometh.

54.

(Matt. xviii. 15, 21-22; Luke xvii. 3-4.)

If thy brother shall trespass against thee, tell him his fault; if he shall hear thee, thou hast gained thy brother . . . How oft shall my brother sin against me and I forgive him? till seven times? Jesus saith unto him: I say not unto thee, Until seven times; but, Until seventy times seven.

55.

(Matt. xvii. 20b; Luke xvii. 6.)

If ye have faith as a grain of mustard seed, ye shall say unto this mountain: Remove from hence to yonder place, and it shall remove.

33.

(Matt. xxiii. 4, 13, 23, 25, 27, 29, 30-32, 34-36; Luke xi. 46, 52, 42, 39, 44, 47-52.)

. . . They bind heavy burdens and lay them on men's shoulders, and they themselves will not move them with one of their fingers.

Woe unto you, Pharisees! for ye shut up the kingdom of God against men; for ye neither go in yourselves, neither suffer ye them that are entering to go in.

Woe unto you, Pharisees! for ye pay tithe of mint and anise and cummin, and have omitted the weightier matters of the law, judgment and mercy.

Now ye Pharisees! ye make clean the outside of the cup and of the platter, but within they are full; of extortion and excess.

(Luke xi. 44.) Woe unto you, for ye are as sepulchers which appear not, and the men that walk over them are not aware of them.

(Matt. xxiii. 27.) (Woe unto you, Pharisees! for ye are like unto whited (white washed) sepulchers, which indeed appear beautiful outward, but within are full of dead men's bones and of all uncleanness.)

Woe unto you! because ye build the tombs of the prophets and say: If we had been in the days of our fathers we would not have been partakers with them in the blood of the prophets. Wherefore ye be witnesses against yourselves that ye are the children of them which killed the prophets, (and now fulfill the measure of your fathers)!

Wherefore also the Wisdom of God said: I send unto you prophets and wise men and scribes; some of them ye shall kill and persecute; that upon you may come all the blood shed upon the earth from the blood of Abel unto the blood of Zacharias, whom ye slew between the temple and the altar. Verily I say unto you, All these things shall come upon this generation.

43.

(Matt. xxiii. 37-39; Luke xiii. 34-35.)

O Jerusalem! Jerusalem! thou that killest the prophets and stonest them which are sent unto thee! How often would I have gathered thy children together, even as a hen (gathereth) her chicks under her wings, and ye would not! Behold your house is left unto you desolate. (For) I say unto you: Ye shall not see me henceforth till (it shall come when) ye shall say: Blessed is he that cometh in the name of the Lord.

56.

(Matt. xxiv. 26-28, 37-41; Luke xvii. 23-24, 37, 26-27, 34-35.)

Wherefore if they shall say unto you: Behold, he is in the desert! Go ye not forth. Behold, he is in the secret chambers! Believe it not. For as the lightning cometh out of the east and shineth even unto the west, so shall also the coming of the Son of man be. For wheresoever the carcase is, there will the eagles be gathered together.

As the days of Noah were, so shall also the coming of the Son of man be. For as in the days that were before the flood they were eating and drinking, marrying and giving in marriage, until the day that Noah entered into the ark, and knew not until the flood came and took them all away, so shall also the coming of the Son of man be. There shall be two in the field, one shall be taken and the other left; two women shall be grinding at the mill, the one shall be taken and the other left.

37.

(Matt. xxiv. 43-51; Luke xii. 39-40, 42-46.)

But know this, that if the goodman of the house had known in what watch the thief would come, he would have watched and would not have suffered his house to be broken up. (Therefore be ye also ready, for in such an hour as ye think not the Son of man cometh.) Who then is a faithful and wise servant whom his lord hath made ruler over his household to give them meat in due season? Blessed is that servant whom his lord when he cometh shall find so doing. Verily I say unto you, that he shall make him rule over all his goods. But and if that (evil) servant shall say in his heart: My lord delayeth his coming, and shall begin to smite his fellow servants, and to eat and drink with the drunken, the lord of that servant shall come in a day when he looketh not for him, and in an hour that he is not aware of, and shall cut him asunder and appoint him his portion with the hypocrites.

58.

(Matt. xxv. 29; Luke xix. 26.)

Unto him (everyone) that hath shall be given, and he shall have abundance; but from him that hath not, shall be taken away even that which he hath.

59.

(Matt. xix. 28; Luke xxii. 28, 30.)

Ye who have followed me . . . shall sit upon twelve thrones. judging the twelve tribes of Israel.

Here is a more modern look at Q using New Revised Standard version of the Bible. Modern and in depth research has yielded a slightly different extraction of Q. The Book of Luke is used as the extraction point:

LUKE 3:7-9 John said to the crowds that came out to be baptized by him, "You brood of vipers! Who warned you to flee from the wrath to come?   8 Bear fruits worthy of repentance. Do not begin to say to yourselves, `We have Abraham as our ancestor'; for I tell you, God is able from these stones to raise up children to Abraham.   9 Even now the ax is lying at the root of the trees; every tree therefore that does not bear good fruit is cut down and thrown into the fire."

3:16-17 John answered all of them by saying, "I baptize you with water; but one who is more powerful than I is coming; I am not worthy to untie the thong of his sandals. He will baptize you with the Holy Spirit and fire.   17 His winnowing fork is in his hand, to clear his threshing floor and to gather the wheat into his granary; but the chaff he will burn with unquenchable fire."

4:1-13 Jesus, full of the Holy Spirit, returned from the Jordan and was led by the Spirit in the wilderness,   2 where for forty days he was tempted by the devil. He ate nothing at all during those days, and when they were over, he was famished.   3 The devil said to him, "If you are the Son of God, command this stone to become a loaf of bread."   4 Jesus answered him, "It is written, `One does not live by bread alone.'"   5 Then the devil led him up and showed him in an instant all the kingdoms of the world.   6 And the devil said to him, "To you I will give their glory and all this authority; for it has been given over to me, and I give it to anyone I please.   7 If you, then, will worship me, it will all be yours."   8 Jesus answered him, "It is written, `Worship the Lord your God, and serve only him.'"   9 Then the devil took him to Jerusalem, and placed him on the pinnacle of the temple, saying to him, "If you are the Son of God, throw yourself down from here,   10 for it is written, `He will command his angels concerning you, to protect you,'   11 and `On their hands they will bear you up, so that you will not dash your foot against a stone.'"   12 Jesus answered him, "It is said, `Do not put the Lord your God to the test.'"   13 When the devil had finished every test, he departed from him until an opportune time.

6:12, 17, 20 Now during those days he went out to the mountain to pray; and he spent the night in prayer to God.   17 He came down with them and stood on a level place, with a great crowd of his disciples and a great multitude of people from all Judea, Jerusalem, and the coast of Tyre and Sidon.   20 Then he looked up at his disciples and said:

6:20-26 "Blessed are you who are poor, for yours is the kingdom of God.   21 "Blessed are you who are hungry now, for you will be filled. "Blessed are you who weep now, for you will laugh.   22 "Blessed are you when people hate you, and when they exclude you, revile you, and defame you on account of the Son of Man.   23

Rejoice in that day and leap for joy, for surely your reward is great in heaven; for that is what their ancestors did to the prophets. 24 "But woe to you who are rich, for you have received your consolation. 25 "Woe to you who are full now, for you will be hungry. "Woe to you who are laughing now, for you will mourn and weep. 26 "Woe to you when all speak well of you, for that is what their ancestors did to the false prophets.

6:27-36 "But I say to you that listen, Love your enemies, do good to those who hate you, 28 bless those who curse you, pray for those who abuse you. 29 If anyone strikes you on the cheek, offer the other also; and from anyone who takes away your coat do not withhold even your shirt. 30 Give to everyone who begs from you; and if anyone takes away your goods, do not ask for them again. 31 Do to others as you would have them do to you. 32 "If you love those who love you, what credit is that to you? For even sinners love those who love them. 33 If you do good to those who do good to you, what credit is that to you? For even sinners do the same. 34 If you lend to those from whom you hope to receive, what credit is that to you? Even sinners lend to sinners, to receive as much again. 35 But love your enemies, do good, and lend, expecting nothing in return. Your reward will be great, and you will be children of the Most High; for he is kind to the ungrateful and the wicked. 36 Be merciful, just as your Father is merciful.

6:37-38 "Do not judge, and you will not be judged; do not condemn, and you will not be condemned. Forgive, and you will be forgiven;

38 give, and it will be given to you. A good measure, pressed down, shaken together, running over, will be put into your lap; for the measure you give will be the measure you get back."

6:39-40 He also told them a parable: "Can a blind person guide a blind person? Will not both fall into a pit?   40 A disciple is not above the teacher, but everyone who is fully qualified will be like the teacher.

6:41-42 Why do you see the speck in your neighbor's eye, but do not notice the log in your own eye?   42 Or how can you say to your neighbor, `Friend, let me take out the speck in your eye,' when you yourself do not see the log in your own eye? You hypocrite, first take the log out of your own eye, and then you will see clearly to take the speck out of your neighbor's eye.

6:43-45 "No good tree bears bad fruit, nor again does a bad tree bear good fruit;   44 for each tree is known by its own fruit. Figs are not gathered from thorns, nor are grapes picked from a bramble bush. 45 The good person out of the good treasure of the heart produces good, and the evil person out of evil treasure produces evil; for it is out of the abundance of the heart that the mouth speaks.

6:46-49 "Why do you call me `Lord, Lord,' and do not do what I tell you?   47 I will show you what someone is like who comes to me, hears my words, and acts on them.   48   That one is like a man building a house, who dug deeply and laid the foundation on rock;

when a flood arose, the river burst against that house but could not shake it, because it had been well built.   49 But the one who hears and does not act is like a man who built a house on the ground without a foundation. When the river burst against it, immediately it fell, and great was the ruin of that house."

7:1-10 After Jesus had finished all his sayings in the hearing of the people, he entered Capernaum.   2 A centurion there had a slave whom he valued highly, and who was ill and close to death.   3 When he heard about Jesus, he sent some Jewish elders to him, asking him to come and heal his slave.   4 When they came to Jesus, they appealed to him earnestly, saying, "He is worthy of having you do this for him,   5 for he loves our people, and it is he who built our synagogue for us."   6 And Jesus went with them, but when he was not far from the house, the centurion sent friends to say to him, "Lord, do not trouble yourself, for I am not worthy to have you come under my roof;   7 therefore I did not presume to come to you. But only speak the word, and let my servant be healed.   8 For I also am a man set under authority, with soldiers under me; and I say to one, `Go,' and he goes, and to another, `Come,' and he comes, and to my slave, `Do this,' and the slave does it."   9 When Jesus heard this he was amazed at him, and turning to the crowd that followed him, he said, "I tell you, not even in Israel have I found such faith."   10 When those who had been sent returned to the house, they found the slave in good health.

7:18-20, 22-23 The disciples of John reported all these things to him.
So John summoned two of his disciples 19 and sent them to the
Lord to ask, "Are you the one who is to come, or are we to wait for
another?" 20 When the men had come to him, they said, "John the
Baptist has sent us to you to ask, `Are you the one who is to come,
or are we to wait for another?'" 22 And he answered them, "Go and
tell John what you have seen and heard: the blind receive their
sight, the lame walk, the lepers are cleansed, the deaf hear, the dead
are raised, the poor have good news brought to them. 23 And
blessed is anyone who takes no offense at me."

7:24-28 When John's messengers had gone, Jesus began to speak to
the crowds about John: "What did you go out into the wilderness to
look at? A reed shaken by the wind? 25 What then did you go out
to see? Someone dressed in soft robes? Look, those who put on fine
clothing and live in luxury are in royal palaces. 26 What then did
you go out to see? A prophet? Yes, I tell you, and more than a
prophet. 27 This is the one about whom it is written, `See, I am
sending my messenger ahead of you, who will prepare your way
before you.' 28 I tell you, among those born of women no one is
greater than John; yet the least in the kingdom of God is greater
than he."

7:31-35 "To what then will I compare the people of this generation,
and what are they like? 32 They are like children sitting in the
marketplace and calling to one another, `We played the flute for

you, and you did not dance; we wailed, and you did not weep.' 33 For John the Baptist has come eating no bread and drinking no wine, and you say, `He has a demon';  34 the Son of Man has come eating and drinking, and you say, `Look, a glutton and a drunkard, a friend of tax collectors and sinners!' 35 Nevertheless, wisdom is vindicated by all her children."

9:57-62 As they were going along the road, someone said to him, "I will follow you wherever you go." 58 And Jesus said to him, "Foxes have holes, and birds of the air have nests; but the Son of Man has nowhere to lay his head." 59 To another he said, "Follow me." But he said, "Lord, first let me go and bury my father." 60 But Jesus said to him, "Let the dead bury their own dead; but as for you, go and proclaim the kingdom of God." 61 Another said, "I will follow you, Lord; but let me first say farewell to those at my home." 62 Jesus said to him, "No one who puts a hand to the plow and looks back is fit for the kingdom of God."

10:2-12 He said to them, "The harvest is plentiful, but the laborers are few; therefore ask the Lord of the harvest to send out laborers into his harvest. 3 Go on your way. See, I am sending you out like lambs into the midst of wolves. 4 Carry no purse, no bag, no sandals; and greet no one on the road. 5 Whatever house you enter, first say, `Peace to this house!' 6 And if anyone is there who shares in peace, your peace will rest on that person; but if not, it will return to you. 7 Remain in the same house, eating and drinking whatever they provide, for the laborer deserves to be paid. Do not move about from house to house. 8 Whenever you enter a town and its people welcome you, eat what is set before you; 9 cure the sick who are there, and say to them, `The kingdom of God has come near to you.' 10 But whenever you enter a town and they do not welcome you, go out into its streets and say, 11 `Even the dust of your town that clings to our feet, we wipe off in protest against you. Yet know this: the kingdom of God has come near.' 12 I tell you, on that day it will be more tolerable for Sodom than for that town.

10:13-15 "Woe to you, Chorazin! Woe to you, Bethsaida! For if the deeds of power done in you had been done in Tyre and Sidon, they would have repented long ago, sitting in sackcloth and ashes. 14 But at the judgment it will be more tolerable for Tyre and Sidon than for you. 15 And you, Capernaum, will you be exalted to heaven? No, you will be brought down to Hades.

10:16 "Whoever listens to you listens to me, and whoever rejects you rejects me, and whoever rejects me rejects the one who sent me."

10:21-22 At that same hour Jesus rejoiced in the Holy Spirit and said, "I thank you, Father, Lord of heaven and earth, because you have hidden these things from the wise and the intelligent and have revealed them to infants; yes, Father, for such was your gracious will. 22 All things have been handed over to me by my Father; and no one knows who the Son is except the Father, or who the Father is except the Son and anyone to whom the Son chooses to reveal him."

10:23-24 Then turning to the disciples, Jesus said to them privately, "Blessed are the eyes that see what you see! 24 For I tell you that many prophets and kings desired to see what you see, but did not see it, and to hear what you hear, but did not hear it."

11:2-4 He said to them, "When you pray, say: Father, hallowed be your name. Your kingdom come. 3 Give us each day our daily bread. 4 And forgive us our sins, for we ourselves forgive everyone indebted to us. And do not bring us to the time of trial."

11:9-13 "So I say to you, Ask, and it will be given you; search, and you will find; knock, and the door will be opened for you. 10 For everyone who asks receives, and everyone who searches finds, and for everyone who knocks, the door will be opened. 11 Is there anyone among you who, if your child asks for a fish, will give a snake instead of a fish? 12 Or if the child asks for an egg, will give a scorpion? 13 If you then, who are evil, know how to give good gifts to your children, how much more will the heavenly Father give the Holy Spirit to those who ask him!"

11:14-23 Now he was casting out a demon that was mute; when the demon had gone out, the one who had been mute spoke, and the crowds were amazed. 15 But some of them said, "He casts out demons by Beelzebul, the ruler of the demons." 17 But he knew what they were thinking and said to them, "Every kingdom divided against itself becomes a desert, and house falls on house. 18 If

Satan also is divided against himself, how will his kingdom stand? -
- for you say that I cast out the demons by Beelzebul. 19 Now if I
cast out the demons by Beelzebul, by whom do your exorcists cast
them out? Therefore they will be your judges. 20 But if it is by the
finger of God that I cast out the demons, then the kingdom of God
has come to you. 21 When a strong man, fully armed, guards his
castle, his property is safe. 22 But when one stronger than he
attacks him and overpowers him, he takes away his armor in which
he trusted and divides his plunder. 23 Whoever is not with me is
against me, and whoever does not gather with me scatters.

11:24-26 "When the unclean spirit has gone out of a person, it
wanders through waterless regions looking for a resting place, but
not finding any, it says, `I will return to my house from which I
came.' 25 When it comes, it finds it swept and put in order. 26
Then it goes and brings seven other spirits more evil than itself, and
they enter and live there; and the last state of that person is worse
than the first."

11:27-28 While he was saying this, a woman in the crowd raised her
voice and said to him, "Blessed is the womb that bore you and the
breasts that nursed you!" 28 But he said, "Blessed rather are those
who hear the word of God and obey it!"

11:16, 29-32 16 Others, to test him, kept demanding from him a sign
from heaven. 29 When the crowds were increasing, he began to say,
"This generation is an evil generation; it asks for a sign, but no sign

will be given to it except the sign of Jonah. 30 For just as Jonah became a sign to the people of Nineveh, so the Son of Man will be to this generation. 31 The queen of the South will rise at the judgment with the people of this generation and condemn them, because she came from the ends of the earth to listen to the wisdom of Solomon, and see, something greater than Solomon is here! 32 The people of Nineveh will rise up at the judgment with this generation and condemn it, because they repented at the proclamation of Jonah, and see, something greater than Jonah is here!

11:33 "No one after lighting a lamp puts it in a cellar, but on the lampstand so that those who enter may see the light.

11:34-36 Your eye is the lamp of your body. If your eye is healthy, your whole body is full of light; but if it is not healthy, your body is full of darkness. 35 Therefore consider whether the light in you is not darkness. 36 If then your whole body is full of light, with no part of it in darkness, it will be as full of light as when a lamp gives you light with its rays."

11:42 "But woe to you Pharisees! For you tithe mint and rue and herbs of all kinds, and neglect justice and the love of God; it is these you ought to have practiced, without neglecting the others.

11:39-41 Then the Lord said to him, "Now you Pharisees clean the outside of the cup and of the dish, but inside you are full of greed and wickedness. 40 You fools! Did not the one who made the outside make the inside also?   41 So give for alms those things that are within; and see, everything will be clean for you.

11:43 Woe to you Pharisees! For you love to have the seat of honor in the synagogues and to be greeted with respect in the marketplaces.

11:44 Woe to you! For you are like unmarked graves, and people walk over them without realizing it."

11:46 And he said, "Woe also to you lawyers! For you load people with burdens hard to bear, and you yourselves do not lift a finger to ease them.

11:47-48 Woe to you! For you build the tombs of the prophets whom your ancestors killed.   48 So you are witnesses and approve of the deeds of your ancestors; for they killed them, and you build their tombs.

11:49-51 Therefore also the Wisdom of God said, `I will send them prophets and apostles, some of whom they will kill and persecute,' 50 so that this generation may be charged with the blood of all the prophets shed since the foundation of the world,   51 from the blood of Abel to the blood of Zechariah, who perished between the altar and the sanctuary. Yes, I tell you, it will be charged against this generation.

11:52 Woe to you lawyers! For you have taken away the key of knowledge; you did not enter yourselves, and you hindered those who were entering."

12:2-3 Nothing is covered up that will not be uncovered, and nothing secret that will not become known. 3 Therefore whatever you have said in the dark will be heard in the light, and what you have whispered behind closed doors will be proclaimed from the housetops.

12:4-7 "I tell you, my friends, do not fear those who kill the body, and after that can do nothing more. 5 But I will warn you whom to fear: fear him who, after he has killed, has authority to cast into hell. Yes, I tell you, fear him! 6 Are not five sparrows sold for two pennies? Yet not one of them is forgotten in God's sight. 7 But even the hairs of your head are all counted. Do not be afraid; you are of more value than many sparrows.

12:8-9 "And I tell you, everyone who acknowledges me before others, the Son of Man also will acknowledge before the angels of God; 9 but whoever denies me before others will be denied before the angels of God.

12:10 And everyone who speaks a word against the Son of Man will be forgiven; but whoever blasphemes against the Holy Spirit will not be forgiven.

12:11-12 When they bring you before the synagogues, the rulers, and the authorities, do not worry about how you are to defend yourselves or what you are to say; 12 for the Holy Spirit will teach you at that very hour what you ought to say."

12:13-14 Someone in the crowd said to him, "Teacher, tell my brother to divide the family inheritance with me." 14 But he said to him, "Friend, who set me to be a judge or arbitrator over you?"

12:16-21 Then he told them a parable: "The land of a rich man produced abundantly. 17 And he thought to himself, `What should I do, for I have no place to store my crops?'  18 Then he said, `I will do this: I will pull down my barns and build larger ones, and there I will store all my grain and my goods. 19 And I will say to my soul, `Soul, you have ample goods laid up for many years; relax, eat, drink, be merry.'  20 But God said to him, `You fool! This very night your life is being demanded of you. And the things you have prepared, whose will they be?' 21 So it is with those who store up treasures for themselves but are not rich toward God."

12:22-31 He said to his disciples, "Therefore I tell you, do not worry about your life, what you will eat, or about your body, what you will wear. 23 For life is more than food, and the body more than clothing. 24 Consider the ravens: they neither sow nor reap, they have neither storehouse nor barn, and yet God feeds them. Of how much more value are you than the birds! 25 And can any of you by worrying add a single hour to your span of life? 26 If then you are not able to do so small a thing as that, why do you worry about the rest? 27 Consider the lilies, how they grow: they neither toil nor spin; yet I tell you, even Solomon in all his glory was not clothed like one of these. 28 But if God so clothes the grass of the field, which is alive today and tomorrow is thrown into the oven, how much more will he clothe you-- you of little faith! 29 And do not keep striving for what you are to eat and what you are to drink, and do not keep worrying. 30 For it is the nations of the world that strive after all these things, and your Father knows that you need them. 31 Instead, strive for his kingdom, and these things will be given to you as well.

12:33-34 Sell your possessions, and give alms. Make purses for yourselves that do not wear out, an unfailing treasure in heaven, where no thief comes near and no moth destroys. 34 For where your treasure is, there your heart will be also.

12:39-40 "But know this: if the owner of the house had known at what hour the thief was coming, he would not have let his house be broken into. 40 You also must be ready, for the Son of Man is coming at an unexpected hour."

12:42-46 And the Lord said, "Who then is the faithful and prudent manager whom his master will put in charge of his slaves, to give them their allowance of food at the proper time? 43 Blessed is that slave whom his master will find at work when he arrives. 44 Truly I tell you, he will put that one in charge of all his possessions. 45

But if that slave says to himself, `My master is delayed in coming,' and if he begins to beat the other slaves, men and women, and to eat and drink and get drunk,   46 the master of that slave will come on a day when he does not expect him and at an hour that he does not know, and will cut him in pieces, and put him with the unfaithful.

12:49, 51-53 "I came to bring fire to the earth, and how I wish it were already kindled! 51 Do you think that I have come to bring peace to the earth? No, I tell you, but rather division!   52 From now on five in one household will be divided, three against two and two against three;   53 they will be divided: father against son and son against father, mother against daughter and daughter against mother, mother-in-law against her daughter-in-law and daughter-in-law against mother-in-law."

12:54-56 He also said to the crowds, "When you see a cloud rising in the west, you immediately say, `It is going to rain'; and so it happens.   55 And when you see the south wind blowing, you say, `There will be scorching heat'; and it happens.   56 You hypocrites! You know how to interpret the appearance of earth and sky, but why do you not know how to interpret the present time?

12:57-59 "And why do you not judge for yourselves what is right? 58 Thus, when you go with your accuser before a magistrate, on the way make an effort to settle the case, or you may be dragged before the judge, and the judge hand you over to the officer, and the officer throw you in prison. 59 I tell you, you will never get out until you have paid the very last penny."

13:18-21 He said therefore, "What is the kingdom of God like? And to what should I compare it? 19 It is like a mustard seed that someone took and sowed in the garden; it grew and became a tree, and the birds of the air made nests in its branches." 20 And again he said, "To what should I compare the kingdom of God? 21 It is like yeast that a woman took and mixed in with three measures of flour until all of it was leavened."

13:24-27 "Strive to enter through the narrow door; for many, I tell you, will try to enter and will not be able. 25 When once the owner of the house has got up and shut the door, and you begin to stand outside and to knock at the door, saying, `Lord, open to us,' then in reply he will say to you, `I do not know where you come from.' 26 Then you will begin to say, `We ate and drank with you, and you taught in our streets.' 27 But he will say, `I do not know where you come from; go away from me, all you evildoers!'

13:28-30 There will be weeping and gnashing of teeth when you see Abraham and Isaac and Jacob and all the prophets in the kingdom of God, and you yourselves thrown out. 29 Then people will come from east and west, from north and south, and will eat in the kingdom of God. 30 Indeed, some are last who will be first, and some are first who will be last."

13:34-35 Jerusalem, Jerusalem, the city that kills the prophets and stones those who are sent to it! How often have I desired to gather your children together as a hen gathers her brood under her wings, and you were not willing!   35 See, your house is left to you. And I tell you, you will not see me until the time comes when you say, `Blessed is the one who comes in the name of the Lord.'"

14:11, 18:14 For all who exalt themselves will be humbled, and those who humble themselves will be exalted."

18:14 I tell you, this man went down to his home justified rather than the other; for all who exalt themselves will be humbled, but all who humble themselves will be exalted."

14:16-24 Then Jesus said to him, "Someone gave a great dinner and invited many.   17 At the time for the dinner he sent his slave to say to those who had been invited, `Come; for everything is ready now.'   18 But they all alike began to make excuses. The first said to him, `I have bought a piece of land, and I must go out and see it; please accept my regrets.'   19 Another said, `I have bought five yoke of oxen, and I am going to try them out; please accept my regrets.'   20 Another said, `I have just been married, and therefore I cannot come.'   21 So the slave returned and reported this to his master. Then the owner of the house became angry and said to his slave, `Go out at once into the streets and lanes of the town and bring in the poor, the crippled, the blind, and the lame.'   22 And the slave said, `Sir, what you ordered has been done, and there is still room.' 23 Then the master said to the slave, `Go out into the roads and lanes, and compel people to come in, so that my house may be filled. 24 For I tell you, none of those who were invited will taste my dinner.'"

14:26-27, 17:33 "Whoever comes to me and does not hate father and mother, wife and children, brothers and sisters, yes, and even life itself, cannot be my disciple. 27 Whoever does not carry the cross and follow me cannot be my disciple.

17:33 Those who try to make their life secure will lose it, but those who lose their life will keep it.

14:34-35 "Salt is good; but if salt has lost its taste, how can its saltiness be restored? 35 It is fit neither for the soil nor for the manure pile; they throw it away. Let anyone with ears to hear listen!"

15:4-10 "Which one of you, having a hundred sheep and losing one of them, does not leave the ninety-nine in the wilderness and go after the one that is lost until he finds it? 5 When he has found it, he lays it on his shoulders and rejoices. 6 And when he comes home, he calls together his friends and neighbors, saying to them, `Rejoice with me, for I have found my sheep that was lost.' 7 Just so, I tell you, there will be more joy in heaven over one sinner who repents than over ninety-nine righteous persons who need no repentance. 8 "Or what woman having ten silver coins, if she loses one of them, does not light a lamp, sweep the house, and search carefully until she finds it? 9 When she has found it, she calls together her friends and neighbors, saying, `Rejoice with me, for I have found the coin that I had lost.' 10 Just so, I tell you, there is joy in the presence of the angels of God over one sinner who repents."

16:13 No slave can serve two masters; for a slave will either hate the one and love the other, or be devoted to the one and despise the other. You cannot serve God and wealth."

16:16 "The law and the prophets were in effect until John came; since then the good news of the kingdom of God is proclaimed, and everyone tries to enter it by force.

16:17 But it is easier for heaven and earth to pass away, than for one stroke of a letter in the law to be dropped.

16:18 "Anyone who divorces his wife and marries another commits adultery, and whoever marries a woman divorced from her husband commits adultery.

17:1-2 Jesus said to his disciples, "Occasions for stumbling are bound to come, but woe to anyone by whom they come! 2 It would be better for you if a millstone were hung around your neck and you were thrown into the sea than for you to cause one of these little ones to stumble.

17:3-4 Be on your guard! If another disciple sins, you must rebuke the offender, and if there is repentance, you must forgive. 4 And if the same person sins against you seven times a day, and turns back to you seven times and says, `I repent,' you must forgive."

17:6 The Lord replied, "If you had faith the size of a mustard seed, you could say to this mulberry tree, `Be uprooted and planted in the sea,' and it would obey you.

17:22-24, 26-30, 34-35, 37 Then he said to the disciples, "The days are coming when you will long to see one of the days of the Son of Man, and you will not see it. 23 They will say to you, `Look there!' or `Look here!' Do not go, do not set off in pursuit. 24 For as the lightning flashes and lights up the sky from one side to the other, so will the Son of Man be in his day. - 26 Just as it was in the days of Noah, so too it will be in the days of the Son of Man. 27 They were eating and drinking, and marrying and being given in marriage, until the day Noah entered the ark, and the flood came and destroyed all of them. 28 Likewise, just as it was in the days of Lot: they were eating and drinking, buying and selling, planting and building, 29 but on the day that Lot left Sodom, it rained fire and sulfur from heaven and destroyed all of them 30 -- it will be like that on the day that the Son of Man is revealed.

 34 I tell you, on that night there will be two in one bed; one will be taken and the other left. 35 There will be two women grinding meal together; one will be taken and the other left." - 37Then they

asked him, "Where, Lord?" He said to them, "Where the corpse is, there the vultures will gather."

19:12-26 So he said, "A nobleman went to a distant country to get royal power for himself and then return. 13 He summoned ten of his slaves, and gave them ten pounds, and said to them, `Do business with these until I come back.'  14 But the citizens of his country hated him and sent a delegation after him, saying, `We do not want this man to rule over us.' 15 When he returned, having received royal power, he ordered these slaves, to whom he had given the money, to be summoned so that he might find out what they had gained by trading. 16 The first came forward and said, `Lord, your pound has made ten more pounds.'  17 He said to him, `Well done, good slave! Because you have been trustworthy in a very small thing, take charge of ten cities.' 18 Then the second came, saying, `Lord, your pound has made five pounds.'  19 He said to him, `And you, rule over five cities.' 20 Then the other came, saying, `Lord, here is your pound. I wrapped it up in a piece of cloth,  21 for I was afraid of you, because you are a harsh man; you take what you did not deposit, and reap what you did not sow.'  22 He said to him, `I will judge you by your own words, you wicked slave! You knew, did you, that I was a harsh man, taking what I did not deposit and reaping what I did not sow? 23 Why then did you not put my money into the bank? Then when I returned, I could have collected it with interest.' 24 He said to the bystanders, `Take the pound from him and give it to the one who has ten pounds.'  25 (And they said to him, `Lord, he has ten pounds!') 26 `I tell you, to all those who have, more will be given; but from those who have nothing, even what they have will be taken away.

22:28-30 "You are those who have stood by me in my trials; 29 and I confer on you, just as my Father has conferred on me, a kingdom, 30 so that you may eat and drink at my table in my kingdom, and you will sit on thrones judging the twelve tribes of Israel.

The Gospel of Thomas

In the winter of 1945, in Upper Egypt, an Arab peasant was gathering fertilizer and topsoil for his crops. While digging in the soft dirt he came across a large earthen vessel. Inside were scrolls containing hitherto unseen books.

The scrolls were discovered near the site of the ancient town of Chenoboskion, at the base of a mountain named Gebel et-Tarif, near Hamra-Dum, in the vicinity of Naj 'Hammadi, about sixty miles from Luxor in Egypt. The texts were written in the Coptic language and preserved on papyrus sheets. The lettering style dated them as having been penned around the third or fourth century A.D. The Gospel of Thomas is the longest of the volumes consisting of between 114 and 118 verses. Recent study indicates that the original works, of which the scrolls are copies, may predate the four canonical gospels of Matthew, Mark, Luke, and John. The origin of The Gospel of Thomas is now thought to be from the first or second century A.D.

The peasant boy who found this treasure stood to be rewarded greatly. This could have been the discovery of a lifetime for his family, but the boy had no idea what he had. He took the scrolls home, where his mother burned some as kindling. Others were sold to the black market antique dealers in Cairo. It would be years until they found their way into the hands of a scholar. Part of the thirteenth codex was smuggled from Egypt to America. In 1955 the existence of the codex had reached the ears of Gilles Quispel, a professor of religion and history in the Netherlands. The race was on to find and translate the scrolls.

The introduction of the collected sayings of Jesus refers to the writer as "Didymus (Jude) Thomas." This is the same Thomas who doubted Jesus and was then told to place his hand within the breach in the side of the Savior. In the Gospel of St. John, he is referred to as "Didymus," which means "twin" in Greek. In Aramaic, the name "Jude" (or Judas) also carries the sense of "twin". The use of this title led some in the apocryphal tradition to believe that he was the brother and confidant of Jesus. However, when applied to Jesus himself, the literal meaning of "twin" must be rejected by orthodox Christianity as well as anyone adhering to the doctrine of the virgin birth of the only begotten son of God. The title is likely meant to signify that Thomas was a close confidant of Jesus.

Ancient church historians mention that Thomas preached to the Parthians in Persia and it is said he was buried in Edessa. Fourth century chronicles attribute the evangelization of India (Asia-Minor or Central Asia) to Thomas.

The text, which some believe predate the four gospels, has a more Eastern flavor than the other gospels. Since it is widely held that the four gospels of Matthew, Mark, and Luke have a common reference in the basic text of Mark, it stands to reason that all follow the same general insight and language. Since scholars believe that the Gospel of Thomas predates the four main gospels, it can be assumed it was written outside the influences common to the other gospels. Although the codex found in Egypt is dated to the fourth century, the actual construction of the text of Thomas is placed by most Biblical scholars at about 50 to 70 A.D. with a few scholars pushing the date out to 150 A.D.

If Thomas wrote his gospel first, without input from Mark, and from the standpoint of Eastern exposure as a result of his sojourn into India, it could explain the "Eastern" quality of the text.

Moreover, there is some speculation that the sayings found in Thomas could be more accurate to the original intent and wording of Jesus than the other gospels. This may seem counter-intuitive until we realize that Christianity itself is an Eastern religion, albeit Middle-Eastern. Although, as it spread west the faith went through many changes to westernize or Romanize it...Jesus was both mystical and Middle-Eastern.

The Gospel of Thomas was most likely composed in Syria, where tradition holds the church of Edessa was founded by Judas Thomas, "The Twin" (Didymus). The gospel may well be the earliest written tradition in the Syriac church

The Gospel of Thomas is sometimes called a Gnostic gospel. The term "Gnostic" derives from "gnosis," which in Greek means "knowledge." Gnostics believed that knowledge is formed or found from a personal encounter with God brought about by inward or intuitive insight. They believed they were privy to a secret knowledge about the divine. It is this knowledge that leads to their name. It is possible that the roots of the Gnostic system pre-dates Christianity and found a suitable home in the mystical side of the Christian faith.

There are numerous references to the Gnostics in second century literature. Their form of Christianity was considered heresy by the early church fathers. It is from the writings condemning the group that we glean most of our information. They are alluded to in the Bible in 1 Tm 1:4 and 1 Tm 6:20, and possibly the entirety of Jude, as the writers of the Bible defended their theology against that of the Gnostics.

The relation between the Gospel of Thomas and the Q document is an interesting one.

The Gospel of Thomas is very different from the gospels that have become part of the New Testament. Like Q, it contains no narrative material, nor is there any story of the birth, the life, or the death of Jesus. It consists only of sayings, 114 in all. The Gospel of Thomas makes a claim in the first page of the text announcing that it is the words of the "living Jesus. The gospel contains the same basic information as Q1 and Q2 of the "three evolutionary stages of Q" hypothesis.

Some of the sayings from the Gospel of Thomas are very much like those found in the gospels of Matthew and Luke.

For New Testament scholars, one of the most interesting things about this gospel is that its author (who calls himself Didymos Judas Thomas) appears to have used sayings from the same collection used by Matthew and Luke. Thus, the Gospel of Thomas may be proof of a central and core collection of sayings directly from the mouth of Jesus. There may have been a small number of these collection, which may have varied slightly in wording and in which sayings were recorded but the source material would have come from Jesus himself. Since the wording of the sayings in Matthew, Mark, Luke, and Thomas were so similar it solidified the belief by some scholars of a center repository of information.

In 1989, a team of researchers led by James M. Robinson of the Institute for Antiquity and Christianity in Claremont, CA, began the "reconstruction" of the Gospel of Q. Robinson and his team are accomplishing this by a highly detailed literary analysis of Matthew, Luke, and Thomas. Their painstaking work goes verse by verse, word by word. Since this respected team has seen fit to use the Gospel of Thomas as part of the collected works for the reconstruction of Q, it may benefit us to examine this book also. As we will see, Thomas, like Q1 and Q2, did not see Jesus in the same light of divinity as Paul and the later Christian movement casts him in.

Based on the fact that there was simply a collection of sayings, which predated the narratives of the resurrection, and based on what those saying were, we can conclude that some Christian communities did not see Jesus as a Messiah. Jesus was not divine, but fully human. To them Jesus was a teacher of wisdom, a man who tried to teach others how to live. The story of the resurrection may have developed a little later in the evolution of the faith and the passion narrative was added to the collection of sayings to yield the gospel we have today.

We have seen the Q collection. Now let us compare it to the sayings collected by Thomas.

The Gospel Of Thomas

These are the secret sayings which the living Jesus has spoken and Judas who is also Thomas (the twin) (Didymos Judas Thomas) wrote.

1. And he said: Whoever finds the interpretation of these sayings will not taste death.

John 8:51 Very truly I tell you, whoever keeps my word will never see death.

2. Jesus said: Let he who seeks not stop seeking until he finds, and when he finds he will be troubled, and when he has been troubled he will marvel (be astonished) and he will reign over all and in reigning, he will find rest.

3. Jesus said: If those who lead you say to you: Behold, the Kingdom is in the sky, then the birds of the sky would enter before you. If they say to you: It is in the sea, then the fish of the

sea would enter ahead you. But the Kingdom of God exists within you and it exists outside of you. Those who come to know (recognize) themselves will find it, and when you come to know yourselves you will become known and you will realize that you are the children of the Living Father. Yet if you do not come to know yourselves then you will dwell in poverty and it will be you who are that poverty.

Luke 17:20 And when he was demanded of by the Pharisees, when the kingdom of God should come, he answered them and said, The kingdom of God cometh not with observation: Neither shall they say, Lo here! Lo There! For, behold, the kingdom of God is within you.

4. Jesus said: The person of old age will not hesitate to ask a little child of seven days about the place of life, and he will live. For many who are first will become last, (and the last will be first). And they will become one and the same.

Mark 9:35 He sat down, called the twelve, and said to them: Whoever wants to be first must be last of all and servant of all. 36 Then he took a little child and put it among them, and taking it in his arms, he said to them: 37 Whoever welcomes one such child in my name welcomes me, and whoever welcomes me welcomes not me but the one who sent me.

5. Jesus said: Recognize what is in front of your face, and what has been hidden from you will be revealed to you. For there is nothing hidden which will not be revealed (become manifest), and nothing buried that will not be raised.

Mark 4:2 For there is nothing hid, except to be made manifest; nor is anything secret, except to come to light.

Luke 12:3 Nothing is covered up that will not be revealed, or hidden that will not be known.

Matthew 10:26 So have no fear of them; for nothing is covered up that will not be uncovered, and nothing secret that will not become known.

6. His Disciples asked Him, how do you want us to fast, and how will we pray? And how will we be charitable (give alms), and what laws of diet will we maintain?

Jesus said: Do not lie, and do not practice what you hate, for everything is in the plain sight of Heaven. For there is nothing concealed that will not become manifest, and there is nothing covered that will not be exposed.

Luke 11:1 He was praying in a certain place, and after he had finished, one of his disciples said to him, Lord, teach us to pray, as John taught his disciples.

7. Jesus said: Blessed is the lion that the man will eat, for the lion will become the man. Cursed is the man that the lion shall eat, and still the lion will become man.

Mathew 26:20-30 He who dipped his hand with me in the dish, the same will betray me. The Son of Man goes, even as it is written of him, but woe to that man through whom the Son of Man is betrayed! It would be better for that man if he had not been born. Judas, who betrayed him, answered, It isn't me, is it, Rabbi? He said to him, You said it. As they were eating, Jesus took bread, gave thanks for it, and broke it. He gave to the disciples, and said, Take, eat; this is my body. He took the cup, gave thanks, and gave to them, saying: All of you drink it, for this is my blood of the new covenant, which is poured out for many for the remission of sins. But I tell you that I will not drink of this fruit of the vine from now on, until that day when I drink it anew with you in my Father's Kingdom. When they had sung a hymn, they went out to the Mount of Olives.

8. And he said: The Kingdom of Heaven is like a wise fisherman who casts his net into the sea. He drew it up from the sea full of small fish. Among them he found a fine large fish. That wise

fisherman threw all the small fish back into the sea and chose the large fish without hesitation. Whoever has ears to hear, let him hear!

Matthew 13:47 Again, the kingdom of heaven is like a net that was thrown into the sea and caught fish of every kind; 48 when it was full, they drew it ashore, sat down, and put the good into baskets but threw out the bad.

9. Jesus said: Now, the sower came forth. He filled his hand and threw (the seeds). Some fell upon the road and the birds came and gathered them up. Others fell on the stone and they did not take deep enough roots in the soil, and so did not produce grain. Others fell among the thorns and they choked the seed, and the worm ate them. Others fell upon the good earth and it produced good fruit up toward the sky, it bore 60 fold and 120 fold.

Matthew 13:3 And he told them many things in parables, saying: Listen! A sower went out to sow. 4 And as he sowed, some seeds fell on the path, and the birds came and ate them up. 5 Other seeds fell on rocky ground, where they did not have much soil, and they sprang up quickly, since they had no depth of soil. 6 But when the sun rose, they were scorched; and since they had no root, they withered away. 7 Other seeds fell among thorns, and the thorns grew up and choked them. 8 Other seeds fell on good soil and brought forth grain, some a hundredfold, some sixty, some thirty.

Mark 4:2 And he taught them many things in parables, and in his teaching he said to them: 3 Behold! A sower went out to sow. 4 And as he sowed, some seed fell along the path, and the birds came and devoured it. 5 Other seed fell on rocky ground, where it had not much soil, and immediately it sprang up, since it had no depth of soil; 6 and when the sun rose it was scorched, and since it had no root it withered away. 7 Other seed fell among thorns and the thorns grew up and choked it, and it yielded no grain. 8 And other seeds fell into good soil and brought forth grain, growing up and increasing and yielding thirty fold and sixty fold and a hundredfold. 9 And he said, He who has ears to hear, let him hear.

Luke 8:4 And when a great crowd came together and people from town after town came to him, he said in a parable: 5 A sower went out to sow his seed; and as he sowed, some fell along the path, and was trodden under foot, and the birds of the air devoured it. 6 And some fell on the rock; and as it grew up, it withered away, because it had no moisture. 7 And some fell among thorns; and the thorns grew with it and choked it. 8 And some fell into good soil and grew, and yielded a hundredfold. As he said this, he called out, He who has ears to hear, let him hear.

10. Jesus said: I have cast fire upon the world and behold, I guard it until it is ablaze.

Luke 12:49 I came to bring fire to the earth, and how I wish it were already kindled.

11. Jesus said: This sky will pass away, and the one above it will pass away. The dead are not alive, and the living will not die. In the days when you consumed what is dead, you made it alive. When you come into the Light, what will you do? On the day when you were united (one), you became separated (two). When you have become separated (two), what will you do?

Matthew 24:35 Heaven and earth will pass away, but my words will not pass away.

12. The Disciples said to Jesus: We know that you will go away from us. Who is it that will be our teacher?

Jesus said to them: Wherever you are (in the place that you have come), you will go to James the Righteous, for whose sake Heaven and Earth were made (came into being).

13. Jesus said to his Disciples: Compare me to others, and tell me who I am like. Simon Peter said to him: You are like a righteous messenger (angel) of God. Matthew said to him: You are like a (wise) philosopher (of the heart). Thomas said to him: Teacher, my mouth is not capable of saying who you are like!

Jesus said: I'm not your teacher, now that you have drunk; you have become drunk from the bubbling spring that I have tended (measured out). And he took him, and withdrew and spoke three words to him: "ahyh ashr ahyh" (I am Who I am).

Now when Thomas returned to his comrades, they inquired of him: What did Jesus say to you? Thomas said to them: If I tell you even one of the words which he spoke to me, you will take up stones and throw them at me, and fire will come from the stones to consume you.

Mark 8:27 Jesus went on with his disciples to the villages of Caesarea Philippi; and on the way he asked his disciples, Who do people say that I am? 28 And they answered him, John the Baptist; and others, Elijah; and still others, one of the prophets. 29 He asked them, But who do you say that I am? Peter answered him, You are the Messiah. 30 And he sternly ordered them not to tell anyone about him.

14. Jesus said to them: If you fast, you will give rise to transgression (sin) for yourselves. And if you pray, you will be condemned. And if you give alms, you will cause harm (evil) to your spirits. And when you go into the countryside, if they take you in (receive you) then eat what they set before you and heal

the sick among them. For what goes into your mouth will not defile you, but rather what comes out of your mouth, that is what will defile you.

Luke 10:8 Whenever you enter a town and its people welcome you, eat what is set before you; 9 Cure the sick who are there, and say to them, The kingdom of God has come near to you.

Mark 7:15 There is nothing outside a person that by going in can defile, but the things that come out are what defile.

Matthew 15:11 Not that what goes into the mouth defiles a man, but what comes out of the mouth, this defiles a man.
Romans 14.14 I know and am persuaded in the Lord Jesus that nothing is unclean in itself; but it is unclean for any one who thinks it unclean.

15. Jesus said: When you see him who was not born of woman, bow yourselves down upon your faces and worship him for he is your Father.

16. Jesus said: People think perhaps I have come to spread peace upon the world. They do not know that I have come to cast dissention (conflict) upon the earth; fire, sword, war. For there will be five in a house. Three will be against two and two against

three, the father against the son and the son against the father. And they will stand alone.

Matthew 10:34 Do not think that I have come to bring peace to the earth; I have not come to bring peace, but a sword. 35 For I have come to set a man against his father, and a daughter against her mother, and a daughter-in-law against her mother-in-law; 36 and one's foes will be members of one's own household.

Luke 12:51 Do you think that I have come to give peace on earth? No, I tell you, but rather division; 52 for henceforth in one house there will be five divided, three against two and two against three; 53 they will be divided, father against son and son against father, mother against daughter and daughter against her mother, mother-in-law against her daughter-in-law and daughter-in-law against her mother-in-law.

17. Jesus said: I will give to you what eye has not seen, what ear has not heard, what hand has not touched, and what has not occurred to the mind of man.

1 Cor 2:9 But, as it is written, What no eye has seen, nor ear heard, nor the human heart conceived, what God has prepared for those who love him.

18. The Disciples said to Jesus: Tell us how our end will come. Jesus said: Have you already discovered the beginning (origin), so that you inquire about the end? Where the beginning (origin) is, there the end will be. Blessed be he who will take his place in the beginning (stand at the origin) for he will know the end, and he will not experience death.

19. Jesus said: Blessed is he who came into being before he came into being. If you become my Disciples and heed my sayings, these stones will serve you. For there are five trees in paradise for you, which are undisturbed in summer and in winter and their leaves do not fall. Whoever knows them will not experience death.

20. The Disciples said to Jesus: Tell us what the Kingdom of Heaven is like. He said to them: It is like a mustard seed, smaller than all other seeds and yet when it falls on the tilled earth, it produces a great plant and becomes shelter for the birds of the sky.

Mark 4:30 He also said, With what can we compare the kingdom of God, or what parable will we use for it? 31 It is like a mustard seed, which, when sown upon the ground, is the smallest of all the seeds on earth; 32 yet when it is sown it grows up and becomes the greatest of all shrubs, and puts forth large branches, so that the birds of the air can make nests in its shade. Matthew 13:31 The kingdom of heaven is like a grain of mustard seed which a man took and sowed in his field; 32 it is the smallest of all seeds, but when it has grown it is the greatest of shrubs and becomes a tree, so that the birds of the air come and make nests in its branches.

Luke 13.18 He said therefore, What is the kingdom of God like? And to what shall I compare it? 19 It is like a grain of mustard seed which a man took and sowed in his garden; and it grew and became a tree, and the birds of the air made nests in its branches.

21. Mary said to Jesus: Who are your Disciples like? He said: They are like little children who are living in a field that is not theirs. When the owners of the field come, they will say: Let us have our field! It is as if they were naked in front of them (They undress in front of them in order to let them have what is theirs) and they give back the field. Therefore I said, if the owner of the house knows that the thief is coming, he will be alert before he arrives and will not allow him to dig through into the house to carry away his belongings. You must be on guard and beware of the world (system). Prepare yourself (arm yourself) with great strength or the bandits will find a way to reach you, for the problems you expect will come. Let there be among you a person of understanding (awareness). When the crop ripened, he came quickly with his sickle in his hand to reap. Whoever has ears to hear, let him hear!

Matthew 24:43 But understand this: if the owner of the house had known in what part of the night the thief was coming, he would have stayed awake and would not have let his house be broken into.

Mark 4:26 He also said, The kingdom of God is as if someone would scatter seed on the ground, 27 and would sleep and rise night and day, and the seed would sprout and grow, he does not know how. 28 The earth produces of itself, first the stalk, then the head, then the full grain in the head. 29 But when the grain is ripe, at once he goes in with his sickle, because the harvest has come.

Luke 12:39 But know this, that if the householder had known at what hour the thief was coming, he would not have left his house to be broken into. 40 You also must be ready; for the Son of man is coming at an unexpected hour.

22. Jesus saw little children who were being suckled. He said to his Disciples: These little children who are being suckled are like those who enter the Kingdom.

They said to him: Should we become like little children in order to enter the Kingdom?

Jesus said to them: When you make the two one, and you make the inside as the outside and the outside as the inside, when you make the above as the below, and if you make the male and the female one and the same (united male and female) so that the man will not be masculine (male) and the female be not feminine (female), when you establish an eye in the place of an eye and a hand in the place of a hand and a foot in the place of a foot and an likeness (image) in the place of a likeness (an image), then will you enter the Kingdom.

Luke 18:16 But Jesus called for them and said, Let the little children come to me, and do not stop them; for it is to such as these that the kingdom of God belongs. 17 Truly I tell you, whoever does not receive the kingdom of God as a little child will never enter it.

Mark 9:43 If your hand causes you to stumble, cut it off; it is better for you to enter life maimed than to have two hands and to go to hell, to the unquenchable fire. 45 And if your foot causes you to stumble, cut it off; it is better for you to enter life lame than to have two feet and to be thrown into hell. 47 And if your eye causes you to stumble, tear it out; it is better for you to enter the kingdom of God with one eye than to have two eyes and to be thrown into hell, 48 where their worm never dies, and the fire is never quenched.

Matthew 18:3 And said, Verily, I say unto you, unless you turn and become like children, you will never enter the kingdom of heaven. 4

Whoever humbles himself like this child, he is the greatest in the kingdom of heaven. 5 Whoever receives one such child in my name receives me;

Matthew 5:29 If your right eye causes you to sin, pluck it out and throw it away; it is better that you lose one of your members than that your whole body be thrown into hell. 30 And if your right hand causes you to sin, cut it off and throw it away; it is better that you lose one of your members than that your whole body go into hell.

23. Jesus said: I will choose you, one out of a thousand and two out of ten thousand and they will stand as a single one.

24. His Disciples said: Show us the place where you are (your place), for it is necessary for us to seek it.

He said to them: Whoever has ears, let him hear! Within a man of light there is light, and he illumines the entire world. If he does not shine, he is darkness (there is darkness).

John13:36 Simon Peter said to him, Lord, where are you going? Jesus answered, Where I am going, you cannot follow me now; but you will follow afterward.

Matthew 6:22 The eye is the lamp of the body. So, if your eye is healthy, your whole body will be full of light; 23 but if your eye is unhealthy, your whole body will be full of darkness. If then the light in you is darkness, how great is the darkness!

Luke 11:34 Your eye is the lamp of your body; when your eye is sound, your whole body is full of light; but when it is not sound, your body is full of darkness. 35 Therefore be careful lest the light in you be darkness. 36 If then your whole body is full of light, having no part dark, it will be wholly bright, as when a lamp with its rays gives you light.

25. Jesus said: Love your friend (Brother) as your soul; protect him as you would the pupil of your own eye.

26. Jesus said: You see the speck in your brother's eye but the beam that is in your own eye you do not see. When you remove the beam out of your own eye, then will you see clearly to remove the speck out of your brother's eye.

Matthew 7:3 Why do you see the speck in your neighbor's eye, but do not notice the log in your own eye? 4 Or how can you say to your neighbor, Let me take the speck out of your eye, while the log is in your own eye? 5 You hypocrite, first take the log out of your own eye, and then you will see clearly to take the speck out of your neighbor's eye.

Luke 6:41 Why do you see the speck that is in your brother's eye, but do not notice the log that is in your own eye? 42 Or how can you say to your brother, Brother, let me take out the speck that is in your eye, when you yourself do not see the log that is in your own eye? You hypocrite, first take the log out of your own eye, and then you will see clearly to take out the speck that is in your brother's eye.

27. Jesus said: Unless you fast from the world (system), you will not find the Kingdom of God. Unless you keep the Sabbath (entire week) as Sabbath, you will not see the Father.

28. Jesus said: I stood in the midst of the world. In the flesh I appeared to them. I found them all drunk; I found none thirsty among them. My soul grieved for the sons of men, for they are blind in their hearts and do not see that they came into the world empty, they are destined (determined) to leave the world empty. However, now they are drunk. When they have shaken off their wine, then they will repent (change their ways).

29. Jesus said: If the flesh came into being because of spirit, it is a marvel, but if spirit came into being because of the body, it would be a marvel of marvels. I marvel indeed at how great wealth has taken up residence in this poverty.

30. Jesus said: Where there are three gods, they are gods (Where there are three gods they are without god). Where there is only one, I say that I am with him. Lift the stone and there you will find me, Split the wood and there am I.

Matthew 18:20 For where two or three are gathered in my name, I am there among them.

31. Jesus said: No prophet is accepted in his own village, no physician heals those who know him.

Mark 6:4 Then Jesus said to them, Prophets are not without honor, except in their hometown, and among their own kin, and in their own house.

Matthew 13:57 And they took offense at him. But Jesus said to them: A prophet is not without honor save in his own country and in his own house.

Luke 4:24 And he said, Truly, I say to you, no prophet is acceptable in his own country.

Joseph Lumpkin

John 4:43 After the two days he departed to Galilee. 44 For Jesus himself testified that a prophet has no honor in his own country.

32. Jesus said: A city being built (and established) upon a high mountain and fortified cannot fall nor can it be hidden.

Matthew 5:14 You are the light of the world. A city built on a hill cannot be hid.

33. Jesus said: What you will hear in your ear preach from your rooftops. For no one lights a lamp and sets it under a basket nor puts it in a hidden place, but rather it is placed upon a lamp-stand so that everyone who comes and goes will see its light.

Matthew 10:27 What I say to you in the dark, tell in the light; and what you hear whispered, proclaim from the housetops.

Luke 8:16 No one after lighting a lamp hides it under a jar, or puts it under a bed, but puts it on a lamp stand, so that those who enter may see the light.

Matthew 5:15 Nor do men light a lamp and put it under a bushel, but on a stand, and it gives light to all in the house.

Mark 4:21 And he said to them, Is a lamp brought in to be put under a bushel, or under a bed, and not on a stand?

Luke 11:33 No one after lighting a lamp puts it in a cellar or under a bushel, but on a stand, that those who enter may see the light.

34. Jesus said: If a blind person leads a blind person, both fall into a pit.

Matthew 15:14 Let them alone; they are blind guides of the blind. And if one blind person guides another, both will fall into a pit.
Luke 6:39 He also told them a parable: Can a blind man lead a blind man? Will they not both fall into a pit?

35. Jesus said: It is impossible for anyone to enter the house of a strong man to take it by force unless he binds his hands, then he will be able to loot his house.

Matthew 12:29 Or how can one enter a strong man's house and plunder his goods, unless he first binds the strong man? Then indeed he may plunder his house.

Luke 11:21 When a strong man, fully armed, guards his own palace, his goods are in peace; 22 but when one stronger than he assails him and overcomes him, he takes away his armor in which he trusted, and divides his spoil.

Mark 3:27 But no one can enter a strong man's house and plunder his property without first tying up the strong man; then indeed the house can be plundered.

36. Jesus said: Do not worry from morning to evening nor from evening to morning about the food that you will eat nor about what clothes you will wear. You are much superior to the lilies which neither card nor spin. When you have no clothing, what do you wear? Who can add time to your life (increase your stature)? He himself will give to you your garment.

Matthew 6:25 Therefore I tell you, do not worry about your life, what you will eat or what you will drink, or about your body, what you will wear. Is not life more than food, and the body more than clothing? 26 Look at the birds of the air; they neither sow nor reap nor gather into barns, and yet your heavenly Father feeds them. Are you not of more value than they? 27 And can any of you by worrying add a single hour to your span of life? 28 And why do you worry about clothing? Consider the lilies of the field, how they grow; they neither toil nor spin, 29 yet I tell you, even Solomon in all his glory was not clothed like one of these. 30 But if God so clothes the grass of the field, which is alive today and tomorrow is thrown into the oven, will he not much more clothe you--you of little faith? 31 Therefore do not worry, saying, What will we eat? or What will we drink? or What will we wear?

Luke 12:22 And he said to his disciples, Therefore I tell you, do not be anxious about your life, what you shall eat, nor about your body, what you shall put on. 23 For life is more than food, and the body more than clothing.

37. His Disciples said: When will you appear to us, and when will we see you?

Jesus said: When you take off your garments without being ashamed, and place your garments under your feet and tread on them as the little children do, then will you see the Son of the Living-One, and you will not be afraid.

38. Jesus said: Many times have you yearned to hear these sayings which I speak to you, and you have no one else from whom to hear them. There will be days when you will seek me but you will not find me.

39. Jesus said: The Pharisees and the Scribes have received the keys of knowledge, but they have hidden them. They did not go in, nor did they permit those who wished to enter to do so. However, you be as wise (astute) as serpents and innocent as doves.

Luke 11:52 Woe to you lawyers! For you have taken away the key of knowledge; you did not enter yourselves, and you hindered those who were entering.

Matthew 10:16 See, I am sending you out like sheep into the midst of wolves; so be wise as serpents and innocent as doves.

Matthew 23.13 But woe unto you, scribes and Pharisees, hypocrites! because you shut the kingdom of heaven against men; for you neither enter yourselves, nor allow those who would enter to go in.

40. Jesus said: A grapevine has been planted outside the (vineyard of the) Father, and since it is not viable (supported) it will be pulled up by its roots and destroyed.

Matthew 15:13 He answered, Every plant that my heavenly Father has not planted will be uprooted.

41. Jesus said: Whoever has (it) in his hand, to him will (more) be given. And whoever does not have, from him will be taken even the small amount which he has.

Matthew 25:29 For to all those who have, more will be given, and they will have an abundance; but from those who have nothing, even what they have will be taken away.

Luke 19:26 I tell you, that to every one who has will more be given; but from him who has not, even what he has will be taken away.

42. Jesus said: Become passers-by.

43. His Disciples said to him: Who are you, that you said these things to us?

Jesus said to them: You do not recognize who I am from what I said to you, but rather you have become like the Jews who either love the tree and hate its fruit, or love the fruit and hate the tree.

John 8:25 They said to him, Who are you? Jesus said to them, Why do I speak to you at all?

Matthew 7:16 You will know them by their fruits. Are grapes gathered from thorns, or figs from thistles? 17 In the same way, every good tree bears good fruit, but the bad tree bears bad fruit. 18 A good tree cannot bear bad fruit, nor can a bad tree bear good fruit. 19 Every tree that does not bear good fruit is cut down and thrown into the fire. 20 Thus you will know them by their fruits.

44. Jesus said: Whoever blasphemes against the Father, it will be forgiven him. And whoever blasphemes against the Son, it will be forgiven him. Yet whoever blasphemes against the Holy Spirit, it will not be forgiven him neither on earth nor in heaven.

Mark 3:28 Truly I tell you, people will be forgiven for their sins and whatever blasphemies they utter; 29 but whoever blasphemes against the Holy Spirit can never have forgiveness, but is guilty of an eternal sin.

Matthew 12:31 Therefore I tell you, every sin and blasphemy will be forgiven men, but the blasphemy against the Spirit will not be forgiven. 32 And whoever says a word against the Son of man will be forgiven; but whoever speaks against the Holy Spirit will not be forgiven, either in this age or in the age to come.

Luke 12:10 And every one who speaks a word against the Son of man will be forgiven; but he who blasphemes against the Holy Spirit will not be forgiven.

45. Jesus said: Grapes are not harvested from thorns, nor are figs gathered from thistles, for they do not give fruit. A good person brings forth goodness out of his storehouse. A bad person brings forth evil out of his evil storehouse which is in his heart, and he speaks evil, for out of the abundance of the heart he brings forth evil.

Luke 6:43 For no good tree bears bad fruit, nor again does a bad tree bear good fruit; 44 for each tree is known by its own fruit. For figs are not gathered from thorns, nor are grapes picked from a bramble bush. 45 The good man out of the good treasure of his heart produces good, and the evil man out of his evil treasure produces evil; for out of the abundance of the heart his mouth speaks.

46. Jesus said: From Adam until John the Baptist there is none born of women who surpasses John the Baptist, so that his eyes should not be downcast (lowered). Yet I have said that whoever among you becomes like a child will know the Kingdom, and he will be greater than John.

Matthew 11:11 Truly I tell you, among those born of women no one has arisen greater than John the Baptist; yet the least in the kingdom of heaven is greater than he.

Luke 7:28 I tell you, among those born of women none is greater than John; yet he who is least in the kingdom of God is greater than he.

Matthew 18:2 He called a child, whom he put among them, 3 and said, Truly I tell you, unless you change and become like children, you will never enter the kingdom of heaven. 18:4 Whoever becomes humble like this child is the greatest in the kingdom of heaven.

47. Jesus said: It is impossible for a man to mount two horses or to draw two bows, and a servant cannot serve two masters, otherwise he will honor the one and disrespect the other. No man drinks vintage wine and immediately desires to drink new wine, and they do not put new wine into old wineskins or they would burst, and they do not put vintage wine into new wineskins or it would spoil (sour). They do not sew an old patch on a new garment because that would cause a split.

Matthew 6:24 No one can serve two masters; for a slave will either hate the one and love the other, or be devoted to the one and despise the other. You cannot serve God and wealth.

Matthew 9:16 No one sews a piece of unshrunk cloth on an old cloak, for the patch pulls away from the cloak, and a worse tear is made. 17 Neither is new wine put into old wineskins; otherwise, the skins burst, and the wine is spilled, and the skins are destroyed; but new wine is put into fresh wineskins, and so both are preserved.

Mark 2:21 No one sews a piece of unshrunk cloth on an old garment; if he does, the patch tears away from it, the new from the old, and a worse tear is made. 22 And no one puts new wine into old wineskins; if he does, the wine will burst the skins, and the wine is lost, and so are the skins; but new wine is for fresh skins.

Luke 5:36 He told them a parable also: No one tears a piece from a new garment and puts it upon an old garment; if he does, he will tear the new, and the piece from the new will not match the old. 37 And no one puts new wine into old wineskins; if he does, the new wine will burst the skins and it will be spilled, and the skins will be destroyed. 38 But new wine must be put into fresh wineskins. 39 And no one after drinking old wine desires new; for he says, The old is good.

48. Jesus said: If two make peace with each other in this one house, they will say to the mountain: Be moved! and it will be moved.

Matthew 18:19 Again, truly I tell you, if two of you agree on earth about anything you ask, it will be done for you by my Father in heaven.

Mark 11:23 Truly I tell you, if you say to this mountain, Be taken up and thrown into the sea, and if you do not doubt in your heart, but believe that what you say will come to pass, it will be done for you. 24 So I tell you, whatever you ask for in prayer, believe that you have received it, and it will be yours.

Matthew 17:20 He said to them, Because of your little faith. For truly, I say to you, if you have faith as a grain of mustard seed, you will say to this mountain, Move from here to there, and it will move; and nothing will be impossible to you.

49. Jesus said: Blessed is the solitary and chosen, for you will find the Kingdom. You have come from it, and unto it you will return.

50. Jesus said: If they say to you: From where do you come? Say to them: We have come from the Light, the place where the Light came into existence of its own accord and he stood and appeared in their image. If they say to you: Is it you? (Who are you?), say: We are his Sons and we are the chosen of the Living Father. If they ask you: What is the sign of your Father in you? Say to them: It is movement with rest. (Peace in the midst of motion.)

51. His Disciples said to him: When will the rest of the dead occur, and when will the New World come? He said to them: That which you look for has already come, but you do not recognize it.

52. His Disciples said to him: Twenty-four prophets preached in Israel, and they all spoke of (in) you. He said to them: You have ignored the Living-One who is in your presence and you have spoken only of the dead.

53. His Disciples said to him: Is circumcision beneficial or not? He said to them: If it were beneficial, their father would beget them already circumcised from their mother. However, the true spiritual circumcision has become entirely beneficial.

54. Jesus said: Blessed be the poor, for yours is the Kingdom of the Heaven.

Matthew 6:20 Then he looked up at his disciples and said: Blessed are you who are poor, for yours is the kingdom of God.

Luke 6:20 And he lifted up his eyes on his disciples, and said: Blessed are you poor, for yours is the kingdom of God.

Matthew 5:3 Blessed are the poor in spirit, for theirs is the kingdom of heaven.

55. Jesus said: Whoever does not hate his father and his mother will not be able to become my Disciple. And whoever does not hate his brothers and his sisters and does not take up his own cross in my way, will not become worthy of me.

Matthew 10:37 Whoever loves father or mother more than me is not worthy of me; and whoever loves son or daughter more than me is not worthy of me; 38 and whoever does not take up the cross and follow me is not worthy of me.

Luke 14:26 If any one comes to me and does not hate his own father and mother and wife and children and brothers and sisters, yes, and even his own life, he cannot be my disciple. 27 Whoever does not bear his own cross and come after me, cannot be my disciple.

56. Jesus said: Whoever has come to understand the world (system) has found a corpse, and whoever has found a corpse, is superior to the world (of him the system is not worthy).

57. Jesus said: The Kingdom of the Father is like a person who has good seed. His enemy came by night and sowed a

weed among the good seed. The man did not permit them to pull up the weed, he said to them: perhaps you will intend to pull up the weed and you pull up the wheat along with it. But, on the day of harvest the weeds will be very visible and then they will pull them and burn them.

Matthew 13:24 He put before them another parable: The kingdom of heaven may be compared to someone who sowed good seed in his field; 25 but while everybody was asleep, an enemy came and sowed weeds among the wheat, and then went away. 26 So when the plants came up and bore grain, then the weeds appeared as well. 27 And the slaves of the householder came and said to him, Master, did you not sow good seed in your field? Where, then, did these weeds come from? 28 He answered, An enemy has done this. The slaves said to him, Then do you want us to go and gather them? 29 But he replied, No; for in gathering the weeds you would uproot the wheat along with them. 30 Let both of them grow together until the harvest; and at harvest time I will tell the reapers, Collect the weeds first and bind them in bundles to be burned, but gather the wheat into my barn.

58. Jesus said: Blessed is the person who has suffered, for he has found life. (Blessed is he who has suffered [to find life] and found life).

Matthew 11:28 Come to me, all you that are weary and are carrying heavy burdens, and I will give you rest.

59. Jesus said: Look to the Living-One while you are alive, otherwise, you might die and seek to see him and will be unable to find him.

John 7:34 You will search for me, but you will not find me; and where I am, you cannot come.

John 13:33 Little children, I am with you only a little longer. You will look for me; and as I said to the Jews so now I say to you, Where I am going, you cannot come.

60. They saw a Samaritan carrying a lamb, on his way to Judea. Jesus said to them: Why does he take the lamb with him? They said to him: So that he may kill it and eat it. He said to them: While it is alive he will not eat it, but only after he kills it and it becomes a corpse. They said: How could he do otherwise? He said to them: Look for a place of rest for yourselves, otherwise, you might become corpses and be eaten.

61. Jesus said: Two will rest on a bed and one will die and the other will live. Salome said: Who are you, man? As if sent by

someone, you laid upon my bed and you ate from my table. Jesus said to her: "I-Am" he who is from that which is whole (the undivided). I have been given the things of my Father. Salome said: I am your Disciple. Jesus said to her: Thus, I say that whenever someone is one (undivided) he will be filled with light, yet whenever he is divided (chooses) he will be filled with darkness.

Luke 17:34 I tell you, on that night there will be two in one bed; one will be taken and the other left.

62. Jesus said: I tell my mysteries to those who are worthy of my mysteries. Do not let your right hand know what your left hand is doing.

Mark 4:11 And he said to them, To you has been given the secret of the kingdom of God, but for those outside, everything comes in parables.

Matthew 6:3 But when you give alms, do not let your left hand know what your right hand is doing.

Luke 8:10 He said, To you it has been given to know the secrets of the kingdom of God; but for others they are in parables, so that seeing they may not see, and hearing they may not understand.

Matthew 13:10 Then the disciples came and said to him, Why do you speak to them in parables? 11 And he answered them, To you it has been given to know the secrets of the kingdom of heaven, but to them it has not been given.

63. Jesus said: There was a wealthy person who had much money, and he said: I will use my money so that I may sow and reap and replant, to fill my storehouses with grain so that I lack nothing. This was his intention (is what he thought in his heart) but that same night he died. Whoever has ears, let him hear!

Luke 12:16 Then he told them a parable: The land of a rich man produced abundantly. 17 And he thought to himself, What should I do, for I have no place to store my crops? 18 Then he said, I will do this: I will pull down my barns and build larger ones, and there I will store all my grain and my goods. 19 And I will say to my soul, Soul, you have ample goods laid up for many years; relax, eat, drink, be merry. 20 But God said to him, You fool! This very night your life is being demanded of you. And the things you have prepared, whose will they be? 21 So it is with those who store up treasures for themselves but are not rich toward God.

64. Jesus said: A person had houseguests, and when he had prepared the banquet in their honor he sent his servant to invite the guests. He went to the first, he said to him: My master invites you. He replied: I have to do business with some merchants. They are coming to see me this evening. I will go to place my orders with them. I ask to be excused from the banquet. He went to another, he said to him: My master has invited you. He replied to him: I have just bought a house and they require me for a day. I will have no spare time. He came to another, he said to him: My master invites you. He replied to him: My friend is getting married and I must arrange a banquet for him. I will not be able to come. I ask to be excused from the banquet. He went to another, he said to him: My master invites you. He replied to him: I have bought a farm. I go to receive the rent. I will not be able to come. I ask to be excused. The servant returned, he said to his master: Those whom you have invited to the banquet have excused themselves. The master said to his servant: Go out to the roads, bring those whom you find so that they may feast. And he said: Businessmen and merchants will not enter the places of my Father.

Luke 14:16 Then Jesus said to him:, Someone gave a great dinner and invited many. 17 At the time for the dinner he sent his slave to say to those who had been invited, Come; for everything is ready now. 18 But they all alike began to make excuses. The first said to him, I have bought a piece of land, and I must go out and see it; please accept my regrets. 19 Another said, I have bought five yoke of oxen, and I am going to try them out; please accept my regrets. 20 Another said, I have just been married, and therefore I cannot come. 21 So the slave returned and reported this to his master. Then the owner of the house became angry and said to his slave, Go out at once into the streets and lanes of the town and bring in the poor, the crippled, the blind, and the lame. 22 And the slave said, Sir, what you ordered has been done, and there is still room. 23 Then the master said to the slave, Go out into the roads and lanes, and compel people to come in, so that my house may be filled. 24 For I tell you, none of those who were invited will taste my dinner.

Matthew 19:23 Then Jesus said to his disciples, Truly I tell you, it will be hard for a rich person to enter the kingdom of heaven.

Matthew 22:3 and sent his servants to call those who were invited to the marriage feast; but they would not come. 4 Again he sent other servants, saying, Tell those who are invited, Behold, I have made ready my dinner, my oxen and my fat calves are killed, and everything is ready; come to the marriage feast. 5 But they made light of it and went off, one to his farm, another to his business, 6 while the rest seized his servants, treated them shamefully, and killed them. 7 The king was angry, and he sent his troops and destroyed those murderers and burned their city. 8 Then he said to his servants, The wedding is ready, but those invited were not worthy. 9 Go therefore to the thoroughfares, and invite to the marriage feast as many as you find. 10 And those servants went out into the streets and gathered all whom they found, both bad and good; so the wedding hall was filled with guests. 11 But when the king came in to look at the guests, he saw there a man who had no wedding garment; 12 and he said to him, Friend, how did *you get in here without a wedding garment? And he was speechless. 13 Then the king said to the attendants, Bind him hand and foot, and cast him into the outer darkness; there men will weep and gnash their teeth. 14 For many are called, but few are chosen.*

65. He said: A kind person who owned a vineyard leased it to tenants so that they would work it and he would receive the fruit from them. He sent his servant so that the tenants would give to him the fruit of the vineyard. They seized his servant and beat him nearly to death. The servant went, he told his master what had happened. His master said: Perhaps they did not recognize him. So, he sent another servant. The tenants beat him also. Then the owner sent his son. He said: Perhaps they will respect my son. Since the tenants knew that he was the heir to the vineyard, they seized him and killed him. Whoever has ears, let him hear!

Matthew 21:33 Listen to another parable. There was a landowner who planted a vineyard, put a fence around it, dug a wine press in it, and built a watchtower. Then he leased it to tenants and went to another country. 34 When the harvest time had come, he sent his slaves to the tenants to collect his produce. 35 But the tenants seized his slaves and beat one, killed another, and stoned another. 36 Again he sent other slaves, more than the first; and they treated them in the same way. 37 Finally he sent his son to them, saying, They will respect my son. 38 But when the tenants saw the son, they said to themselves, This is the heir; come, let us kill him and get his inheritance. 39 So they seized him, threw him out of the vineyard, and killed him.

Mark 12:1 And he began to speak to them in parables. A man planted a vineyard, and set a hedge around it, and dug a pit for the wine press, and built a tower, and let it out to tenants, and went into another country. 2 When the time came, he sent a servant to the tenants, to get from them some of the fruit of the vineyard. 3 And they took him and beat him, and sent him away empty-handed. 4 Again he sent to them another servant, and they wounded him in the head, and treated him shamefully. 5 And he sent another, and him they killed; and so with many others, some they beat and some they killed. 6 He had still one other, a beloved son; finally he sent him to them, saying, They will respect my son. 7 But those tenants said to one another, This is the heir; come, let us kill him, and the inheritance will be ours. 8 And they took him and killed him, and cast him out of the vineyard. 9 What will the owner of the vineyard do? He will come and destroy the tenants, and give the vineyard to others.

Luke 20:9 And he began to tell the people this parable: A man planted a vineyard, and let it out to tenants, and went into another country for a long while. 10 When the time came, he sent a servant to the tenants, that they should give him some of the fruit of the vineyard; but the tenants beat him, and sent him away empty-handed. 11 And he sent another servant; him also they beat and treated shamefully, and sent him away empty-handed. 12 And he sent yet a third; this one they wounded and cast out. 13 Then the owner of the vineyard said, What shall I do? I will send my beloved son; it may be they will respect him. 14 But when the tenants saw him, they said to themselves, This is the heir; let us kill him, that the inheritance may be ours. 15 And they cast him out of the vineyard and killed him. What then will the owner of the vineyard do to them? 16 He will come and destroy those tenants, and give the vineyard to others. When they heard this, they said, God forbid!

66. Jesus said: Show me the stone which the builders have rejected. It is that one that is the cornerstone (keystone).

Matthew 21:42 Jesus said to them, Have you never read in the scriptures: The very stone which the builders rejected has become the head of the corner; this was the Lord's doing, and it is marvelous in our eyes?

Mark 12:10 Have you not read this scripture: The very stone which the builders rejected has become the head of the corner; 11 this was the Lord's doing, and it is marvelous in our eyes?

Luke 20:17 But he looked at them and said, What then does this text mean: The stone that the builders rejected has become the cornerstone?

67. Jesus said: Those who know everything but themselves, lack everything. (whoever knows the all and still feels a personal lacking, he is completely deficient).

68. Jesus said: Blessed are you when you are hated and persecuted, but they themselves will find no reason why you have been persecuted.

Matthew 5:11 Blessed are you when people revile you and persecute you and utter all kinds of evil against you falsely on my account.

Luke 6:22 Blessed are you when men hate you, and when they exclude you and revile you, and cast out your name as evil, on account of the Son of man!

69. Jesus said: Blessed are those who have been persecuted in their heart these are they who have come to know the Father in truth. Jesus said: Blessed are the hungry, for the stomach of him who desires to be filled will be filled.

Matthew 5:8 Blessed are the pure in heart, for they will see God.

Luke 6:21 Blessed are you who are hungry now, for you will be filled.

70. Jesus said: If you bring forth what is within you, it will save

you. **If you do not have it within you to bring forth, that which you lack will destroy you.**

71. Jesus said: I will destroy this house, and no one will be able to build it again.

Mark 14:58 We heard him say, I will destroy this temple that is made with hands, and in three days I will build another, not made with hands.

72. A person said to him: Tell my brothers to divide the possessions of my father with me. He said to him: Oh man, who made me a divider? He turned to his Disciples, he said to them: I'm not a divider, am I?

Luke 12:13 Someone in the crowd said to him, Teacher, tell my brother to divide the family inheritance with me. 14 But he said to him, Friend, who set me to be a judge or arbitrator over you? 15 And he said to them, Take care! Be on your guard against all kinds of greed; for one's life does not consist in the abundance of possessions.

73. Jesus said: The harvest is indeed plentiful, but the workers are few. Ask the Lord to send workers for the harvest.

Matthew 9:37 Then he said to his disciples, The harvest is plentiful, but the laborers are few; 38 therefore ask the Lord of the harvest to send out laborers into his harvest.

74. He said: Lord, there are many around the well, yet there is nothing in the well. How is it that many are around the well and no one goes into it?

75. Jesus said: There are many standing at the door, but only those who are alone are the ones who will enter into the Bridal Chamber.

Matthew 22:14 For many are called, but few are chosen.

76. Jesus said: The Kingdom of the Father is like a rich merchant who found a pearl. The merchant was prudent. He sold his fortune and bought the one pearl for himself. You also, seek for his treasure which does not fail, which endures where no moth can come near to eat it nor worm to devour it.

Matthew 13:45 Again, the kingdom of heaven is like a merchant in search of fine pearls; 46 on finding one pearl of great value, he went and sold all that he had and bought it.

Matthew 6:19 Do not store up for yourselves treasures on earth, where moth and rust consume and where thieves break in and steal; 20 but store up for yourselves treasures in heaven, where neither moth nor rust consumes and where thieves do not break in and steal.

77. Jesus said: "I-Am" the Light who is over all things, "I-Am" the All. From me all came forth and to me all return (The All came from me and the All has come to me). Split wood, there am I. Lift up the stone and there you will find me.

John 8:12 Again Jesus spoke to them, saying, I am the light of the world. Whoever follows me will never walk in darkness but will have the light of life.
John 1:3 All things came into being through him, and without him not one thing came into being.

78. Jesus said: Why did you come out to the wilderness; to see a reed shaken by the wind? And to see a person dressed in fine (soft – plush) garments like your rulers and your dignitaries? They are clothed in plush garments, and they are not able to

recognize (understand) the truth.

Matthew 11:7 As they went away, Jesus began to speak to the crowds about John: What did you go out into the wilderness to look at? A reed shaken by the wind? 8 What then did you go out to see? Someone dressed in soft robes? Look, those who wear soft robes are in royal palaces. 9 What then did you go out to see? A prophet? Yes, I tell you, and more than a prophet.

79. A woman from the multitude said to him: Blessed is the womb which bore you, and the breasts which nursed you! He said to her: Blessed are those who have heard the word (meaning) of the Father and have truly kept it. For there will be days when you will say: Blessed be the womb which has not conceived and the breasts which have not nursed.

Luke 11:27 While he was saying this, a woman in the crowd raised her voice and said to him, Blessed is the womb that bore you and the breasts that nursed you! 28 But he said, Blessed rather are those who hear the word of God and obey it!

Luke 23:29 For the days are surely coming when they will say, Blessed are the barren, and the wombs that never bore, and the breasts that never nursed.

80. Jesus said: Whoever has come to understand (recognize) the world (world system) has found a corpse, and whoever has found the corpse, of him the world (world system) is not worthy.

81. Jesus said: Whoever has become rich should reign, and let whoever has power renounce it.

82. Jesus said: Whoever is close to me is close to the fire, and whoever is far from me is far from the Kingdom.

83. Jesus said: Images are visible to man but the light which is within them is hidden. The light of the father will be revealed, but he (his image) is hidden in the light.

84. Jesus said: When you see your reflection, you rejoice. Yet when you perceive your images which have come into being before you, which neither die nor can be seen, how much will you have to bear?

85. Jesus said: Adam came into existence from a great power and a great wealth, and yet he was not worthy of you. For if he had been worthy, he would not have tasted death.

86. Jesus said: The foxes have their dens and the birds have their nests, yet the Son of Man has no place to lay his head for rest.

Matthew 8:20 And Jesus said to him, Foxes have holes, and birds of the air have nests; but the Son of Man has nowhere to lay his head.

87. Jesus said: Wretched is the body which depends upon another body, and wretched is the soul which depends on these two (upon their being together).

88. Jesus said: The angels and the prophets will come to you, and what they will give you what belongs to you. And you will give them what you have, and say among yourselves: When will they come to take (receive) what belongs to them?

89. Jesus said: Why do you wash the outside of your cup? Do you not understand (mind) that He who creates the inside is also He who creates the outside?

Luke 11:39 Then the Lord said to him, Now you Pharisees clean the outside of the cup and of the dish, but inside you are full of greed and wickedness. 40 You fools! Did not the one who made the outside make the inside also?

90. Jesus said: Come unto me, for my yoke is comfortable (natural) and my lordship is gentle— and you will find rest for yourselves.

Matthew 11:28 Come to me, all you that are weary and are carrying heavy burdens, and I will give you rest. 29 Take my yoke upon you, and learn from me; for I am gentle and humble in heart, and you will find rest for your souls. 30 For my yoke is easy, and my burden is light.

91. They said to him: Tell us who you are, so that we may believe

in you. He said to them: You examine the face of the sky and of the earth, yet you do not recognize Him who is here with you, and you do not know how to seek in (to inquire of Him at) this moment (you do not know how to take advantage of this opportunity).

John 9:36 He answered, And who is he, sir? Tell me, so that I may believe in him.

Luke 12:54 He also said to the crowds, When you see a cloud rising in the west, you immediately say, It is going to rain; and so it happens. 55 And when you see the south wind blowing, you say, There will be scorching heat; and it happens. 56 You hypocrites! You know how to interpret the appearance of earth and sky, but why do you not know how to interpret the present time?

92. Jesus said: Seek and you will find. But in the past I did not answer the questions you asked. Now I wish to tell them to you, but you do not ask about (no longer seek) them.

Matthew 7:7 Ask, and it will be given you; search, and you will find; knock, and the door will be opened for you.

93. Jesus said: Do not give what is sacred to the dogs, lest they throw it on the dung heap. Do not cast the pearls to the swine, lest they cause it to become dung (mud).

Matthew 7:6 Do not give what is holy to dogs; and do not throw your pearls before swine, or they will trample them under foot and turn and maul you.

94. Jesus said: Whoever seeks will find. And whoever knocks, it will be opened to him.

Matthew 7:8 For everyone who asks receives, and everyone who searches finds, and for everyone who knocks, the door will be opened.

95. Jesus said: If you have money, do not lend at interest, but rather give it to those from whom you will not be repaid.

Luke 6:34 If you lend to those from whom you hope to receive, what credit is that to you? Even sinners lend to sinners, to receive as much again. 35 But love your enemies, do good, and lend, expecting nothing in return. Your reward will be great, and you will be children of the Most High; for he is kind to the ungrateful and the wicked.

96. Jesus said: The Kingdom of the Father is like a woman who has taken a little yeast and hidden it in dough. She produced large loaves of it. Whoever has ears, let him hear!

Matthew 13:33 He told them another parable: The kingdom of heaven is like yeast that a woman took and mixed in with three measures of flour until all of it was leavened.

97. Jesus said: The Kingdom of the Father is like a woman who was carrying a jar full of grain. While she was walking on a road far from home, the handle of the jar broke and the grain poured out behind her onto the road. She did not know it. She had noticed no problem. When she arrived in her house, she set the jar down and found it empty.

98. Jesus said: The Kingdom of the Father is like someone who wished to slay a prominent person. While still in his own house

he drew his sword and thrust it into the wall in order to test whether his hand would be strong enough. Then he slew the prominent person.

99. His Disciples said to him: Your brethren and your mother are standing outside. He said to them: Those here who do my Father's desires are my Brethren and my Mother. It is they who will enter the Kingdom of my Father.

Matthew 12:46 While he was still speaking to the crowds, his mother and his brothers were standing outside, wanting to speak to him. 47 Someone told him, Look, your mother and your brothers are standing outside, wanting to speak to you. 48 But to the one who had told him this, Jesus replied, Who is my mother, and who are my brothers? 49 And pointing to his disciples, he said, Here are my mother and my brothers! 50 For whoever does the will of my Father in heaven is my brother and sister and mother.

100. They showed Jesus a gold coin, and said to him: The agents of Caesar extort taxes from us. He said to them: Give the things of Caesar to Caesar, give the things of God to God, and give to me what is mine.

Mark 12:14 Is it lawful to pay taxes to the emperor, or not? 15 Should we pay them, or should we not? But knowing their hypocrisy, he said to them,

Why are you putting me to the test? Bring me a denarius and let me see it. 16 And they brought one. Then he said to them, Whose head is this, and whose title? They answered, The emperor's. 12:17 Jesus said to them, Give to the emperor the things that are the emperor's, and to God the things that are God's. And they were utterly amazed at him.

101. Jesus said: Whoever does not hate his father and his mother as I do, will not be able to become my Disciple. And whoever does not love his Father and his Mother as I do, will not be able to become my Disciple. For my mother bore me, yet my true Mother gave me the life.

Matthew 10:37 Whoever loves father or mother more than me is not worthy of me; and whoever loves son or daughter more than me is not worthy of me.

102. Jesus said: Damn these Pharisees. They are like a dog sleeping in the feed trough of oxen. For neither does he eat, nor does he allow the oxen to eat.

Matthew 2:.13 But woe unto you, scribes and Pharisees, hypocrites! because you shut the kingdom of heaven against men; for you neither enter yourselves, nor allow those who would enter to go in.

103. Jesus said: Blessed is the person who knows at what place of the house the bandits may break in, so that he can rise and collect his things and prepare himself before they enter.

Matthew 24:43 But understand this: if the owner of the house had known in what part of the night the thief was coming, he would have stayed awake and would not have let his house be broken into.

104. They said to him: Come, let us pray today and let us fast. Jesus said: What sin have I committed? How have I been overcome (undone)? When the Bridegroom comes forth from the Bridal Chamber, then let them fast and let them pray.

105. Jesus said: Whoever acknowledges (comes to know) father and mother, will be called the son of a whore.

106. Jesus said: When you make the two one, you will become Sons of Man (children of Adam), and when you say to the mountain: Move! It will move.

Mark 11:23 Truly I tell you, if you say to this mountain, Be taken up and thrown into the sea, and if you do not doubt in your heart, but believe that what you say will come to pass, it will be done for you.

107. Jesus said: The Kingdom is like a shepherd who has a hundred sheep. The largest one of them went astray. He left the ninety-nine and sought for the one until he found it. Having searched until he was weary, he said to that sheep: I desire you more than the ninety-nine.

Matthew 18:12 What do you think? If a shepherd has a hundred sheep, and one of them has gone astray, does he not leave the ninety-nine on the mountains and go in search of the one that went astray? 13 And if he finds it, truly I tell you, he rejoices over it more than over the ninety-nine that never went astray.

108. Jesus said: Whoever drinks from my mouth will become like me. I will become him, and the secrets will be revealed to him.

109. Jesus said: The Kingdom is like a person who had a treasure hidden in his field and knew nothing of it. After he died, he bequeathed it to his son. The son accepted the field knowing nothing of the treasure. He sold it. Then the person who bought it came and plowed it. He found the treasure. He began to lend money at interest to whomever he wished.

Matthew 13:44 The kingdom of heaven is like treasure hidden in a field, which someone found and hid; then in his joy he goes and sells all that he has and buys that field.

110. Jesus said: Whoever has found the world (system) and becomes wealthy (enriched by it), let him renounce the world (system).

Mark 10:21 Then Jesus beholding him loved him, and said unto him, One thing thou lackest: go thy way, sell whatsoever thou hast, and give to the poor, and thou shalt have treasure in heaven: and come, take up the cross, and follow me. 22 And he was sad at that saying, and went away grieved: for he had great possessions. 23 And Jesus looked round about, and saith unto his disciples, How hardly shall they that have riches enter into the kingdom of God!

111. Jesus said: Heaven and earth will roll up before you, but he who lives within the Living-One will neither see nor fear death. For, Jesus said: Whoever finds himself, of him the world is not worthy.

112. Jesus said: Damned is the flesh which depends upon the soul. Damned is the soul which depends upon the flesh.

113. His Disciples said to him: When will the Kingdom come?

Jesus said: It will not come by expectation (because you watch or wait for it). They will not say: Look here! or: Look there! But the Kingdom of the Father is spread upon the earth, and people do not realize it.

Luke 17:20 And when he was demanded of by the Pharisees, when the kingdom of God should come, he answered them and said, The kingdom of God cometh not with observation: Neither shall they say, Lo-Here! Lo-There! For, behold, the kingdom of God is within you.

(Saying 114 was written later and was added to the original text.)
114. Simon Peter said to them: Send Mary away from us, for women are not worthy of this life. Jesus said: Behold, I will draw her into me so that I make her male, in order that she herself will become a living spirit like you males. For every female who becomes male will enter the Kingdom of the Heavens.

The Passion Narrative

According to tradition, Mark was not one of the original apostles, but rather a follower of one of them. Church historians tell us he followed Peter. One account places Mark in Rome, but another has him located at Alexandria. Since Mark supposedly wrote and translated for Peter, the story that we call Mark's gospel could have been derived from Peter. Whoever wrote the gospel attributed to Mark used several oral traditions, some of which had passed into written form, as components to construct the story. One of these sources is called the Passion Narrative.

Judging from its language and content, most scholars believe The Passion Narrative was written between 30 A.D. and 60 A.D. Mark used the document to construct the story of Jesus' trial, crucifixion, and burial. In Mark we can see the chronology behind the text.

There is lack of historical consistency between John and the other gospels. Because of the apparent discrepancy between the synoptic Gospels of Matthew, Mark and Luke and the Gospel of John one could argue there is evidence of differences in sources between John on one hand, and the synoptic gospels on the other. Since there are great differences it leaves one to hypothesize there could be at least two oral traditions containing the passion of Jesus. Either or both stories could have been preserved in written form and used by Mark, with his source and John with his separate source.

138

One such variance is the day Jesus died.

In the synoptic Gospels, Jesus offers the Lord's Supper "on the first day of unleavened bread, when they sacrificed the Passover lamb" (Mark 14:12; cf. Matt. 26:17, Luke 22:7). That would mean Jesus said the first Mass on Thursday, the fourteenth of Nisan. This was "the day of preparation" for the Passover when the lambs were slain and the meal prepared to be eaten in the evening according to Ex. 12:6. However, John tells us that Jesus was crucified on the "day of preparation" in John 19:31. That would seem to make Friday, the fourteenth of Nisan, the day of preparation. Saturday would then have been both the Sabbath and the Passover.

John's gospel is different in many respects from Matthew, Mark and Luke.

In John's gospel Jesus tells no parables, and speaks in a poetic style very different from his "voice" in the synoptic gospels. Another difference: in Matthew, Mark and Luke, the central moment of Jesus' "last supper" comes when he takes bread and wine and says "This is my body, this is my blood." This event isn't even mentioned in the gospel of John, which instead speaks of Jesus' washing his disciples' feet as the significant moment of this final meal.

In John's gospel, the "last supper" is described as a meal that takes place before the Passover (John 13:1). In John's gospel, Jesus dies on the cross on Passover. This enables John to make the theological and spiritual point that Jesus, the true "Lamb of God," dies at the exact hour the lambs that will be used for the Passover meals are being sacrificed in the Temple.

Although some have speculated that Jesus may have followed the Jewish sect called the Essenes, and they celebrated the Passover on a slightly different date, this would assume the authors jumped back and forth regarding dates without mentioning why or even mentioning the small sect at all. Even if it is true that all Jews in Jerusalem would not have been eating their Passover meal on exactly the same evening, it may not excuse the differences between the gospels.

The discrepancy in dating is perhaps best explained with the realization that the author of the gospel of John was using a different source in the writing of his gospel.

There is some evidence the source used by Mark, and carried over into Matthew, was Aramaic in origin.

When Jesus cries out to God, saying "My God, My God, why have you forsaken me, he uses the words "ELOI, ELOI, LAMA SABACHTHA or ELI, ELI, LAMA SABACHTHANI.

e'-loi, e-lo'i, la'-ma, sa-bakh-tha'-ni, or (Eloi, eloi, lama sabachthanei):

The forms of the first word as translated vary in the two narratives between Mark and Matthew.

The utterance is a variance of form probably from Psalms 22:1 ('eli 'eli lamah `azabhtani).

Psalm 22

New King James Version (NKJV)

The Suffering, Praise, and Posterity of the Messiah

To the Chief Musician. Set to "The Deer of the Dawn." A Psalm of David.

22 My God, My God, why have You forsaken Me?

Why are You so far from helping Me,

And from the words of My groaning?

O My God, I cry in the daytime, but You do not hear;

And in the night season, and am not silent.

The statement uttered by Jesus on the cross minutes before his death, just as from King David, is translated, "My God, my God, why hast thou forsaken me?" (Matthew 27:46; Mark 15:34). But there is a problem with this passage. There seems to be a mixture of Aramaic and Hebrew words.

The first two words, whether in Hebrew or Aramaic have different meanings to the crowd to warrant the jeer that Jesus was calling upon Elias, and not God. Mark gives the phrase and then explains to those who do not fully understand the language, that he was not calling on Elias, but on God.

According to Westcott and Hort's, *The New Testament in Greek*:

"The forms lema and lama used in Matthew and Mark respectively represent the various possible forms, the first in Aramaic, and the second in Hebrew.

The various readings and translations of the latter word, sabachthani, certainly has the influence of the Aramaic. Aramaic plays such a large part in the translation and transmission of the original meaning that it has led some to speculate that Mark's source for the passion of Jesus was likely in Aramaic. Mark would have written the phrase for the edification of the readers, not to confuse them."

There are other differences, between the synoptic gospels and John, which indicate not only a different source, but also a period of time the sources were written. One such point is the way Pilate is treated. Writers were well advised not to mention the names of powerful people in a negative context". By contrast, as shown by Philo and Josephus, Pilate "was the subject of more negative tradition than many other prefects and procurators," and so the creators of the original passion narrative had no reason not to mention Pilate by name and to place blame upon him. This situation is changed in the period after the First Jewish Revolt in the writings of Matthew and Luke, in which Pilate is exonerated and the high priest is named without hesitation.

On the naming of "James the younger," Theissen writes, "It would have been particularly necessary in Jerusalem to distinguish a 'James the younger' (or 'the less') from the 'older' (or 'greater') bearers of that name in the period circa 30-65 C.E."

Concerning the story of Barabbas, Theissen comments, "the text speaks quite simply of '*the* rebels,' who were taken prisoner during '*the* insurrection.' . . . We can only suppose that the text was composed before the next great uprising; after that, the author would have 'historicized' the account by distinguishing the previous 'stasis' from the more recent one. The next unrest with bloody clashes that struck Jerusalem was the appearance of Theudas under Cuspius Fadus (44-45 C.E.; cf. Acts 5:36, *Ant.* 20.97-98)."

Finally, there are two anonymous people in the story: the bystander who cuts off the ear of the high priest's slave with a sword (Mk 14:47) and a young man who escapes arrest by running away (Mk 14:51-52). Theissen writes (pp. 186-187):

"It seems to me that the narrative motive for this anonymity is not hard to guess: both of them run afoul of the "police." The one who draws his sword commits no minor offense when he cuts off someone's ear. Had the blow fallen only slightly awry, he could have wounded the man in the head or throat. This blow with a sword is violence with possibly mortal consequences. The anonymous young man has also offered resistance. In the struggle, his clothes are torn off, so that he has to run away naked. Both these people were in danger in the aftermath. As long as the high priest's slave was alive (and as long as the scar from the sword cut was visible) it would have been inopportune to mention their names; it would not even have been wise to identify them as members of the early Christian community. Their anonymity is for their protection, and the obscuring of their positive relationship to Jesus is a strategy of caution. Both the teller and the hearers know more about these two people. Only they could tell us who they were, whether Peter was the one with the sword, whether both are the same person, and whether reference was made to them in order to make the story of Jesus' end more credible."

Later, John would reveal it was Peter that cut the ear off the man, as we read in John 18:26-27. Being written around 130 A.D, enough time had passed there was no danger to Peter if the details were revealed or a name was added to the story.

Theissen writes: "If we are correct in our hypothesis of protective anonymity, the location of the Passion tradition would be unmistakable. Only in Jerusalem was there reason to draw a cloak of anonymity over followers of Jesus who had endangered themselves by their actions. The date could also be pinpointed: parts of the Passion account would have to have been composed within the generation of the eyewitnesses and their contemporaries, that is, somewhere between 30 and 60 C.E."

Although any one of these lines of evidence could be dismissed as coincidence, Theissen manages to create a series of plausible connections that make a case as a whole for the existence of an early pre-Markan passion narrative.

Where the passion story, or its source, ends is the final question. There are two theories. The first one is that it ended with the confession of the centurion. The second one is that the story ended with the appearance of Jesus to the disciples, which took place in Galilee.

By examining the language, word choices, structure, and flow of the Gospel of Mark, scholars have attempted to reconstruct the passion source.

Now, let us take a look at the Passion Narrative. The following depends on the Young's Literal Translation of the passion narrative in the Gospel of Mark, verses 14:32-15:47.

The Passion Narrative of Mark

Mark 14:32 And they come to a spot, the name of which [is] Gethsemane, and he saith to his disciples, `Sit ye here till I may pray;'

14:33 and he taketh Peter, and James, and John with him, and began to be amazed, and to be very heavy,

14:34 and he saith to them, `Exceeding sorrowful is my soul -- to death; remain here, and watch.'

14:35 And having gone forward a little, he fell upon the earth, and was praying, that, if it be possible the hour may pass from him,

14:36 and he said, `Abba, Father; all things are possible to Thee; make this cup pass from me; but, not what I will, but what Thou.'

14:37 And he cometh, and findeth them sleeping, and saith to Peter, `Simon, thou dost sleep! thou wast not able to watch one hour!

14:38 Watch ye and pray, that ye may not enter into temptation; the spirit indeed is forward, but the flesh weak.'

14:39 And again having gone away, he prayed, the same word saying;

14:40 and having returned, he found them again sleeping, for their eyes were heavy, and they had not known what they might answer him.

14:41 And he cometh the third time, and saith to them, `Sleep on henceforth, and rest -- it is over; the hour did come; lo, the Son of Man is delivered up to the hands of the sinful;

14:42 rise, we may go, lo, he who is delivering me up hath come nigh.'

14:43 And immediately -- while he is yet speaking -- cometh near Judas, one of the twelve, and with him a great multitude, with swords and sticks, from the chief priests, and the scribes, and the elders;

14:44 and he who is delivering him up had given a token to them, saying, `Whomsoever I shall kiss, he it is, lay hold on him, and lead him away safely,'

14:45 and having come, immediately, having gone near him, he saith, `Rabbi, Rabbi,' and kissed him.

14:46 And they laid on him their hands, and kept hold on him;

14:47 and a certain one of those standing by, having drawn the sword, struck the servant of the chief priest, and took off his ear.

14:48 And Jesus answering said to them, `As against a robber ye came out, with swords and sticks, to take me!

14:49 daily I was with you in the temple teaching, and ye did not lay hold on me -- but that the Writings may be fulfilled.'

14:50 And having left him they all fled;

14:51 and a certain young man was following him, having put a linen cloth about [his] naked body, and the young men lay hold on him,

14:52 and he, having left the linen cloth, did flee from them naked.

14:53 And they led away Jesus unto the chief priest, and come together to him do all the chief priests, and the elders, and the scribes;

14:54 and Peter afar off did follow him, to the inside of the hall of the chief priest, and he was sitting with the officers, and warming himself near the fire.

14:55 And the chief priests and all the sanhedrim were seeking against Jesus testimony -- to put him to death, and they were not finding,

14:56 for many were bearing false testimony against him, and their testimonies were not alike.

14:57 And certain having risen up, were bearing false testimony against him, saying --

14:58 `We heard him saying -- I will throw down this sanctuary made with hands, and by three days, another made without hands I will build;'

14:59 and neither so was their testimony alike.

14:60 And the chief priest, having risen up in the midst, questioned Jesus, saying, `Thou dost not answer anything! what do these testify against thee?'

14:61 and he was keeping silent, and did not answer anything. Again the chief priest was questioning him, and saith to him, `Art thou the Christ -- the Son of the Blessed?'

14:62 and Jesus said, `I am; and ye shall see the Son of Man sitting on the right hand of the power, and coming with the clouds, of the heaven.'

14:63 And the chief priest, having rent his garments, saith, `What need have we yet of witnesses?

14:64 Ye heard the evil speaking, what appeareth to you?' and they all condemned him to be worthy of death,

14:65 and certain began to spit on him, and to cover his face, and to buffet him, and to say to him, `Prophesy;' and the officers were striking him with their palms.

14:66 And Peter being in the hall beneath, there doth come one of the maids of the chief priest,

14:67 and having seen Peter warming himself, having looked on him, she said, `And thou wast with Jesus of Nazareth!'

14:68 and he denied, saying, `I have not known [him], neither do I understand what thou sayest;' and he went forth without to the porch, and a cock crew.

14:69 And the maid having seen him again, began to say to those standing near -- `This is of them;'

14:70 and he was again denying. And after a little again, those standing near said to Peter, `Truly thou art of them, for thou also art a Galilean, and thy speech is alike;'

14:71 and he began to anathematize, and to swear -- `I have not known this man of whom ye speak;'

14:72 and a second time a cock crew, and Peter remembered the saying that Jesus said to him -- `Before a cock crow twice, thou mayest deny me thrice;' and having thought thereon -- he was weeping.

15:1 And immediately, in the morning, the chief priests having made a consultation, with the elders, and scribes, and the whole sanhedrim, having bound Jesus, did lead away, and delivered [him] to Pilate;

15:2 and Pilate questioned him, `Art thou the king of the Jews?' and he answering said to him, `Thou dost say it.'

15:3 And the chief priests were accusing him of many things, [but he answered nothing.]

15:4 And Pilate again questioned him, saying, `Thou dost not answer anything! lo, how many things they do testify against thee!'

15:5 and Jesus did no more answer anything, so that Pilate wondered.

15:6 And at every feast he was releasing to them one prisoner, whomsoever they were asking;

15:7 and there was [one] named Barabbas, bound with those making insurrection with him, who had in the insurrection committed murder.

15:8 And the multitude having cried out, began to ask for themselves as he was always doing to them,

15:9 and Pilate answered them, saying, `Will ye [that] I shall release to you the king of the Jews?'

15:10 for he knew that because of envy the chief priests had delivered him up;

15:11 and the chief priests did move the multitude, that he might rather release Barabbas to them.

15:12 And Pilate answering, again said to them, `What, then, will ye [that] I shall do to him whom ye call king of the Jews?'

15:13 and they again cried out, `Crucify him.'

15:14 And Pilate said to them, `Why -- what evil did he?' and they cried out the more vehemently, `Crucify him;'

15:15 and Pilate, wishing to content the multitude, released to them Barabbas, and delivered up Jesus -- having scourged [him] -- that he might be crucified.

15:16 And the soldiers led him away into the hall, which is Praetorium, and call together the whole band,

15:17 and clothe him with purple, and having plaited a crown of thorns, they put [it] on him,

15:18 and began to salute him, `Hail, King of the Jews.'

15:19 And they were smiting him on the head with a reed, and were spitting on him, and having bent the knee, were bowing to him,

15:20 and when they [had] mocked him, they took the purple from off him, and clothed him in his own garments, and they led him forth, that they may crucify him.

15:21 And they impress a certain one passing by -- Simon, a Cyrenian, coming from the field, the father of Alexander and Rufus -- that he may bear his cross,

15:22 and they bring him to the place Golgotha, which is, being interpreted, `Place of a skull;'

15:23 and they were giving him to drink wine mingled with myrrh, and he did not receive.

15:24 And having crucified him, they were dividing his garments, casting a lot upon them, what each may take;

15:25 and it was the third hour, and they crucified him;

15:26 and the inscription of his accusation was written above -- `The King of the Jews.'

15:27 And with him they crucify two robbers, one on the right hand, and one on his left,

15:29 And those passing by were speaking evil of him, shaking their heads, and saying, `Ah, the thrower down of the sanctuary, and in three days the builder!

15:30 save thyself, and come down from the cross!'

15:31 And in like manner also the chief priests, mocking with one another, with the scribes, said, `Others he saved; himself he is not able to save.

15:32 The Christ! the king of Israel -- let him come down now from the cross, that we may see and believe;' and those crucified with him were reproaching him.

15:33 And the sixth hour having come, darkness came over the whole land till the ninth hour,

15:34 and at the ninth hour Jesus cried with a great voice, saying, `Eloi, Eloi, lamma sabachthani?' which is, being interpreted, `My God, my God, why didst Thou forsake me?'

15:35 And certain of those standing by, having heard, said, `Lo, Elijah he doth call;'

15:36 and one having run, and having filled a spunge with vinegar, having put [it] also on a reed, was giving him to drink, saying, `Let alone, let us see if Elijah doth come to take him down.'

15:37 And Jesus having uttered a loud cry, yielded the spirit,

15:38 and the veil of the sanctuary was rent in two, from top to bottom,

15:39 and the centurion who was standing over-against him, having seen that, having so cried out, he yielded the spirit, said, `Truly this man was Son of God.'

15:40 And there were also women afar off beholding, among whom was also Mary the Magdalene, and Mary of James the less, and of Joses, and Salome,

15:41 (who also, when he was in Galilee, were following him, and were ministering to him,) and many other women who came up with him to Jerusalem.

15:42 And now evening having come, seeing it was the preparation, that is, the fore-sabbath,

15:43 Joseph of Arimathea, an honourable counsellor, who also himself was waiting for the reign of God, came, boldly entered in unto Pilate, and asked the body of Jesus.

15:44 And Pilate wondered if he were already dead, and having called near the centurion, did question him if he were long dead,

15:45 and having known [it] from the centurion, he granted the body to Joseph.

15:46 And he, having brought fine linen, and having taken him down, wrapped him in the linen, and laid him in a sepulchre that had been hewn out of a rock, and he rolled a stone unto the door of the sepulchre,

15:47 and Mary the Magdalene, and Mary of Joses, were beholding where he is laid.

Mark

We have covered much regarding Mark, but let us recap briefly. The Gospel of Mark was written between 60 and 100 A.D. (with most scholars agreeing on 65 – 75 AD) by a person calling himself Mark, to whom Peter was recounting memories of his time with Jesus. Peter's memory, like most of ours, was freely running from one memory to another, as memories are chained together loosely and not in chronological order.

It also appears that Mark had access to the first parts of Q, or Q1 and maybe Q2, but not Q3. This leads us to wonder how much of Mark was built upon Peter's dictation and how much was taken from Q. It also appears that the Passion Narrative was used to set the times and order for the suffering and death of Jesus. Again, the question occurs of why the narrative was used and how much Peter remembered on his own. One could also ask the question suggesting that Peter or one of his acquaintances in the Jesus movement wrote part of Q and/or the Passion Narrative.

Justin Martyr spoke of Mark as being the memoirs of Peter (Dial. 106.3). In Acts 10:34-40, Peter's speech serves as a good summary of the Gospel of Mark, "beginning in Galilee after the baptism that John preached."

The NAB introduction to Mark says: "Petrine influence should not, however, be exaggerated. The evangelist has put together various oral and possibly written sources--miracle stories, parables, sayings, stories of controversies, and the passion--so as to speak of the crucified Messiah for Mark's own day."

John P. Meier states, "Prior to Mark's Gospel there seems to have been two cycles of traditions about Jesus' ministry in Galilee, each one beginning with one version of the feeding miracle (Mk 6:32-44 and Mk 8:1-10). Before these cycles were created, the two versions of the feeding would have circulated as independent units, the first version attracting to itself the story of Jesus' walking on the water (a development also witnessed in John 6), while the second version did not receive such an elaboration. Behind all three versions of the miracle story would have stood some primitive form."

Randel Helms writes concerning Mark 11:1 (Who Wrote the Gospels?, p. 6): "Anyone approaching Jerusalem from Jericho would come first to Bethany and then Bethphage, not the reverse. This is one of several passages showing that Mark knew little about Palestine; we must assume, Dennis Nineham argues, that 'Mark did not know the relative positions of these two villages on the Jericho road' (1963, 294-295). Indeed, Mark knew so little about the area that he described Jesus going from Tyrian territory 'by way of Sidon to the Sea of Galilee through the territory of the Ten Towns' (Mark 7:31). The simplist solution, says Nineham, is that 'the evangelist was not directly acquainted with Palestine'"

Although most place the date of Mark to be around 70 A.D. Others point to a single verse, which, if interpreted in a certain light would advance the date greatly. Verse 14 says: "When you see the 'Abomination of Desecration' standing where it should not be - let the reader take note! - those in Judea must flee to the mountains." The parenthetical comment to "let the reader take note" underscores the fact that this speech was written for the Christians of Mark's time. The contemporary audience of Mark would understand very well what he was talking about, although the 'Abomination of Desecration' is a cryptic reference to modern readers. The phrase is borrowed from Dn 9:27, where it refers to Antiochus profaning the Temple of Jerusalem c. 165 BC (probably with an image of Zeus), although it has been adapted to the evangelist's times. In the context of the First Jewish Revolt, this probably refers to the profanation of the Temple by the Romans. Josephus tells us that the victorious soldiers raised their imperial standards and worshiped them in the holy place (Wars of the Jews 6.6.1).

There is a significant modification to the end of Mark. Some time, just after it was penned and before many copies were made, through accident or mistreatment, the last page of one of the few copies of Mark was destroyed. New endings were added to several of the manuscripts as the damaged manuscript was copied. No less than four different endings have been found to the Gospel of Mark. It is thought the gospel ended simply, with the disciples going forth to teach and preach. The earliest manuscripts and some other ancient witnesses do not have verses 9–20.

Mark 16:9 When Jesus rose early on the first day of the week, he appeared first to Mary Magdalene, out of whom he had driven seven demons. 10 She went and told those who had been with him and who were mourning and weeping. 11 When they heard that Jesus was alive and that she had seen him, they did not believe it.

12 Afterward Jesus appeared in a different form to two of them while they were walking in the country. 13 These returned and reported it to the rest; but they did not believe them either.

14 Later Jesus appeared to the Eleven as they were eating; he rebuked them for their lack of faith and their stubborn refusal to believe those who had seen him after he had risen.

15 He said to them, "Go into all the world and preach the gospel to all creation. 16 Whoever believes and is baptized will be saved, but whoever does not believe will be condemned. 17 And these signs will accompany those who believe: In my name they will drive out demons; they will speak in new tongues; 18 they will pick up snakes with their hands; and when they drink deadly poison, it will not hurt them at all; they will place their hands on sick people, and they will get well."

19 After the Lord Jesus had spoken to them, he was taken up into heaven and he sat at the right hand of God. 20 Then the disciples went out and preached everywhere, and the Lord worked with them and confirmed his word by the signs that accompanied it.

Some manuscripts have the following ending between verses 8 and 9, and one manuscript has it after verse 8 (omitting verses 9-20):

Then they quickly reported all these instructions to those around Peter. After this, Jesus himself also sent out through them from east to west the sacred and imperishable proclamation of eternal salvation. Amen.

The church settled on the ending of Mark we now use because it was powerful and it became the best known ending. The fact it did not appear in the original version may explain why every year the snake handling churches bury members who have died from snake bite and drinking poison.

Matthew

If Matthew used Mark as a source, the Gospel of Matthew must have been written after Mark. Scholars place the writing of Matthew between 80 and 100 A.D.

Matthew was written in Greek using Mark, Q , and the Septuagint as its sources. This is not what Eusebias tells us Papias said in his book. But then Eusebias tells us Papias was not very intelligent, and in Eusebias' opinion Papias was wrong in some of his assumptions, having misinterpreted information from various interviews of visitors to his area. No evidence has been found that points to Matthew being written in Hebrew, but it is not impossible that someone translated the book into Hebrew for their own use but it is more likely that the person referred to by Papias is not the Matthew we know.

Having first seen the construction of Mark, using the narrative Peter gave dictated to him, and part of the Q document to spur memory, we can now turn to Matthew and Luke, who used Mark as their foundation.

In 1951 B.H. Streeter set about to find how much of the Gospel of Mark was within the Gospel of Matthew. Taking a fresh approach to the language and structure he found that out of 666 verses in Mark, 600 of them occurred in Matthew. Hundreds of times the same words were used in the same order. Matthew is an expansion of Mark.

Herman N. Ridderbos writes (Matthew, p. 7):

This means, however, that we can no longer accept the traditional view of Matthew's authorship. At least two things forbid us to do so. First, the tradition maintains that Matthew authored an Aramaic writing, while the standpoint I have adopted does not allow us to regard our Greek text as a translation of an Aramaic original. Second, it is extremely doubtful that an eyewitness like the apostle Matthew would have made such extensive use of material as a comparison of the two Gospels indicates. Mark, after all, did not even belong to the circle of the apostles. Indeed Matthew's Gospel surpasses those of the other synoptic writers neither in vividness of presentation nor in detail, as we would expect in an eyewitness report, yet neither Mark nor Luke had been among those who had followed Jesus from the beginning of His public ministry.

J. C. Fenton argues (The Gospel of Saint Matthew, p. 12):

It is usually thought that Mark's Gospel was written about A.D. 65 and that the author of it was neither one of the apostles nor an eyewitness of the majority of the events recorded in his Gospel. Matthew was therefore dependent on the writing of such a man for the production of his book. What Matthew has done, in fact, is to produce a second and enlarged edition of Mark. Moreover, the changes which he makes in Mark's way of telling the story are not those corrections which an eyewitness might make in the account of one who was not an eyewitness. Thus, whereas in Mark's Gospel we may be only one removed from eyewitnesses, in Matthew's Gospel we are at one removed further still.

Francis Write Beare notes (The Gospel according to Matthew, p. 7):

But the dependence of the book upon documentary sources is so great as to forbid us to look upon it as the work of any immediate disciple of Jesus. Apart from that, there are clear indications that it is a product of the second or third Christian generation. The traditional name of Matthew is retained in modern discussion only for convenience.

As for dating of the Gospel of Matthew, J.C. Fenton summarizes the evidence for the dating of Matthew as follows (op. cit., p. 11):

The earliest surviving writings which quote this Gospel are probably the letters of Ignatius, the Bishop of Antioch, who, while being taken as prisoner from the East to Rome about A.D. 110, wrote to various churches in Asia and Asia Minor and to the church at Rome. Ignatius refers to the star which appeared at the time of the birth of Jesus, the answer of Jesus to John the Baptist, when he was baptized, and several sayings of Jesus which are recorded only in this Gospel (12:33, 15:13, 19:12). It seems almost certain that Ignatius, and possibly the recipients of his letters also, knew this

Gospel, and thus that it was written before A.D. 110. But how long before?

Here we cannot be so certain. But it is possible that we can find evidence that Matthew was writing after the war between the Romans and the Jews which ended in the destruction of the temple at Jerusalem in A.D. 70. See, for example, 22:7: The king was angry, and he sent his troops and destroyed those murderers and burned their city; and compare also 21:41, 27:25. Similarly, Matthew's Gospel contains a strongly anti-Jewish note running through it, from the teaching not to do as the hypocrites do in Chapter 6, to the Woes on the scribes and Pharisees in Chapter 23; and this may point to a date after c. A.D. 85 when the Christians were excluded from the Jewish synagogues. It is worth noting here that Matthew often speaks of their synagogues (4:23, 9:35, 10:17, 12:9, 13:54), as if to distinguish Christian meetings and meeting places from those of the Jews, from which the Christians had now been turned out.

When a source is used the author will attempt to make the scenes, meanings, and information clearer and sharper to the reader. Ambiguities will be removed and meanings sharpened. One can see this in the scene of Jesus' baptism.

In Q (or the Sayings Gospel), as in Thomas, we see Jesus as a wise teacher. Mark reveals him as a "secret messiah." He is a teacher with divine guidance. In Matthew we see Jesus becoming divine.

Mark has the voice of God saying, "This is my beloved son. Listen to him."

Matthew writes the scene with the voice saying, "This is my beloved son on whom my favor rests."

Matthew attempts to make sure the readers understand this is God's messianic stamp of approval on Jesus.

In Mark we see Jesus in the tutelage of John the Baptist. In Matthew, John is simple there to announce Jesus' arrival and perform his baptism as a divine directive.

There are dozens of such re-interpretations, rewording, and embellishments between Mark and the other two synoptic gospels.

Luke

Most scholars place the dating of Luke between 80 and 130 A.D. The first element that stands out in Luke is that it is the men who do not believe in the resurrection of Jesus and it is the men who do not understand the significance. Although Luke follows Mark's account of the three women at the tomb, Luke tells us the women did not run and it was the women who reported it all to the men who did not believe them. Luke stresses the depth of wisdom and faith of the women. Luke even hints that the delay of the spirit at Pentecost may have been due to the fact that the men did not fully accept the resurrection. Further, passages, such as Luke 8:23 suggests there may have been more women than men in the crowd of believers.

These facts have led scholars, such as Randel McGraw Helms and others to speculate the writer of Luke may have been a woman.

From the outset, the author of Luke tells us that he or she was not an eyewitness, but was exposed to sources of information.

Luke 1:1 Forasmuch as many have taken in hand to set forth in order a declaration of those things which are most surely believed among us,

2 Even as they delivered them unto us, which from the beginning were eyewitnesses, and ministers of the word;

3 It seemed good to me also, having had perfect understanding of all things from the very first, to write unto thee in order, most excellent Theophilus,

4 That thou mightest know the certainty of those things, wherein thou hast been instructed.

These sources appear to be the Gospel of Mark and the Q document. Luke wrongly assumes, as we have also done, that Mark was an eyewitness. However, Mark wrote down what Peter told him about the events.

Luke was a native of the Hellenistic city of Antioch in Syria. Within scholarly circles, both secular and religious, there is lack of evidence as to the identity of the author of Luke. Luke is mentioned briefly a few times, and referred to as a doctor in the Pauline epistle to the Colossians. He is thought by most scholars to have been both a physician and a disciple of Paul. Luke was not an apostle but was probably a follower of Paul. This does not mean we should toss out the idea that Luke may have been a woman. After all, according to the book "The Acts of Paul and Thecla" (c.a.190A.D.) women were a large part of the Christian movement and there were no shortage of strong, intelligent, and wealthy women.

The author of Luke was very likely also the author of Acts. This has come to be so widely accepted that the two books are referred to as a single volume of Luke-Acts.

Edgar Goodspeed, in his book, The Work of Luke, tells us: "Luke and Acts are not two books, written at different times, but two volumes of a single work, conceived and executed as a unit. This distinction may not seem significant, but it is, as a matter of fact, of the utmost importance. It is one thing to write a pamphlet or a book;

it implies a certain degree of reflection, research, and organization. It is a very different thing to plan a book in two volumes, each in some degree a unit in itself but even more an integral part of a larger whole. Further, to recognize that Luke and Acts form two volumes of a single work enables us, so to speak, to gather all the light that each one of them has to throw on authorship, purpose, sources, date interest, etc., and focus it upon both of them."

Goodspeed goes on to say: " We have seen that the idea of writing such a work as Luke-Acts on the beginnings of the Christian movement could hardly have occurred to anyone until the Greek mission was a marked success and a great future had begun to open before the Christian faith. And wherever we test the book, it gives unmistakable signs of lateness of date, such as:

1. Its literary form is carefully organized into two volumes, each with its own distinct sphere and field and yet integrated with the other so as to be practically inseparable.

2. Its literary features are the preface, dedication, account of sources, purpose, and method.

3. Its infancy interest is pushed back to the birth of John. One is reminded that in the Book of James (the Protevangelium), half a century or more later, this infancy interest is pushed still farther back to the nativity of the Virgin herself.

4. Its resurrection interest include a whole series of appearances, visits, eatings, penetration of locked doors, protracted through forty days. This is in marked contrast to Matthew's (which was probably

also Mark's) account and is much nearer to the second-century representations of Jesus' long post-resurrection conversations with the apostles, e.g., the Epistle of the Apostles, ca. A.D. 150.

5. Its doctrine of the Holy Spirit pervades both volumes. The Holy Spirit is to come over Mary, 1:35; it fills Elizabeth, 1:42, and Zechariah, 1:67. It came down upon Jesus, 3:22; he was full of the Holy Spirit, 4:1. It is on almost every page of the Acts, the whole narrative of which seems to float upon a sea of it. Luke evidently has a definite and developed doctrine of the holy Spirit, which was the fruit of no little religious reflection.

6. The interest in punitive miracles is a feature conspicuous in the Elijah-Elisha cycles of Kings but wholly wanting from Mark and Matthew. It marks the opening scene of Luke (Zechariah is struck dumb) and plays a prominent part in the Acts: Ananias and Sapphira are struck dead, 5:5, 10; Elymas is struck blind, 13:11; compare 12:23. In this trait we are on our way to the fondness for punitive miracles in the infancy gospels of the second century, which also found it edifying, e.g., the Gospel of Thomas.

7. The passing of the Jewish controversy; this interest, so acute in Paul's day, has become a dead issue when Luke is written.

8. The interest in Christian psalmody. Luke preserves hymn after hymn, 1:42, 46, 68; 2:14, 29-the Magnificat, the Benedictus, the Gloria in Excelsis, the Nunc Dimittis. Nowhere else do we find any such early interest in Christian writings, except in Eph. 5:14 and in the arias, choruses, and antiphonies of the Revelation. Already that

liturgical endowment, which Walter Pater once said was one of the special gifts of the early church, was beginning to appear.

9. Church organization consists of the Twelve appear in the Acts as a sort of college of apostles, stationed in Jerusalem, watching over the progress of the Christian mission. With them are associated the elders, 15:2, 6, 22; 16:4, etc. Paul is represented as appointing elders in each church, 14:23, so the presbyteral organization is recognized as established, though Paul himself in his list of types of Christian leadership in I Cor. 12:28 says nothing about elders. The office of deacon is also traced back to the earliest days of the church and given added dignity and luster by the story of Stephen, chapters 6, 7. Luke's account of Ananias and Sapphira shows an interest in church funds when he wrote the Acts, and the story of Dorcas sewing for the poor, 9:39, also points to a considerable degree of organization. The point made here is not as to the fact of such embezzlement or charitable doings in the church, but of the writer's interest in recording them. Here belongs also the emphasis upon baptism as a condition of church membership, forgiveness, and salvation that is so characteristic of the Acts. 2:38; 8:12, 36; 9:18; 10:47; 16:15, 33.

10. The Speaking with Tongues was simply ecstatic utterance with Paul, I Corinthians, chapters 12-14, but in the Acts it has come to be a miraculous endowment with the power to speak foreign languages, Acts 2:4-11.

11. The circumstances of Paul's dead is that he is still living when the curtain falls upon the Acts in 28:30, 31, is outweighed by his

farewell to the Ephesian elders, 20:25, with its solemn declaration that none of them would ever see his face again, underscored by its repetition in 20:38: "they were especially saddened at his saying that they would never see his face again." Such presentiments are remembered and recorded only when they have proven true.

12. Paul has risen to hero stature. He is not only dead; he has become a hallowed memory. He is no longer a man struggling and grappling with difficulties, as in his letters; he has become a heroic figure and towers above priests, officers, governors, and kings. This is simply the retrospect of history. Lincoln rose in a generation into a heroic figure, very different from the man his contemporaries knew. The manner of his death no doubt contributed to this, but Paul's death too made its contribution to the reverence in which he came to be held, for he was probably the first of the Roman martyrs. Time has to play its part in the development of these attitudes. The success of the Greek mission naturally drew attention to the figure of the leader of that movement.

13. In the emergence of the sects, men of their own number were appearing and teaching perversions of the truth in order to draw the disciples away after them, 20:30. Apart from this reference to them in Acts the first we hear of the sects is in Eph. 4:14; compare 4:3-6, and in the Revelation, where the mysterious sect of the Nicolaitans is mentioned with abhorrence, 2:6, 15. Early in the second century the Docetists appear (cf. I, II John, Ignatius), then the Marcionites and Gnostics, and then the Montanists. Here, again, Acts seems to belong to the time of Ephesians and the Revelation.

14. Nonacquaintance with Paul's collected letters. The letters of Paul would have been of great value to the writer of the Acts; if he had known them, he could not have helped making use of them along with the numerous sources he mentions in his preface. It is next to impossible, if one knows Paul's letters, not to reveal the fact when writing about his life and work. They are ideal materials for such a task. But the Acts nowhere betrays any knowledge of them.

15. The situation presupposed by the conception of such a work-the wide success achieved by the Greek mission.

Luke-Acts might be still more definitely dated if it could be shown that Luke made use in it of the Antiquities of Josephus, which appeared in A.D. 93. The chief points of resemblance are the Theudas-Judas passage, Ant. xx. 5. 1, 2 (cf. Acts 5:36, 37), and the Lysanias reference, Ant. xx. 7. 1 (cf. Luke 3:1, 2), but, in both, matters are so very differently understood and stated in the Acts that it seems more probable that the two accounts are not immediately related to each other. If Luke used Josephus, he put Judas in the time of Quirinius' census after the Theudas of the times of Fadus, forty years later, and represented Lysanias as still tetrarch of Abilene sixty-five years after his death. Even the best of modern critical writers do not always escape just such errors, but it would be strange for Luke to do this if he really had Josephus.

It is not too much to say that, wherever we sound the book of Acts, the result is the same; it reveals itself as a work of the last decade of the first century. Even two or three of the considerations just listed would make such a date highly probable, but taken altogether they are overwhelming. Such points are too often dismissed as "difficulties" or dealt with atomistically-one at a time-the others being momentarily put aside. But it is their cumulative effect that is so significant. They are, as a matter of fact, clues to the solution of the problem of the date of the two volumes, and they may fairly be said to demonstrate that Acts (and Luke of course with it), was written about A.D. 90, about the time of Ephesians and Revelation but probably before the regulations of Domitian had brought the church acutely into collision with the empire over the matter of emperor worship." (This ends the quote from Goodspeed.)

Thus, we know with some certainty that the Gospel of Luke was written after 93 A.D. since Luke, whoever he or she may be, used the works of Josephus and Luke refers to emperor worship as a point of contention with Rome and the cause of execution of many Christians.

Tradition has Luke dying in Greece around 74 A.D. The conclusion hardly needs pointing out that the dates set here exclude Luke from being the author of the Gospel bearing his or her name.

Thus far we have Mark, who was not an eyewitness, but was writing down what Peter remembered, although his memory did not allow things to be written in chronological order. We believe Mark has access to the first two layers of Q but not the complete document. We have Luke admitting from the start he or she was not an eyewitness but was combining sources. And we have Matthew, who obviously used Mark's Gospel and Q, along with their personal additions, to write his gospel.

The further back we go the more important Q becomes.

John

The Gospel of John, of course, stands apart from the other gospels because Matthew and Luke use common sources. They both use the gospel of Mark. They both use the so-called Q, or the synoptic sayings gospel. Similarities are evident, particularly the outline of the ministry of Jesus. The Gospel of John uses another source, called Signs Source. John also has some relationships to the sources used by the other gospels. He seems to use the same passion narrative as in Mark, Matthew, Luke and in the Gospel of Peter. The other thing that is common with the other gospels is a chain of miracle stories.

The major speeches in the gospel of John are developed out of traditional sayings materials but many of the sayings or monologs John records have parallels in the Gospel of Thomas. So John draws on a different set of traditional sayings of Jesus than do the first three gospels of the New Testament.

The personality and teachings of Jesus are quite different in John. Here, Jesus is in hostile opposition to the established Jewish leaders. It is likely the Christian faith was developing its own identity and breaking away from mainline Jewish worship, and thus being persecuted for it.

In John, Jesus explains who and what he is, revealing his theological place more than in the other Gospels. This developed theological reflection grows out of a different circle and tradition. The world was a Greek world with Greek sensibilities and Greek philosophies. Matthew, Mark , and Luke were plain, unadorned gospels. Their opening statements would have left Greek readers yawning, but John begins like a Greek would have written it. Indications are that the church was beginning to put together its complex doctrine, which would be influenced by the soaring Greek thoughts and pros.

John seems thoroughly Greek in character . Its thought and its literary and dialogue styles are thoroughly Greek. It has comparatively limited use of the Jewish scriptures (roughly about one-fifth of Matthew's). Its definite purpose, to strip Christianity of its Jewishness and give it a Greek face. This is also backed up by its anti-Jewish feeling, and its great debt to the mystery. Greeks loved a good mystery religion. Indications are the writer was a Greek, not a Jew.

Alfred Loisy, in his work, "The Origins of the New Testament" states: "The first publication can hardly have been effected before 135-140 (A.D.); the additions and retouches on synoptic lines will have been introduced soon afterwards when Asiatic Christianity was uniting with that of other churches to make common front against the flood of gnosticism and especially against Marcion. It is none the less true that the fourth Gospel is, essentially, a gnostic document, although its structure-form proclaims it a Christian catechism: moreover it has absorbed a number of gnostic pieces, rhythmic utterances of mystic teaching, originally composed outside the Gospel framework and incorporated with it by methods to be indicated presently, just as the Synoptics have incorporated many a fragment of the earlier eschatological teaching. The result is that the Johannine catechesis is hardly less complex than the synoptic."

Loisy continues, "Towards the end of the first century or the beginning of the second there lived a mystic prophet, a master of gnosis rather than an apostle of the faith, from whom came forth the hymns and symbolic visions on which the fourth Gospel is founded. A little later, towards 135-140, his sublime meditations were collected and framed in a Gospel story, to be used as a manual of initiation into the Christian faith, like other books of similar form already in circulation among the churches. The chronological framework was probably fixed at the same time and a part of the borrowings made from the synoptic tradition. At this stage and in this form the book had no author's name attached to it and its diffusion was limited, or nearly so, to the province of Asia. Some fifteen or twenty years later, towards 150-160, the Marcionite heresy having broken out, this Asiatic book was amended, completed and more or less worked over, not only by the addition of chapter xxi, but by other retouches and additions in the main body; it was then boldly presented as the work of an apostle. But everything was welcome that gave satisfaction to faith, and the result just described was accepted by those whose will-to-believe found the truth in it. Thus it came to pass that, when the Montanist controversy broke out, the adversaries of these pretended writings of the apostle John found nobody to listen to them. When later, towards 190, the great controversy arose about the keeping of Easter, the Roman Church failed to perceive, or pretended not to perceive that, while the

Synoptics supported the ritual tradition of Rome and of most other Christian churches, the fourth Gospel supported the different tradition followed by the churches of Asia." (This ends the quotes from Loisy.)

It is widely accepted that the source material of John is different from the synoptic gospels. Scholars believe he used something called the Signs Gospel. Let us look at the hypothetical source as scholars have used linguistics and comparisons of writing styles to pull from John's Gospel his source.

The Signs Gospel

The Signs Gospel is a hypothetical document, which recorded the life of Jesus. Some scholars believe it to be a primary source document used by John as the foundational information for the writing of the Gospel of John. As with the hypothesis of the Q and Passion sources, this theory has its basis in source criticism. In 1941 the scholar, Rudolf Bultmann, put forth a theory called the Hypothesis of a Semeia (signs or miracles) Source. The idea has gained wide acceptance.

Just as Q was written in layers over time and Mark depended on Q as his foundational information, Bultmann's hypothesis holds that the Gospel of John was composed in layers over a period of time with the author (or authors) of John building upon the previous work of the Signs author, who wrote an earlier, and likely more lean account of the life and miracles of Jesus.

The "Signs Gospel" was independent of, and not used by, the authors of the synoptic gospels, which is why the Gospel of John is so different in content and tone from Matthew, Mark, and Luke.

It is believed the Signs Gospel was circulating before the year 70 A.D. and was probably written between 50 and 70 A.D. The fact that John may not have been the final author of the Gospel of John does not mean he was not a contributor to the Gospel. The Gospel of John is dated between 90 and 120 A.D. and thus not likely written by the disciple. Raymond Edward Brown believed that the original author of the Signs Gospel to be John the Beloved Disciple.

D. Moody Smith comments (*Johannine Christianity*, p. 63): "It is now rather widely agreed that the Fourth Evangelist drew upon a miracle tradition or written source(s) substantially independent of the synoptics, whether or not he had any knowledge of one or more of those gospels. Since the epoch-making commentary of Rudolf Bultmann, the hypothesis of a *semeia-* (or miracle) source has gained rather wide acceptance."

Norman Perrin writes (*The New Testament: An Introduction*, p. 225): "But there is one source whose use must be recognized: a signs source.
In 2:11 Jesus' miracle at Cana is described as "the first of his signs." Further signs are mentioned in general terms in 2:23, and in 4:54 the

healing of the official's son at Capernaum is described as "the second sign that Jesus did when he had come from Judea to Galilee." Then 12:37 says, "Though he had done so many signs before them, yet they did not believe in him," and this note is sounded again in the closing summary of the gospel proper, 20:30-31: "Now Jesus did many other signs in the presence of the disciples, which are not written in this book; but these are written that you may believe. . . ." The possibility that in his narrative up to 12:37 the evangelist had used a source other than the synoptic gospels or the tradition represented by those gospels is strengthened since all the other miracles in John that are not paralleled in the synoptic gospels occur before 12:37: the healing at the pool of Bethzatha (5:1-9); the healing of the blind man (9:1-12); the raising of Lazarus (11:1-44). These miracles are generally on a grander and more elaborate scale than those in the synoptic gospels and seem to go further in presenting Jesus as a Hellenistic "divine man." Throughout the gospel until 12:37-38, and again in 20:30-31, the miracles are presented as intending to call forth faith: 2:11; 4:53; 6:14; 7:31; 11:45, 47b-48; 12:37-38; 20:31. Whereas in the synoptic gospels the emphasis is on faith as the prerequisite for miracles (e.g., Mark 6:5-6), here in the gospel of John miracles induce faith. These references not only contrast with the synoptic gospels, they also contrast with the remainder of the gospel of John itself. In 2:23-25 as in 4:48, Jesus repudiates the kind of faith induced by signs. The conversation with Nicodemus contrasts such faith unfavorably with rebirth "from above" and "of the spirit" (3:2, 3, 5-6). These factors make it very probable that the author of the gospel of John is

184

using as a source and *reinterpreting* a book of signs that presents Jesus as a Hellenistic "divine man" whose miracles induce faith."

Kysar writes (*The Anchor Bible Dictionary*, v. 3, pp. 921-922): "The most widely held proposal for a literary source is that of a *signs source*. A number of things in the gospel contribute to the effort to reconstruct such a source: The presence of the series of wonder stories in the narrative, the unique use of the word, *semeia* ("signs"), to designate such wonders, the numbering of the signs in 2:11 and 4:54, and the reference to signs in the conclusion of the gospel. ...What is proposed is that there was a collection of the wonders of Jesus circulating within the Johannine community prior to the writing of the gospel. Efforts to reconstruct such a signs source from the gospel vary. At one extreme is the argument that it contained not only the wonders narrated in the gospel, but also the calling of the disciples in 1:19-51 and a passion story. At the other extreme is the suggestion that the collection was little more than seven wonder stories told consecutively. Some such theory is embraced by a large number of Johannine scholars, but by no means has agreement been reached on such a proposal."

Fortna states (op. cit., p. 19): "The following deeds of Jesus, less the Johannine insertions they now contain, would have comprised the bulk of SQ: changing water into wine (2:1-11), healing an official's son (4:46-54) and a lame man (5:2-9), feeding the multitude (6:1-14) - probably together with crossing the sea (6:15-25), giving sight to a blind man (9:1-8), and raising Lazarus (11:1-45). (Some would also include the catch of fish now found at 21:1-14.) An articulated series emerges from the reconstruction, not merely a gather of miracle stories, and a few other passages are also to be included: part of chap. 1 (at least the gathering of the first disciples in vv 35-49) as introduction and, as conclusion, 20:30-31a, and perhaps also parts of 12:37-41."

Did the Signs Gospel contain only miracles or was it a book recounting the teachings of Jesus also? Did it include his discourses and sermons, or was the author simply reporting miracles in order to evoke faith and wonder in the reader? The Signs Gospel (or SQ as some have designated it) is used to transmit to us that feeling seen in the stories when those who were exposed to his miracles and wonders knew immediately by their power that the man performing them was indeed the one so long anticipated. The messiah.

After concluding there is a high probability that the Signs Gospel exists, and is embedded within the Gospel of John, the most difficult task remaining is the parsing of the Gospel of John to expose the Signs Gospel within it. This is done by using clues within the Gospel of John, such as phrases indicating "this is the first sign (miracle or wonder)" and other such interesting hints that may lead to the conclusion the information was pulled from a source containing a list of stories. Another clue is a shift on wording, voice, tone, and even cadence of speech, which would occur as the Gospel of John shifts from one writer to another.

We will rely on Robert Fortuna's work for this parsing. A copy of this is found in Andrew Bernhard's book, The Lost Gospels. In Bernhard's book he states, "The following reconstruction of the hypothetical source employed by the author of the fourth gospel is derived from the analysis found in Robert Fortna's The Fourth Gospel and Its Predecessor. The text of the Signs Gospel has been reconstructed using the New Revised Standard Version (NRSV) of the Gospel of John; differences between the text of the Signs Gospel and the NRSV are printed in italics."

Verses are in the order in which they were thought to occur in the original Signs Gospel.

The Signs Gospel

John 1

(6) There was a man sent from God, whose name was John. (7) He came as a witness, so that all might believe through him.

(19) This is the testimony given by John when priests and Levites *came* to ask him, "Who are you?"

(20) *He* confessed, "I am not the Messiah."

(21) And they asked him, "What then? Are you Elijah?"

He said, "I am not."

"Are you the prophet?"

He answered, "No."

(22) Then they said to him, "Who are you? What do you say about yourself?"

(23) He said, "I am the voice of one crying out in the wilderness, 'Make straight the way of the Lord,' " as the prophet Isaiah said. I baptize with water. Among you stands (27) the one who is coming after me; I am not worthy to untie the thong of

his sandal."

(28) He saw Jesus coming toward him and declared, "Here is the Lamb of God. I came for this reason, that he might be revealed to Israel. I saw the Spirit descending from heaven like a dove on him. (34) And I myself have seen and have testified that this is the Son of God."

(35) *Now* John was standing with two of his disciples *who* heard him say this, and they followed Jesus. (38) They said to him, "Rabbi, where are you staying?"
(39) He said to them, "Come and see." They came and saw where he was staying, and they remained with him that day. It was about four o'clock in the afternoon.
(40) One of the two who heard John speak and followed him was Andrew. (41) He first found his brother Simon and said to him, "We have found the Messiah." (42) He brought Simon to Jesus, who looked at him and said, "You are Simon son of John. You are to be called Cephas."
He found Philip and *Jesus* said to him,

"Follow me." (44) Now Philip was from Bethsaida, the city of Andrew and Peter. (45) Philip found Nathanael and said to him, "We have found him about whom Moses in the law wrote, Jesus son of Joseph from Nazareth."

(46) Nathanael said to him, "Can anything good come out of Nazareth?" Philip said to him, "Come and see."

(47) When Jesus saw Nathanael coming toward him, he said of him, "Here is truly an Israelite."

(49) Nathanael replied, "Rabbi, you are the Son of God! You are the King of Israel!"

John 2

(1) There was a wedding in Cana, and the mother of Jesus was there. (2) Jesus and his disciples had also been invited to the wedding. (3) When the wine gave out, the mother of Jesus said to the servants, "Do whatever he tells you." (6) Now standing there were six stone water jars, each holding twenty or thirty gallons.

(7) Jesus said to them, "Fill the jars with water." And they filled them up to the

brim.

(8) He said to them, "Now draw some out, and take it to the chief steward." So they took it.

(9) When the steward tasted the water that had become wine, the steward called the bridegroom (10) and said to him, "Everyone serves the good wine first, and then the inferior wine after the guests have become drunk. But you have kept the good wine until now."

(11) Jesus did this, the first of his signs; and his disciples believed in him.

(12) After this he went down to Capernaum with his disciples.

John 4 (46) Now there was a royal official whose son lay ill in Capernaum. (47) He went and said to him, "Sir, come down before my little boy dies."

(50) Jesus said, "Go; your son will live." The man started on his way. (51) As he was going down, his slaves met him and told him that his child was alive. (52) So he asked them the hour when he began to recover, and they said to him, "Yesterday at one in the afternoon the fever left him."

(53) So he himself believed, along with his whole household.

(54) Now this was the second sign that Jesus did.

John 21

(2) Gathered there together were Simon Peter, Thomas called the Twin, Nathanael of Cana, the sons of Zebedee. (3) Simon Peter said to them, "I am going fishing." They said to him, "We will go with you." They went out and got into the boat, but that night they caught nothing.

(4) Just after daybreak, Jesus stood on the beach. (6) He said to them, "Cast the net to the right side of the boat, and you will find some."

So they cast it, and now they were not able to haul it in because there were so many fish. (7) Simon Peter put on some clothes and jumped into the sea (8) for they were not far from the land, only about a hundred yards off. (11) So Simon Peter went *ashore* and hauled the net ashore, full of large fish, a hundred fifty-three of them; and though there were so many, the net was not torn. (14) This was now the third *sign* that Jesus *did before* the disciples.

John 6   (1) After this Jesus went to the other side of the Sea of Tiberias. (3) *He* went up the mountain and sat down there with his disciples. (5) When he looked up and saw a large crowd coming toward him, Jesus said to Philip, "Where are we to buy bread for these people to eat?"

(7) Philip answered him, "Six months' wages would not buy enough bread for each of them to get a little."

(8) One of his disciples said to him, (9) "There is a boy here who has five barley loaves and two fish. But what are they among so many people?"

(10) Jesus said, "Make the people sit down." Now there was a great deal of grass in the place; so they sat down, about five thousand in all. (11) Then Jesus took the loaves, and when he had given thanks, he distributed them to those who were seated; so also the fish, as much as they wanted.

(13) And from the fragments of the five

barley loaves, left by those who had
eaten, they filled twelve baskets. (14)
When the people saw the sign that he had
done, they began to say, "This is indeed
the prophet who is to come into the
world."

(15) *Jesus* withdrew again to the mountain
by himself. (16) When evening came, his
disciples went down to the sea, (17) got
into a boat, and started across the sea to
Capernaum. (18) The sea became rough
because a strong wind was blowing. (19)
When they had rowed about three or four
miles, they saw Jesus walking on the sea,
and they were terrified. (20) But he said to
them, "It is I; do not be afraid." (21) And
immediately the boat reached the land
toward which they were going.

John 11

(1) Now a certain Mary; (2) her brother
Lazarus was ill. (3) *She* sent a message to
Jesus, "Lord, he whom you love is ill."
(7) He said to the disciples, "Our friend
Lazarus has fallen asleep. Let us go to
him."
(17) When Jesus arrived, he found that

Lazarus had already been in the tomb four days. (32) When Mary saw him, she knelt at his feet and said to him, "Lord, if you had been here, my brother would not have died."

(33) When Jesus saw her weeping, he was greatly disturbed in spirit and deeply moved. (34) He said, "Where have you laid him?"

They said to him, "Lord, come and see."

(38) Then Jesus came to the tomb. It was a cave, and a stone was lying against it. (39) Jesus said, "Take away the stone." *Then* he cried with a loud voice, "Lazarus, come out!"

(44) The dead man came out, his hands and feet bound with strips of cloth, and his face wrapped in a cloth. Jesus said to them, "Unbind him, and let him go."

(45) *Those who* had seen what Jesus did, believed in him.

John 9

(1) As he walked along, he saw a man blind from birth. (6) He spat on the ground and made mud with the saliva and spread the mud on the man's eyes, (7)

saying to him, "Go, wash in the pool of Siloam." Then he went and washed and came back able to see. (8) The neighbors and those who had seen him before as a beggar began to ask, "Is this not the man who used to sit and beg?"

John 5

(2) Now in Jerusalem by the Sheep Gate there is a pool, called in Hebrew Beth-zatha, which has five porticoes. (3) In these lay many invalids—blind, lame, and paralyzed. (5) One man was there who had been ill for thirty-eight years. (6) When Jesus saw him lying there and knew that he had been there a long time, he said to him, "Do you want to be made well?"

(7) The sick man answered him, "Sir, I have no one to put me into the pool when the water is stirred up; and while I am making my way, someone else steps down ahead of me."

(8) Jesus said to him, "Stand up, take your mat and walk."

(9) At once the man was made well, and he took up his mat and began to walk.

John 2

(14) In the temple *Jesus* found people selling cattle, sheep, and doves, and the money changers seated at their tables. (15) Making a whip of cords, he drove all of them out of the temple, both the sheep and the cattle. He also poured out the coins of the money changers and overturned their tables. (16) He told those who were selling the doves, "Take these things out of here! Stop making my Father's house a marketplace!"
(18) The Jews then said to him, "What sign can you show us for doing this?"
19 Jesus answered them, "Destroy this temple, and in three days I will raise it up."

John 11

(47) So the chief priests called a meeting of the council, and said, "This man is performing many signs. (48) If we let him go on like this, everyone will believe in him, and the Romans will come and destroy our nation."
(49) But one of them, Caiaphas, who was

high priest that year, said to them, (50) "It is better for you to have one man die for the people than to have the whole nation destroyed." (53) So from that day on they planned to put him to death.

John 12

(37) Although he had performed so many signs, they did not believe in him. (38) This was to fulfill the word spoken by the prophet Isaiah: "Lord, who has believed our message, and to whom has the arm of the Lord been revealed?" (39) And so they could not believe, because Isaiah also said, (40) "He has blinded their eyes and hardened their heart, so that they might not look with their eyes, and understand with their heart and turn— and I would heal them."

(1) Six days before the Passover Jesus came to Bethany, the home of Lazarus, whom he had raised from the dead. (2) There they gave a dinner for him. Martha served, and Lazarus was one of those at the table with him. (3) Mary took a pound of costly perfume made of pure nard, anointed Jesus, and wiped them with her

hair. The house was filled with the fragrance of the perfume.

(4) But Judas Iscariot, one of his disciples, said, (5) "Why was this perfume not sold for three hundred denarii and the money given to the poor?"

(7) Jesus said, "She bought it so that she might keep it for the day of my burial. (8) You always have the poor with you, but you do not always have me."

(12) The next day the great crowd that had come to the festival heard that Jesus was coming to Jerusalem. (13) So they took branches of palm trees and went out to meet him, shouting, "Hosanna! Blessed is the one who comes in the name of the Lord — the King of Israel!"

(14) Jesus found a young donkey and sat on it; as it is written: (15) "Do not be afraid, daughter of Zion. Look, your king is coming, sitting on a donkey's colt!"

John 13

(1) Now before the festival of the Passover, Jesus knew that his hour had

come to depart from this world and go to the Father. Having loved his own who were in the world, he loved them to the end. (2) The devil had already put it into the heart of Judas son of Simon Iscariot to betray him. And during supper (3) Jesus, knowing that the Father had given all things into his hands, and that he had come from God and was going to God, (4) got up from the table, took off his outer robe, and tied a towel around himself. (5) Then he poured water into a basin and began to wash the disciples' feet and to wipe them with the towel that was tied around him. (6) He came to Simon Peter, who said to him, "Lord, are you going to wash my feet?"

(7) Jesus answered, "You do not know now what I am doing, but later you will understand."

(8) Peter said to him, "You will never wash my feet."

Jesus answered, "Unless I wash you, you have no share with me."

(9) Simon Peter said to him, "Lord, not my feet only but also my hands and my head!"

(10) Jesus said to him, "One who has bathed does not need to wash, except for the feet, but is entirely clean. And you are clean, though not all of you." (11) For he knew who was to betray him; for this reason he said, "Not all of you are clean." (12) After he had washed their feet, had put on his robe, and had returned to the table, he said to them, "Do you know what I have done to you? (13) You call me Teacher and Lord — and you are right, for that is what I am. (14) So if I, your Lord and Teacher, have washed your feet, you also ought to wash one another's feet. (15) For I have set you an example, that you also should do as I have done to you. (16) Very truly, I tell you, servants are not greater than their master, nor are messengers greater than the one who sent them. (17) If you know these things, you are blessed if you do them. (18) I am not speaking of all of you; I know whom I have chosen. But it is to fulfill the scripture, 'The one who ate my bread has lifted his heel against me.' (19) I tell you this now, before it occurs, so that when it does occur, you may believe that I am he.

(20) Very truly, I tell you, whoever receives one whom I send receives me; and whoever receives me receives him who sent me."

John 18

(1) Jesus went out with his disciples across the Kidron valley to a place where there was a garden. (2) Now Judas, who betrayed him, also knew the place, because Jesus often met there with his disciples. (3) So Judas brought a detachment of soldiers together with police from the chief priests, and they came there with lanterns and torches and weapons. (4) Then Jesus asked them, "Whom are you looking for?"

(5) They answered, "Jesus of Nazareth." Jesus replied, "I am he."

(10) Then Simon Peter, who had a sword, drew it, struck the high priest's slave, and cut off his right ear. The slave's name was Malchus.

(11) Jesus said to Peter, "Put your sword back into its sheath. Am I not to drink the cup that the Father has given me?" (12) So the soldiers, their officer, and the Jewish

police arrested Jesus and bound him.

(13) First they took him to Annas, who was the father-in-law of Caiaphas, the high priest that year. (15) Simon Peter and another disciple followed Jesus. Since that disciple was known to the high priest, he went with Jesus into the courtyard of the high priest, (16) but Peter was standing outside at the gate. So the other disciple, who was known to the high priest, went out, spoke to the woman who guarded the gate, and brought Peter in.

(17) The woman said to Peter, "You are not also one of this man's disciples, are you?"

He said, "I am not."

(18) Now the slaves and the police had made a charcoal fire because it was cold, and they were standing around it and warming themselves. Peter also was standing with them and warming himself. (19) Then the high priest questioned Jesus about his teaching. (20) Jesus answered, "I have always taught in the temple, where all come together. (21) Why do you ask

me?"

(22) When he had said this, one of the
police standing nearby struck Jesus on the
face, saying, "Is that how you answer the
high priest?"

(24) Then Annas sent him bound to
Caiaphas the high priest. (25)They asked
him, "You are not also one of his disciples,
are you?"

He denied it and said, "I am not."

(26) One of the slaves of the high priest, a
relative of the man whose ear Peter had
cut off, asked, "Did I not see you in the
garden with him?"

(27) Again Peter denied it, and at that
moment the cock crowed.

(28) Then they took Jesus from Caiaphas
to Pilate's headquarters. It was early in
the morning. (29) Pilate said, "What
accusation do you bring against this
man?"

(33) Then Pilate summoned Jesus and
asked him, "Are you the King of the
Jews?"

Jesus answered, "You say that I am a

king."

(38) He told them, "I find no case against him. (39) But you have a custom that I release someone for you at the Passover. Do you want me to release for you the King of the Jews?"

(40) They shouted in reply, "Not this man, but Barabbas!" Now Barabbas was a bandit.

John 19

(1) Then Pilate took Jesus and had him flogged. (2) And the soldiers wove a crown of thorns and put it on his head, and they dressed him in a purple robe. (3) They kept coming up to him, saying, "Hail, King of the Jews!" and striking him on the face.

(6) And the police saw him, they shouted, "Crucify him! Crucify him!" Pilate said to them, "I find no case against him."

(13) Pilate brought Jesus outside and sat on the judge's bench at a place called The Stone Pavement, or in Hebrew Gabbatha. (14) Now it was the day of Preparation; and it was about noon. (16) Then he handed him over to them to be crucified.

So they took Jesus. (17) He went out to what is called The Place of the Skull, which in Hebrew is called Golgotha. (18) There they crucified him, and with him two others, one on either side. (19) *And there was written*, "Jesus of Nazareth, the King of the Jews." (20) And it was written in Hebrew, in Latin, and in Greek.

(23) When the soldiers had crucified Jesus, they took his clothes and divided them into four parts, one for each soldier. They also took his tunic; now the tunic was seamless, woven in one piece from the top. (24) So they said to one another, "Let us not tear it, but cast lots for it to see who will get it." This was to fulfill what the scripture says, "They divided my clothes among themselves, and for my clothing they cast lots."

(25) And that is what the soldiers did. Meanwhile, standing near the cross of Jesus were his mother, and his mother's sister, Mary the wife of Clopas, and Mary Magdalene. (28) After this, he said (in order to fulfill the scripture), "I am thirsty."

(29) A jar full of sour wine was standing there. So they put a sponge full of the wine on a branch of hyssop and held it to his mouth.

(30) When Jesus had received the wine, he said, "It is finished." Then he bowed his head and gave up his spirit.

(31) Since it was the day of Preparation, the Jews did not want the bodies left on the cross during the sabbath. So they asked Pilate to have the legs of the crucified men broken and the bodies removed. (32) Then the soldiers came and broke the legs of the first and of the other who had been crucified with him. (33) But when they came to Jesus and saw that he was already dead, they did not break his legs. (34) Instead, one of the soldiers pierced his side with a spear, and at once blood and water came out. (36) These things occurred so that the scripture might be fulfilled, "None of his bones shall be broken."

(37) And again another passage of scripture says, "They will look on the one whom they have pierced." (38) After these things, Joseph of Arimathea, who was a

disciple of Jesus, asked Pilate to let him
take away the body of Jesus. Pilate gave
him permission; so he came and removed
his body and wrapped it with the spices
in linen cloths.

(41) Now there was a garden in the place
where he was crucified, and in the garden
there was a new tomb in which no one
had ever been laid. (42) And so, because it
was the day of Preparation, and the tomb
was nearby, they laid Jesus there.

John 20

(1) Early on the first day of the week,
Mary Magdalene came to the tomb and
saw that the stone had been removed
from the tomb. (2) So she ran and went to
Simon Peter and said, "They have taken
the Lord out of the tomb, and we do not
know where they have laid him."
(3) Then Peter set out and went toward
the tomb and went into the tomb. (9) For
as yet they did not understand the
scripture, that he must rise from the dead.
(10) Then *he* returned to *his* home.
(11) But Mary stood weeping outside the
tomb. As she wept, she bent over to look

into the tomb; (12) and she saw two angels in white, sitting where the body of Jesus had been lying, one at the head and the other at the feet. (14) She turned around and saw Jesus standing there. (15) Jesus said to her, "Whom are you looking for, Mary?"

She said to him in Hebrew, "Rabbouni!."

(17) Jesus said to her, "Do not hold on to me. But go to my brothers."

(18) Mary Magdalene went and announced to the disciples, "I have seen the Lord."

(19) When it was evening on that day and the doors of the house where the disciples had met were locked, Jesus came and stood among them and said, "Peace be with you." (20) He showed them his hands and his side. Then the disciples rejoiced when they saw the Lord.

(22) He breathed on them and said to them, "Receive the Holy Spirit."

(30) Now Jesus did many other signs in the presence of his disciples, which are not written in this book. (31) But these are written so that you may come to believe that Jesus is the Messiah, the Son of God.

Conclusion of Sources

Let us first state an obvious but often missed fact – None of the Gospels claim authorship. Nowhere in the Gospels are we told who the authors were. Names assigned to the gospels were done so after the fact, by the church, according to tradition, as a way of labeling the books. The books were simply given those titles. The Gospels have no signature of authorship. As a reminder, let us look at the opening statements of each gospel. In them we will find no statement of authorship.

Mark 1
1 The beginning of the good news about Jesus the Messiah, the Son of God

Matthew 1
1 This is the genealogy of Jesus the Messiah the son of David, the son of Abraham:

Luke 1
1 Many have undertaken to draw up an account of the things that have been fulfilled among us, 2 just as they were handed down to us by those who from the first were eyewitnesses and servants of the word.

John 1

1 In the beginning was the Word, and the Word was with God, and the Word was God. 2 He was with God in the beginning.

With the possible exception of Mark, there is little possibility that any of the gospels were written by the people whose names are attached to them as authors. Matthew, Luke, and John were probably not the authors of the books bearing their names. If they were they would not have had to use source materials. The fact that Matthew and Luke used Mark as a source may indicate they thought Mark was authentic, but it also proves they were not eyewitnesses and probably not the real Matthew or Luke. Since Mark admits to not being an eyewitness but instead being a scribe for Peter, we have at best a second hand account of events a decade or two past from a man whose memory was fading. The Gospels are not books written in a single sitting by a single person. They are collections of available information. Indeed, if we believe Mark used what was available from Q at the time, we are left wondering why an eyewitness used a list of sayings. Q1 was the only part of Q we are reasonably certain was available at the time and the only reliable repository of the sayings of Jesus. But that would only be needed if the writer did not remember or did not witness the events at all.

If everyone who wrote the gospels had written what he or she remembered the wording, events, and emphasis of each would have been markedly different. Instead, the three synoptic gospels are so much alike it leaves little doubt they used the same cheat sheets.

As it turns out, Mark may have actually borrowed from Paul, since the first letter to the Corinthian Church was written prior to the Gospel of Mark. It is only in the last part of Mark that we see the idea of the blood sacrifice, and it is connected to the Lord's Supper.

At this point we should examine the fact that the idea of the blood sacrifice appears at the end of the Gospel of Mark, and is propagated into Matthew and Luke. Here is how Mark puts it:

And as they were eating, he took bread, and after blessing it broke it and gave it to them, and said, "Take; this is my body." And he took a cup, and when he had given thanks he gave it to them, and they all drank of it. And he said to them, "This is my blood of the covenant, which is poured out for many" (Mark 14:22-24).

Mark was written around 65 to 100 A.D. with most scholars placing it at around 68 A.D. But Mark, like all the Gospels, is a collection of traditions available at the time. Mark, as it turns out, is echoing what Paul put forth in 1 Corinthians some twenty years earlier.

First Corinthians is one of the four letters of Paul which are universally accepted to be authentic. The letter is usually dated c. 54/55 A.D. Werner Georg Kummel states (Introduction to the New Testament, p. 275): "The genuineness of I Cor is not disputed: the letter is already clearly known in I Clem 37:5; 47:1-3; 49:5; Ign., Eph 16:1; 18:1; Rom 5:1; Phila 3:3." Chronologically, this may be the first mention of the blood sacrifice. Paul says he got the idea from "the Lord" and explains it this way:

For I received from the Lord what I also handed on to you, that the Lord Jesus on the night when he was betrayed took bread, and when he had given thanks, he broke it, and said, "This is my body which is [broken] for you. Do this in remembrance of me." In the same way also he took the cup, after supper, saying, "This cup is the new covenant in my blood. Do this, as often as you drink it, in remembrance of me" (1 Corinthians 11:23-25).

The verbal similarities between these two accounts are remarkable and cannot be discounted. Paul's version of the Last Supper in 1 Corinthians was written at least twenty years earlier than Mark's. Gospel. The doctrine was not built into the new faith. The first generation of elders controlling the church after the death of Jesus were not teaching this doctrine. Paul plainly says it is his own idea. He states: "For I received from the Lord what I handed on to you." His language is clear. He did not say he received it from one of the apostles or he learned it in Jerusalem from James. He states he got it "from the Lord." Paul uses the same language to defend his revelation and his new beliefs and thus the actions that followed, some of which went contrary to the doctrines of James and the first apostles who actually lived with Jesus. He says he did not receive it from any man, nor was he taught it, but swears with an oath, "I received it through a revelation of Jesus Christ" (Galatians 1:11-12).

New King James Version (NKJV)

Galatians 1:11 But I make known to you, brethren, that the gospel which was preached by me is not according to man. 12 For I neither received it from man, nor was I taught it, but it came through the revelation of Jesus Christ.

This means the idea of the blood sacrifice and its relation to the Lord's Supper with bread and wine representing the Flesh and Blood of Jesus comes to us from Paul. Mark, being a collection of traditions, was echoing it from Paul and Paul alone. Prior to Paul the tradition and doctrine did not exist. Matthew and Luke picked up the teaching from Mark, who got it from Paul, who never met Jesus outside of metaphysical encounters in the desert. It would not be long until the idea of the virgin birth would follow. After all, if the exsanguination of one person was going to cover the sins of all mankind to come, that blood had to be pure and sinless, maybe even supernatural. Maybe even from God. Further. If God found a woman to impregnate that woman would have to be very special, thus the idea of Mary's immaculate conception would be raised.

Is there no eyewitness among any of the Gospel writers? No, not one. Our hope of knowing anything from witnesses close to Jesus come down, not to the gospels but to the sources from which they used to write the gospels.

Dating Q is difficult, since it continued to be expanded and revised. Q1 was likely written around 40 to 50 A.D. Additions continued until 80 A.D. This would seem to fit generally since Thomas was written around 50 to 70 A.D. The Passion Narrative was written between 30 to 60 A.D. The Signs Gospel was likely written between 50 and 70 A.D. This means the first written account comes from a time ten to twenty years after Jesus, at the absolute earliest.

It is possible, just possible, that the authors of these source documents may have actually been witnesses to the life of Jesus. However, there is no way of knowing. They could have collected stories, folklore, and sayings from others, who themselves could have heard stories told, or could have been blessed to touch the hem of his garment.

At best, our gospels are second and third hand accounts with redactions throughout. Yet, in the Q1 Gospel, The Passion Narrative, The Gospel of Thomas, and the Signs Gospel we come closest to the person, theology, and history of Jesus.

The Gospel of Thomas and Q1 are the earliest recorded and unaltered saying of Jesus. Q1 may have influenced the Gospel of

Mark. Q1, which was the earliest recorded sayings of Jesus could have been used as a source document for Mark. The entire Q document, Q1,Q2, and Q3, was used as the basis of Luke and Matthew's Gospels. If we look at Q1 we should be closer to the real words of Jesus, without redactions and additions. In Q1 we should be able to see his teachings. Keeping in mind Q1 was written about 10 to 20 years after the death of Jesus, what we are seeing is a collection of memorable quotes, but at least some of these could be first hand testimonies. The words are pulled from the Gospel of Luke.

The translation is by Wim van der Dugen. The (K) designation indicates inclusion in Kloppenborg's edition.

Q1
ca.50 A.D.

These are the words of Jesus.
Seeing the crowds he said to his disciples :
Luke 6:20-21 (K8)

1 "How fortunate are the poor ; they have the Kingdom of Elohim.
2 How fortunate the hungry ; they will be fed.
3 How fortunate those who weep ; they will laugh."

Luke 6:27-35 (K9)

4 "But to you who hear, I say : love your enemies, bless those who curse you, and pray for those who mistreat you.

5 If someone slaps you on the cheek, offer the other as well. If anyone grabs your coat, let him have your shirt as well.

6 Give to anyone who asks, and if someone takes away which is yours, do not ask to have it back.

7 As you want people to treat you, do the same to them.

8 For if you love those who love you, what credit is that to you ? Even tax collectors love those who love them, do they not ?

9 And if you embrace only your brothers, what credit is that to you. Doesn't everybody do that ?

10 And if you lend to those from whom you hope to receive, what credit is that to you ? For wrongdoers also lend to their kind because they expect to be repaid.

11 On the contrary, love your enemies, do good and lend without expecting anything in return. Your reward will be great, and you will be children of Elohim. For He makes His sun rise on the evil and on the good ; He sends rain on the just and on the unjust."

Luke 6:36-38 - Mt.7:1-2 (K10)

12 "Be merciful even as your Father is merciful.

13 Judge not, and you will not be judged.

14 For you will be judged with the standard you judge with."

Luke 6:39-40 (K11)

15 He gave them a parable : "Can the blind lead the blind ? Will they not both fall into a pit ?

16 A student is not above his teacher. It is enough for a student to be like his teacher."

Luke 6:41-42 (K12)

17 "How can you look for the splinter in your brother's eye, and not notice the stick in your own eye ?

18 How can you say to your brother : 'Brother, let me pull out the splinter in your eye', when you do not see the stick in your own eye? You hypocrite ! First take the stick from your own eye, and then you can see to remove the splinter that is in your brother's eye."

Luke 6:43-45 (K13)

19 "A good tree does not bear rotten fruit ; a rotten tree does not bear good fruit.

20 Are figs gathered from thorns, or grapes from thistles ? Every tree is known by its fruit.

21 The good man produces good things from his store of goods and treasures ; and the evil man evil things. For the mouth speaks from a full heart !"

Luke 6:46-49 (K14)

22 "And why do you call me 'Master, master', and do not do what I say ?

23 Everyone who hears my words and does them, I will show you to whom he is like.

24 He is like a man who built a house on a rock. The rain fell, a torrent broke against the house, and it did not fall, for it had a rock foundation.

25 But everyone who hears my words but does not do them, is like a man who built a house on sand. The rain came, the torrent broke against it, and it collapsed. The ruin of that house was great."

Luke 9:57-62 (K21)

26 When someone said to Him : "Master, I will follow you wherever you go."

27 Jesus answered : "Foxes have holes, and birds of the air have nests, but the Son of Man has nowhere to lay his head."

28 When another said : "Let me first go and bury my father."

29 Jesus said : "Leave the dead to bury their dead."

30 Yet another said : "I will follow you, Master, but first let me say farewell to my family."

31 Jesus said to him : "No one who puts his hand to the plow and then looks back is fit for the Kingdom of Elohim."

Luke 10:2-11 (K22)

32 He said : "The harvest is great, but the workers are few ; beg therefore the Master of the harvest to send out workers into His harvest.

33 Go your ways : look, I send you out as lambs among wolves.

34 Do not carry purse, or bag, or sandals, or staff ; and do not greet anyone on the road.

35 Whatever house you enter, say : 'Peace be to this house !'

36 And if a child of peace is there, your peace will rest on him ; if not, let your peace return to you.

37 And stay in the same house, eating and drinking whatever they provide, for the worker deserves his wages. Do not go from house to house.

38 And if you enter a town, and they receive you, eat what is set before you,

39 heal the sick there, and say to them : 'The Kingdom of Elohim has come near to you.'

40 But if you enter a town and they do not receive you, as you leave, shake the dust from your feet and say :

41 'Nevertheless, be sure of this, the Kingdom of Elohim has come to you.'"

Luke 11:2-4 (K27)

42 He said to them : "When you pray, say : 'Father, may your name be holy. May your rule take place.

43 Always give us our bread.

44 Forgive us our debts, for we ourselves forgive everyone that is indebted to us. And lead us away from a trying situation'." (Some have – Deliver us from the evil one.)

Luke 11:9-11 (K28)

45 "Ask and it will be given to you ; seek and you will find ; knock and the door will be opened for you.

46 For everyone who asks receives, and the one who seeks finds, and to the one who knocks the door will be opened.

47 What father of yours, if his son ask for a loaf of bread, will give him a stone ?

48 Or if he ask for a fish, will give him a snake ?

49 So, if you, although you are not good, know how to give good gifts to your children, how much more will the Father above give good things to those who ask Him ?"

Luke 12:2-3 (K35)

50 "For nothing is hidden that will not be made known, or secret that will not come to light.

51 What I tell you in the dark, speak in the light, and what you hear as a whisper, proclaim on the housetops."

Luke 12:4 & 12:6-7 (K36)

52 "I say to you my friends : be not afraid of those that kill the body, and after that have nothing more to do.

53 Are five sparrows not sold for two cents ? Yet Elohim does not forget one of them.

54 Even the hairs of your head are all numbered. So don't be afraid. You are worth more than many sparrows."

Luke 12:13-21 (K40)

55 Someone from the crowd said to him : "Teacher, tell my brother to divide the inheritance with me."

56 He said to him : "Man, who made me your judge or divider ?"

57 He told them a parable, saying : "The land of a certain rich man produced in abundance.

58 And he thought to himself, saying : 'What should I do, for I have nowhere to store my crops ?'

59 And he said : 'This will I do. I will pull down my barns, and build larger ones, and there I will store all my wheat and my goods,

60 and I will say to my soul : Soul, you have ample goods stored up for many years. Take it easy, eat, drink, and be merry.'

61 But Elohim said to him : 'Foolish man ! This very night you will have to give back your soul. The things you produced, whose will they be ?'

62 That is what happens to he who stores up treasure for himself and is not rich in the sight of Elohim."

Luke 12:22-31 (K41)

63 And he said to his disciples : "I am telling you : do not worry about your life, what you will eat, or about your body, what you will wear.

64 Life is more than food, and the body is more than clothing.

65 Consider the ravens : they do not sow nor reap, they have neither storehouse nor barn, and Elohim feeds them. How much more are you worth than the birds ?

66 Which one of you can add a single day to his life by worrying ?

67 Consider the lilies how they grow : they toil not, they spin not. Yet I say to you, that Solomon in all his splendor was not arrayed like one of these.

68 If then Elohim so clothes the grass that is in the field today and thrown into the oven tomorrow, won't He put clothes on you, faint hearts ?

69 And you, seek not what you will eat or what you will drink, neither be disquieted.

70 For those of the world seek these things, and your Father knows that you need these things.

71 But rather seek the Kingdom of Elohim, and all these things will be yours as well.

Luke 12:33-34 (K42)

72 "Sell your possessions and give alms. Store up a treasure in the heavens for yourselves, where no thief can break in and steal and no moth consumes.

73 For where your treasure is, there your heart will also be."

Luke 13:18-21 (K49)

74 He said : "What is the Kingdom of Elohim like ? To what should I compare it ?

75 It is like a grain of mustard which a man took and sowed in his garden, it grew, became a great tree, and the birds of the air made nests in its branches."

76 He also said : "The Kingdom of Elohim is like yeast, which a woman took and hid in three measures of flour, till the whole was leavened."

Luke 14:11 (K54)

77 "He who glorifies himself will be humiliated, and he who humbles himself will be praised."

Luke 14:16-22 (K55)

78 "A man once gave a great supper, and invited many.

79 At the time of the banquet he sent his servant to say to those who had been invited : 'Come, for everything is now ready.'

80 But they all began to make excuses. The first said to him : 'I have bought a piece of ground, and I must go and see it. Please excuse me.'

81 And another said : 'I have bought five pair of oxen and I need to check them out. Please excuse me.'

82 And another said : 'I have married a woman and so I can't come.'

83 When the servant came home he reported this to his master. Then the master of the house in anger said to his servant : 'Go out quickly to the streets of the town and bring in as many people as you find.

84 And the servant went out into the streets and brought together everybody he could find.

85 That way the house was filled with guests.'"

Luke 14:26-27 & 17:33 (K56)

86 "Whoever does not hate his father and mother will not be able to learn from me.

Whoever does not hate his son and daughter cannot belong to my school.

87 Whoever does not bear his cross and just follows me, cannot be one of my disciples.

88 Whoever seeks to save his life will lose it ; but whoever loses his life on account of me will preserve it."

Luke 14:34-35 (K57)

89 "Salt is good : but if salt loses its taste, how to restore it ?

90 It is not good for either the land or the dunghill : people just throw it out.

91 Whoever has ears to hear, let him hear !"

(End Q1)

The teachings that set the world ablaze, when broken down, are childishly simple, yet impossibly difficult to perform. Jesus made them very plain. Religion clouded the issue. Jesus preached an inclusive gospel. Religion made this gospel exclusive, for the sake of control.

How much more simple could his teachings be? How much more difficult can they be to perform all the time, every day? But if they were put to use the world would change over night.

Seek to know God's love

Seek to show love and mercy.

Do not judge.

Do not do anything to others you would not want done to you.

Help the poor.

Pray for the sick.

Don't worry about the future or material possessions.

Fully commit to this way of life.

Expect that when you do people will not like you because you will be different.

Do not fear death. God awaits his children.

Do not fear life. God's kingdom is near.

Do these things. The rest is commentary.

Dating Ancient Manuscripts

Scholars use a number of methods to establish the date of manuscripts. Contrary to what some think, Carbon-14 dating is only accurate within a fifty to one-hundred year period on items of recent history. The older the object the wider the possible dating error, because error rates are calculated in percentage. Since Carbon-14 dating needs material from the item it necessitates the destruction of part of the item for sampling. For ancient papyrus or vellum or other very precious material this may not be possible. For this reason, generally more indirect methods of dating are used.

Perspectives change in time. One way to set a date is to look at events mentioned in the text. If some event is mentioned or described the text must have been written after the date of occurrence. What is said about an occurrence could also help date and place the author. The recent wars in the Middle East, the first one ending in 1991 and the second continuing at the writing of this chapter, was thought to be a good idea, but after the U.S. went on to free Afghanistan it was understood by most that the actions unleashed a backlash of resistance and terrorism, which has called into question the wisdom of either war. Distance in time clarifies events.

Language and word choices are other indicators of date. Let us take a few recent examples. The words "transistor, computer, and data are recent occurrences. We know that computers have only been around as home appliances since the late 1980's. Floppy drives have already come and gone. Words come into style and go out in a matter of a generation. We no longer use the words snazzy, hep, or groovy. Use of these words would date the writing to within just a few years. Languages change and morph. Ours does, and so does any language in constant use. This simple idea can be clouded when manuscripts are added to and changed over time as words and ideas outside the original timeframe are introduced to older writings.

Writing styles change. The way letters are formed change over period of time. *from one script or style to another script, or to another style,* scripts change over time. Even the alphabet itself changes. The letter "W" was not used before the 7th century A.D. and did not see common use until the 11th century A.D.

The letter 'J' emerged in Middle High German. Gian Giorgio Trissino (1478–1550) was the first to explicitly distinguish I and J as representing separate sounds, in Trissino's epistle about the letters recently added in the Italian language" of 1524.

Even the way sentences and paragraphs are written change over time. The ancient Greeks did not have any equivalent to our modern devices of punctuation. Punctuation was invented several centuries after the time of Christ. The oldest copies of both the Greek New Testament and the Hebrew Old Testament were written with no punctuation at all. The ancient Greeks used no spaces between words or paragraphs. Texts were a continuous string of letters, without spaces or punctuation. Early Greeks had only one case of letters. Texts were written in what we would think of as all capitals.

The writing instruments and mediums are indicators of general timeframes in which the production of a document occurred. Papyrus was first manufactured in Egypt and Southern Sudan as far back as the fourth millennium BC. The earliest archaeological evidence of papyrus was excavated in 2012-2013 at Wadi al-Jarf, an ancient Egyptian harbor located on the Red Sea coast. These documents date from ca. 2560-2550 BC (end of the reign of Khufu).

Between 100 B.C. to 100 A.D. parchment began to rival papyrus. Parchment was prepared from animal skins. Sheets of parchment were folded to form quires from which book-form codices were fashioned. Early Christian writers soon adopted the codex form, and in the Græco-Roman world, it became common to cut sheets from papyrus rolls to form codices. The latest certain dates for the use of papyrus are 1057 for a papal decree (typically conservative, all papal bulls were on papyrus until 1022), under Pope Victor II, and 1087 for an Arabic document. Its use in Egypt continued until it was replaced by more inexpensive paper introduced by Arabs.

Papyrus was replaced in Europe by the cheaper parchment and vellum, of significantly higher durability in moist climates.

The term parchment is a general term for an animal skin which has been prepared for writing or printing. Parchment has been made for centuries, and is usually calf, goat, or sheep skin. The term vellum from the French veau refers to a parchment made from calf skin.

By examining the materials used to produce the manuscript, such as the ink and parchment, scholars can start with a general span of time. Then by looking at the letters, style of script, use of word choices, and sentence structures scholars continue to narrow the dating possibility. The content and occurrences written about in the text puts the finishing boundaries on the document's date.

Although there are many other considerations, these are the main items examined when dating a codex.

It is easy to see how controversies could exist between scholars when it comes to placing dates on ancient writings.

Reading the Words of Jesus From the Bible

Joseph Lumpkin

Preface

We have seen how the oral traditions spoken by Jesus were recalled and recorded to become the source material used to produce the Gospels. After reading these sources and understanding how they evolved and combined to yield the four Gospels, we can now look at all of the words of Jesus found in what became the Gospels of the New Testament .

In 1927, Arthur Hinds produced a simple yet comprehensive list of the sayings of Jesus. The guide was used by such great men as Norman Vincent Peale and has served as a layman's reference to all the words spoken by Jesus in the New Testament. As we have traced the words of Jesus through oral traditions and into various sources, we now see the end result. Wisdom taught and proclaimed by Jesus over two-thousand years ago, heard by common men and women and recorded by a few inspired souls became the gospels used by millions today. Below is a reproduction of the work of Arthur Hinds, which catalogs the words of Jesus throughout the New Testament of the Holy Bible.

The Complete Sayings of Jesus, by Arthur Hinds, [1927]

The number of words in the New Testament is 181,253. Only 36,450 of these 181,253 words are the words of Christ--barely over 20 per cent. Considered as verses, the New Testament has 7,959 verses, of which but 1,599 are sayings of Christ.

These relatively few sayings of Jesus have not a place apart, but run in an uneven distribution through the four Gospels (a few in other Books); and in each of the four Gospels--Matthew, Mark, Luke, John--the "sayings" are unevenly distributed through the narrative. Often a "saying" recorded, it may be, by Matthew, is paraphrased, or even duplicated, by one or more of the other three biographers, none of whom seems to have intended either a chronological harmony with the others, or even a sustained sequence of his own.

Accordingly, only the devoted reader of the New Testament, the habitual reader, is sufficiently the delver to have become familiar with Christ's sayings--really familiar--familiar with the sayings not only as severally set down by the four evangels, but also as one message, one gospel proclaiming the Saviour's great objective.

If relatively few persons in a Christian country are habitual readers of the sayings of Christ, that may be because relatively few persons are delvers.

The publisher is convinced that this book provides the means for the nonreaders of the New Testament to become familiar with Jesus the Christ, his sayings, and his great purpose, without delving-- indeed without effort, so engaging is the story here recorded--a glowing short story.

THE COMPILER'S PURPOSE

THE shelves of the libraries and of the bookstores bend beneath the tomes of the sayings, the bare sayings, of all the other great men; but one will not find in library or bookstore, in any published book, the complete sayings of Jesus, the bare sayings in simple sequence, Christ's own words, separate.

This compiler's purpose has been to enable any reader, whether confirmed Christian or inquiring pagan, or a frankly detached, to get him a book of CHRIST'S OWN WORDS, "divested," so runs the title page, "of the context, excepting those brief portions of the gospel narratives retained to establish the place, the time, or occasion, or a question the reply to which is the Master's own answer."

Many a reader, arrived at FINIS in the New Testament itself, has but a hazy picture of Christ on his daily walks as a circuit preacher everywhere within walking distance; has but a sketchy outline of the times and occasions--so many biographers!--Matthew, Mark, Luke, John, Paul--each essaying not a biography as such, not the record of the Teacher's sayings as such, but intent upon launching each his own conception of Christ's mission.

Christ's sayings complete, brought into a sequence of times and occasions, but lifted out of contexts alien to the present purpose, may prove to be a glowing story new not only to the non-reader, but new even to the whilom New-Testament readers who have not as yet discerned the "continuities."

Devoted readers will not be diverted from the Great Text. Perhaps other readers--the casual New-Testament reader and the non-reader--after enjoying these pages may venture the greater enjoyment: the attentive perusal of all the gospels and all the epistles, perhaps of all the New Testament.

A. H.

Joseph Lumpkin

This introduction appeared in later editions of this book. I was unable to find any evidence of a separate copyright.--JBH.

INTRODUCTION
BY NORMAN VINCENT PEALE, D.D.

ONE of the high spiritual moments which have enriched my life came the day I read this book at one sitting. It was a moving and unforgettable experience in which I had the feeling of actually being in the presence of Jesus. It produced a strange compelling identification with the sights, sounds and atmosphere of those times and the Lord's presence was profoundly realistic. When I finished the book I came back to present reality with a start. This effect was created by the fact that here we have every recorded word spoken by Jesus and in the sequence in which he uttered them.

This little volume offers an amazing reading experience, one in which the reader follows the Master through the villages and about the lake and into the cities, hearing his priceless comments to individuals and his sermons to vast multitudes. The reading of all of his words at one time and in chronological order produces an effect quite different from that which is attained by reading isolated Scripture passages in which his spoken words appear, as profoundly helpful as these are. The impact upon mind and heart, of his whole massage, affects one profoundly.

This book gives a panoramic concept of the thoughts and teachings of Jesus. And so grand and noble is the impression made upon the mind that the reader has an enhanced understanding of the purpose of this the greatest life ever lived. For mental stimulation, heartfelt comfort, and soul satisfaction, THE COMPLETE SAYINGS OF JESUS is unique.

I shall always be grateful that Lunsford P. Yandell made this little volume known to me years ago. He explained that a friend of his, a businessman, Arthur Hinds, sensed the importance of bringing the words of Jesus together in chronological form so that the full sweep and completeness of the immortal message might more effectively be felt and comprehended. These laymen had a keen consciousness of the ineffable power of the words of Jesus and, in a desire to relate them more widely to busy modern people, arranged them in this convenient and readable form. For many years this book has been made available through the literature sales organization of the Marble Collegiate Church. The thousands who have read the book, through our recommendation, have reported that it has brought great spiritual blessing to them. I commend this new edition to all who desire the creative touch of Christ upon their lives.

LINEAGE OF JESUS

I

LINEAGE OF JESUS--BORN IN BETHLEHEM

FROM NARRATIVES OF MATTHEW AND LUKE

Matthew 1, 1-2; 6-7; 11-12; 16-17.

The book of the generation of Jesus Christ, the son of David, the son of Abraham:

Abraham begat Isaac; and Isaac begat . . . .

. . .. And Jesse begat David the king; and David the king begat Solomon; and Solomon begat . . . .

. . .. And Josias begat Jechonias and his brethren, about the time they were carried away to Babylon; and Jechonias begat . . . .

. . .. And Jacob begat Joseph the husband of Mary, of whom was born Jesus who is called Christ.

So all the generations from Abraham to David are [**] fourteen generations; and from David until the carrying away into Babylon are fourteen generations; and from the carrying away into Babylon unto Christ are fourteen generations.

Luke 2, 1-12; 16-21.

It came to pass in those days, that there went out a decree from Cesar Augustus, that all the world should be taxed. And all went to be taxed, every one into his own city.

Joseph also went up from Galilee, out of the city of Nazareth, into Judea, unto the city of David which is called Bethlehem (because he was of the house and lineage of David), to be taxed with Mary his espoused wife, being great with child.

So it was, that, while they were there, the days were accomplished that she should be delivered. She brought forth her firstborn son, and wrapped him in swaddling clothes, and laid him in a manger; because there was no room for them in the inn. Dec. B.C. 5. [*+]

There were in the same country shepherds abiding in the field, keeping watch over their flock by night. And, lo, the angel of the Lord came upon them, and said, Behold, I bring you good tidings of great joy, which shall be to all people. For unto you is born this day in the city of David a Savior, which is Christ the Lord. Ye shall find the babe wrapped in swaddling clothes, lying in a manger.

And they came with haste, and found Mary, and Joseph, and the babe lying in a manger.

When eight days were accomplished for the circumcising of the child, his name was called JESUS, which was so named of the angel before he was conceived in the womb.

Footnotes

^5:* Like this "are," all the words which are italicized in the King James text are set in italics throughout this book also.
The punctuations also are, throughout, the punctuations of the King James text.

^5:+ It happens that dates "from the birth of Christ" did not begin to be cast until centuries after Christ's day. The monk said to be then responsible for the calculations made a mistake. The consensus of informed opinion now is that the "birth" of Jesus is to be set back four years. Accordingly the boy Jesus was "five years old" in December of what would have been the first year of the anno Domini calendar if that calendar had been started on the day of his birth: that is, five years and one week old on New Year's Day, A.D. 2.

II

THE ESCAPE FROM HEROD--AGAIN IN GALILEE AT NAZARETH

FROM MATTHEW'S NARRATIVE

B.C. 4

Matthew 2, 1-5; 7-15; 19-23.

NOW when Jesus was born in Bethlehem of Judea in the days of Herod the king, behold, there came wise men from the east to Jerusalem, saying, Where is he that is born King of the Jews? for we have seen his star in the east, and are come to worship him.

When Herod the king had heard these things, he was troubled. And when he had gathered the chief priests and scribes of the people together, he demanded of them where Christ should be born. They said, In Bethlehem of Judea.

Then Herod privily called the wise men, and inquired of them what time the star appeared. He sent them to Bethlehem, and said, Search diligently for the child; and when ye have found him, bring me word, that I may come and worship him also.

The wise men departed; and, lo, the star, which they saw in the east, went before them, till it stood over where the child was. They rejoiced with exceeding great joy.

And when they saw the child with Mary his mother, they worshipped him: and they opened their treasures, and presented unto him gifts, gold, and frankincense, and myrrh.

Warned of God in a dream that they should not return to Herod, the wise men departed into their own country another way.

When the wise men were departed, behold, the angel of the Lord appeareth to Joseph in a dream, saying, Arise, take the child and his mother, and flee into Egypt and be thou there until I bring thee word: for Herod will seek the child to destroy him.

Joseph arose, took the child and his mother by night, and departed into Egypt: and was there until the death of Herod.

When Herod was dead, behold, an angel of the Lord appeareth in a dream to Joseph in Egypt, saying, Arise, and take the child and his mother, and go into the land of Israel.

But Joseph heard that Archelaus did reign in Judea in the room of his father Herod: he was afraid to go thither: he turned aside into the parts of Galilee: and he came and dwelt in Nazareth.

III

THE BOY JESUS: AT TWELVE, VISITS JERUSALEM--TARRIES BEHIND--TALKS IN TEMPLE WITH THE DOCTORS--SPEAKS TO HIS MOTHER
 HIS FIRST RECORDED WORDS

A.D. 8. Age 12. Nazareth. Jerusalem

Luke 2, 40-52.

THE child grew, and waxed strong in spirit, filled with wisdom: and the grace of God was upon him.

Now his parents went to Jerusalem every year at the feast of the passover. When Jesus was twelve years old, they went up to Jerusalem after the custom of the feast.

They fulfilled the days, and as they returned, the child Jesus tarried behind in Jerusalem; and Joseph and his mother knew not of it. They, supposing him to have been in the company, went a day's journey and [then] they sought him among their kinsfolk and acquaintance. When they found him not, they turned back to Jerusalem, seeking him.

After three days they found him in the temple, sitting in the midst of the doctors, both hearing them, and asking questions. All that heard him were astonished at his understanding and answers.

His mother said unto him, Son, why hast thou thus dealt with us? behold, thy father and I have sought thee sorrowing. Jesus said unto them, How is it that ye sought me? wist ye not that I must be about my Father's business? And they understood not.

He went down with them to Nazareth, and was subject into them: but his mother kept all these sayings in her heart.

And Jesus increased in wisdom and stature, and in favor with God and man. [**]

Footnotes

^7:* Note that the curtain drops here, as it were, on the drama of Jesus at the age of twelve, not to rise again till the age of thirty.

IV

JESUS AT THIRTY--BAPTIZED BY JOHN
A.D. 27. Age 30 Judea: Jordan.
Matthew 3, 1-6; 13-17: Mark 1, 10-11; Luke 3, 22-23.

In those days came John the Baptist, preaching in the wilderness of Judea, saying, Repent ye: for the kingdom of heaven is at hand.

This is he that was spoken of by the prophet Esaias, saying, The voice of one crying in the wilderness, Prepare ye the way of the Lord, make his paths straight.

John had his raiment of camel's hair, and a leathern girdle about his loins; and his meat was locusts and wild honey.

Then went out to him Jerusalem, and all Judea, and all the region round about Jordan, and were baptized of him in Jordan, confessing their sins.

Then cometh Jesus from Galilee to Jordan unto John, to be baptized of him. But John forbade him, saying, I have need to be baptized of thee, and comest thou to me?

Jesus answering said unto him, Suffer it to be so now: for thus it becometh us to fulfill all righteousness.

Then John suffered him. And Jesus, when he was baptized, went up straightway out of the water: and praying, lo, the heavens were opened unto him, and he saw the Spirit of God descending in a bodily shape like a dove, and lighting upon him; and to a voice from heaven, saying, This is my beloved Son, in whom I am well pleased.

And Jesus himself began to be about thirty years of age.

V

CHRIST'S LONG FAST IN THE WILDERNESS--SATAN'S FUTILE WILES

A.D. 27. Age 30. Judea.
Matthew 4, 1-11: Mark 1, 13: Luke 4, 1-13.

THEN was Jesus led up of the Spirit into the wilderness to be tempted of the devil. He was there in the wilderness forty days, and was with the wild beasts. In those days he did eat nothing. And when he had fasted forty days and forty nights, he was a hungered.

The tempter came: he said, If thou be the Son of God, command that these stones be made bread. But Jesus answered, It is written, Man shall not live by bread alone, but by every word that proceedeth out of the mouth of God.

Then, in Jerusalem, the holy city, on a pinnacle of the temple, the devil saith unto Jesus, If thou be the Son of God, cast thyself down from hence: for it is written, He shall give his angels charge concerning thee, to keep thee: and in their hands they shall bear thee up, lest at any time thou dash they foot against a stone.

Jesus answering said, It is written again, Thou shalt not tempt the Lord thy God.

Again, up an exceeding high mountain, the devil sheweth him, in a moment of time, all the kingdoms of the world, and the glory of them, and saith unto Jesus, All these things will I give thee; all this power, and the glory of them: if thou wilt fall down and worship me, all shall be thine.

And Jesus answered, Get thee behind me, Satan; get thee hence: for it is written, Thou shalt worship the Lord thy God, and him only shalt thou serve.
Then the devil leaveth him.

VI

JOHN ANSWERS THE PRIESTS--"BEHOLD THE LAMB OF GOD"--JESUS HAILS ANDREW, SIMON, PHILIP, AND NATHANAEL

A.D. 27 Age 30. Bethabara

Joseph Lumpkin

John, 1, 19-20 . . . 22-29 . . . 37-51.

JOHN, when the Jews sent priests and Levites from Jerusalem to ask him, Who art thou? confessed, I am not the Christ. I am the voice of one crying in the wilderness, Make straight the way of the Lord.

They asked him, Why baptizest thou then, if thou be not that Christ?

John answered, I baptize with water: but there standeth one among you, whom ye know not; he it is, who coming after me is preferred before me, whose shoe's latchet I am not worthy to unloose.

These things were done in Bethabara beyond Jordan, where John was baptizing.

The next day after, John stood, and two of his disciples; and looking upon Jesus as he walked, he saith, Behold the Lamb of God, which taketh away the sin of the world.

The two disciples heard John speak, and they followed Jesus. He saw them following, and saith, What seek ye?

They answered, Rabbi (which is to say, Master), where dwellest thou? Jesus saith, Come and see.

They came and saw where he dwelt, and they abode with him that day. One of the two was Andrew, Simon Peter's brother. He first findeth Simon, and saith unto him, We have found the Messias. [**]

Andrew brought Simon to Jesus. And when Jesus beheld Simon, he said, Thou art Simon the son of Jona: thou shalt be called Cephas.

Cephas is, by interpretation, A stone. [*+]

The day following, Jesus would go forth into Galilee, and findeth Philip: he was of Bethsaida, the city of Andrew and Simon Peter. And Jesus saith unto Philip, Follow me.

Philip findeth Nathanael, and saith unto him, We have found him of whom Moses did write, Jesus of Nazareth, the son of Joseph. And Nathanael said, Can there any good thing come out of Nazareth? Philip said, Come and see.

Jesus saw Nathanael coming, and saith of him, Behold an Israelite indeed, in whom is no guile!

Nathanael saith, Whence knowest thou me? Jesus answered, Before that Philip called thee, when thou wart under the fig tree, I saw thee.

Nathanael answered, Master, thou art the Son of God; thou art the King of Israel. Jesus said, Because I said unto thee, I saw thee under the fig tree, believest thou? thou shalt see greater things than these. Verily, verily, I say unto you, Hereafter ye shall see heaven open, and the angels of God ascending and descending upon the Son of man.

Footnotes

^9:* ". . . which is, being interpreted, the Christ."

^9:+ The Revised Version has it: ". . . which is by interpretation, Peter." Both words, Peter and Cephas, have the meaning, rock, stone.

VII

JESUS' MOTHER AND THE WATER CHANGED TO WINE--HE DRIVES THE MONEYMAKERS FROM THE TEMPLE--TEMPLE OF THE BODY

A.D. 27. Age 30. Cana. Jerusalem.
John 2, 1-9; 12-16; 18-21.

THE third day, there was a marriage in Cana of Galilee. Both Jesus was called, and his disciples, to the marriage; and the mother of Jesus was there.

When they wanted wine, his mother saith unto Jesus, They have no wine. Jesus saith, Woman, what have I to do with thee? mine hour is not yet come.

His mother saith unto the servants, Whatsoever he saith, do it.

There were set there six waterpots of stone containing two or three firkins apiece. Jesus saith, Fill the waterpots with water.

They filled them to the brim. And he saith, Draw out now, and bear unto the governor of the feast.

And they bare it. The ruler of the feast tasted. The water was made wine.

After this he went to Capernaum, Jesus, and his mother, and his brethren, and his disciples; and they continued there not many days.

The Jews' passover was at hand: Jesus went up to Jerusalem.

[**]He found in the temple those that sold oxen and sheep and doves; and the changers of money sitting: and when he had made a scourge of small cords, he drove them all out of the temple, and the sheep, and the oxen; and poured out the changers' money, and overthrew the tables; and said unto them that sold doves,

Take these things hence, make not my Father's house a house of merchandise.

Then the Jews said unto Jesus, What sign shewest thou unto us, seeing that thou doest these things? He answered, Destroy this temple, and in three days I will raise it up. [*+]

Then said the Jews, Forty and six years was this temple in building, and wilt thou rear it up in three days?
But Jesus spake of the temple of his body.

Footnotes

^11:* John 2, 14-16. Matthew and Mark tell of a similar encounter (turn to LXV of this book).

^11:+ Symbolism: For other examples turn to XXXVI and XLV in this book.

VIII

NIGHTTIME VISIT OF NICODEMUS--CHRIST ENLIGHTENS HIM

April, A.D. 27 Age 30. Jerusalem.

John 3, 1-21.

A MAN of the Pharisees, named Nicodemus, a ruler of the Jews, came to Jesus by night, and said unto him, Master, we know that thou art a teacher come from God: for no man can do these miracles that thou doest, except God be with him. Jesus answered, Verily, verily, I say unto thee, Except a man be born again, he cannot see the kingdom of God.

Nicodemus saith unto him, How can a man be born when he is old? Jesus answered, Verily, verily, I say unto thee, Except a man be born of water and of the Spirit, he cannot enter into the kingdom of God. That which is born of the flesh is flesh: and that which is born of the Spirit is spirit.

Marvel not that I said unto thee, Ye must be born again. The wind bloweth where it listeth, and thou hearest the sound thereof, but canst not tell whence it cometh, and whither it goeth: so is every one that is born of the Spirit.

Nicodemus said, How can these things be? Jesus answered, Art thou a master of Israel, and knowest not these things? Verily, verily, I say unto thee, We speak that we do know, and testify that we have seen; and ye receive not our witness.

If I have told you earthly things, and ye believe not, how shall ye believe, if I tell you of heavenly things? And no man hath ascended up to heaven, but he that came down from heaven, even the Son of man which is in heaven.

And as Moses lifted up the serpent in the wilderness, even so must the Son of man be lifted up: that whosoever believeth in him should not perish, but have eternal life.

For God so loved the world, that he gave his only begotten Son, that whosoever believeth in him should not perish, but have everlasting life. For God sent not his Son into the world to condemn the world; but that the world through him might be saved.

He that believeth on him is not condemned; but he that believeth not is condemned already, because he hath not believed in the name of the only begotten Son of God.

And this is the condemnation, that light has come into the world, and men loved darkness rather than light, because their deeds were evil. For every one that doeth evil hateth the light, neither cometh to the light, lest his deeds should be reproved. But he that doeth truth cometh to the light, that his deeds may be made manifest, that they are wrought in God. [**]

Footnotes

^12:* Nicodemus appears again in the story (in LXXXVII in this book).

IX

JOHN EXTOLS JESUS--THE WOMAN AT THE WELL--"ONE SOWETH, AND ANOTHER REAPETH"

A.D. 27. Age 30. Samaria: Sychar.

John 3, 22 . . . 28; 1-40.

AFTER these things came Jesus and his disciples into the land of Judea. John was baptizing in Enon near to Salim. For John was not yet cast into prison.

There arose a question between some of John's disciples and the Jews. They came unto John, saying, Rabbi, he that was with thee beyond Jordan, to whom thou barest witness, behold, the same baptizeth, and all men come to him.

John said, Ye yourselves bear me witness, that I said, I am not the Christ, but that I am sent before him.

When Jesus knew how the Pharisees had heard that he made and baptized more disciples than John (though Jesus himself baptized not, but his disciples), he left Judea, and departed again into Galilee. And he must needs go through Samaria.

Then cometh he to a city of Samaria called Sychar, near to the parcel of ground that Jacob gave to his son Joseph.

Now Jacob's well was there. Jesus being wearied with his journey, sat on the well.

There cometh a woman of Samaria to draw water: Jesus saith unto her, Give me to drink.

The woman saith, How is it that thou, being a Jew, asketh drink of me, a woman of Samaria? for the Jews have no dealings with the Samarians. Jesus answered, If thou knewest the gift of God, and who it is that saith to thee, Give me to drink; thou wouldest have asked of him, and he would have given thee living water.

The woman saith, Sir, thou hast nothing to draw with, and the well is deep: from whence then hast thou that living water? Art thou greater than our father Jacob, which gave us the well, and drank thereof himself, and his children, and his cattle? Jesus said, Whosoever drinketh of this water shall thirst again; but whosoever drinketh of the water that I shall give him shall never thirst; but the water that I shall give him shall be in him a well of water springing up into everlasting life.

The woman answered, Sir, give me this water, that I thirst not, neither come hither to draw. Jesus saith, Go, call thy husband, and come hither.

The woman answered, I have no husband. Jesus said, Thou hast well said, I have no husband: for thou hast had five husbands; and he whom thou now hast is not thy husband: in that saidst thou truly.

The woman saith, Sir, I perceive that thou art a prophet. Our fathers worshipped in this mountain; and ye say, that in Jerusalem is the place where men ought to worship. Jesus saith, Woman, believe me, the hour cometh, when ye shall neither in this mountain, nor yet at Jerusalem, worship the Father. Ye worship ye know not what: we know what we worship; for salvation is of the Jews.

But the hour cometh, and now is, when the true worshippers shall worship the Father in spirit and in truth: for the Father seeketh such to worship him.

God is a Spirit: and they that worship him must worship him in spirit and in truth.

The woman saith, I know that Messias cometh, which is called Christ: when he is come, he will tell us all things. Jesus saith, I that speak unto thee am he.

The woman went her way into the city, and saith to the men, Come, see a man, which told me all things that ever I did: is not this the Christ?

In the mean while his disciples prayed him, saying, Master, eat. But he said, I have meat to eat that ye know not of.

Therefore said the disciples one to another, Hath any man brought him aught to eat? Jesus saith unto them, My meat is to do the will of him that sent me, and to finish his work.

Say not ye, There are yet four months, and then cometh harvest? Behold, I say unto you, Lift up your eyes, and look on the fields; for they are white already to harvest. And he that reapeth receiveth wages, and gathereth fruit unto life eternal: that both he that soweth and he that reapeth may rejoice together.

And herein is that saying true, One soweth, and another reapeth.

I sent you to reap that whereon ye bestowed no labor: other men labored, and ye are entered into their labor.

Many of the Samaritans of that city believed on him for the saying of the woman, which testified, He told me all that ever I did.

So they besought Jesus that he would tarry with them: and he abode there two days.

X

CHRIST IN CANA CURES NOBLEMAN'S SON AT CAPERNAUM

A.D. 27. Age 30. Galilee: Cana (again).

John 4, 43-53.

AFTER two days Jesus went into Galilee: for Jesus himself testified, that a prophet hath no honor in his own country.

The Galileans received him, having seen all the things that he did at Jerusalem at the feast: for they also went unto the feast.

So Jesus came again into Cana of Galilee, where he [had] made the water wine.

And there was a certain nobleman, whose son was sick at Capernaum. He went unto Jesus, and besought him that he would come down, and heal his son: for he was at the point of death. Then said Jesus unto him, Except ye see signs and wonders, ye will not believe.

The nobleman saith, Sir, come down ere my child die. Jesus answered, Go thy way: thy son liveth.

The man believed, and went his way. And going down, his servants met him, and told him, Thy son liveth.

Then inquired he of them the hour when the child began to amend. They said, Yesterday at the seventh hour the fever left him.

So the father knew that it was at the same hour, in the which Jesus said unto him, Thy son liveth.

XI

AT THE POOL: THE IMPOTENT MAN CURED--SABBATH HEALING JUSTIFIED--JESUS' SONSHIP SET FORTH--"SEARCH THE SCRIPTURES"

A.D. 27. Age 30. Jerusalem: Pool of Bethesda.

John 5, 1-47.

AFTER this there was a feast of the Jews; and Jesus went up to Jerusalem.

At Jerusalem there is a pool, called Bethesda, having five porches. In these lay impotent folk: blind, halt, withered, waiting for the moving of the water. For an angel went down at a certain season into the pool, and troubled the water: whosoever then first after the troubling of the water stepped in was made whole of whatever disease he had.

A certain man was there, which had an infirmity thirty and eight years. When Jesus saw him lie, and knew that he had been now a long time in that case, he saith unto him, Wilt thou be made whole?

The impotent man answered, Sir, I have no man, when the water is troubled, to put me into the pool: but while I am coming, another steppeth down before me. Jesus saith unto him, Rise, take up thy bed, and walk.

Immediately the man was made whole, and took up his bed, and walked: and on the same day was the sabbath.

The Jews therefore said unto him that was cured, It is the sabbath day: it is not lawful for thee to carry thy bed.

He answered, He that made me whole, the same said unto me, Take up thy bed, and walk.

Then they asked him, What man is that? And he that was healed wist not who it was: for Jesus had conveyed himself away, a multitude being in that place.

Afterward Jesus findeth him in the temple, and said unto him,

Joseph Lumpkin

Behold, thou art made whole: sin no more, lest a worse thing come unto thee.

The man departed, and told the Jews that it was Jesus, which had made him whole. And the Jews sought to slay Jesus, because he had done these things on the sabbath day.

But Jesus answered them, My Father worketh hitherto, and I work.

The Jews sought the more to kill him, because he not only had broken the sabbath, but said also that God was his Father, making himself equal with God. Then Jesus said unto them, Verily, verily, I say unto you, The Son can do nothing of himself, but what he seeth the Father do: for what things soever he doeth, these also docth the Son likewise. For the Father loveth the Son, and sheweth him all things that himself doeth: and he will shew him greater works than these, that ye may marvel.

For as the Father raiseth up the dead, and quickeneth them; even so the Son quickeneth whom he will.

For the Father judgeth no man, but hath committed all judgment unto the Son; that all men should honor the Son, even as they honor the Father. He that honoreth not the Son honoreth not the Father which hath sent him.

263

Verily, verily, I say unto you, He that heareth my word, and believeth on him that sent me, hath everlasting life, and shall not come into condemnation; but is passed from death unto life.

Verily, verily, I say unto you. The hour is coming, and now is, when the dead shall hear the voice of the Son of God: and they that hear shall live. For as the Father hath life in himself; so hath he given to the Son to have life in himself; and hath given him authority to execute judgment also because he is the Son of man. Marvel not at this: for the hour is coming, in the which all that are in the graves shall hear his voice, and shall come forth; they that have done good, unto the resurrection of life; and they that have done evil, unto the resurrection of damnation.

I can of mine own self do nothing: as I hear, I judge: and my judgment is just; because I seek not mine own will, but the will of the Father which hath sent me. If I bear witness of myself, my witness is not true.

There is another that beareth witness of me; and I know that the witness which he witnesseth of me is true.

Ye sent unto John, and he bare witness unto the truth. But I receive not testimony from man: but these things I say, that ye might be saved. He was a burning and a shining light: and we were willing for a season to rejoice in his light.

But I have greater witness than that of John: for the works which the Father hath given me to finish, the same works that I do, bear witness of me, that the Father hath sent me. And the Father himself, which hath sent me, hath borne witness of me. Ye have neither heard his voice at any time, nor seen his shape. And ye have not his word abiding in you: for whom he hath sent, him ye believe not.

Search the Scriptures; for in them ye think ye have eternal life: and they are they which testify of me. And ye will not come to me, that ye might have life.

I receive not honor from men. But I know you, that ye have not the love of God in you. I am come in my Father's name, and ye receive me not: if another shall come in his own name, him ye will receive. How can ye believe, which receive honor one of another, and seek not the honor that cometh from God only?

Do not think that I will accuse you to the Father: there is one that accuseth you, even Moses, in whom ye trust. For had ye believed Moses, ye would have believed me: for he wrote of me. But if ye believe not his writings, how shall ye believe my words?

XII

CHRIST READS IN SYNAGOGUE AT NAZARETH--ELUDES ANGRY HEARERS--BEGINS TO PREACH REPENTANCE

A.D. 28. Age 31. Nazareth. Capernaum.

Luke 4, 16-31; Mark 1, 15; Matthew 4, 17.

JESUS came to Nazareth, where he had been brought up: and, as his custom was, he went into the synagogue on the sabbath day, and stood up for to read. When he had opened the book, he found the place where it was written,

[**]The Spirit of the Lord is upon me, because he hath anointed me to preach the gospel to the poor; he hath sent me to heal the brokenhearted, to preach deliverance to the captives, and recovering of sight to the blind, to set at liberty them that are bruised, to preach the acceptable year of the Lord.

He closed the book, gave it again to the minister, and sat down. The eyes of all them that were in the synagogue were fastened on him: and he began to say unto them, This day is this Scripture fulfilled in your ears.

And all bare witness, and wondered at the gracious words which pro-ceded out of his mouth. They said, Is not this Joseph's son? And Jesus said, Ye will surely say unto me this proverb, Physician, heal thyself: whatsoever we have heard done in Capernaum, do also here in thy country.

And he said, Verily I say unto you, No prophet is accepted in his own country.

But I tell you of a truth, many widows were in Israel in the days of Elias, when the heaven was shut up three years and six months, when great famine was throughout all the land; but unto none of them was Elias sent, save unto Sarepta, a city of Sidom, unto a woman that was a widow.

And many lepers were in Israel in the time of Eliseus the prophet: and none of them was cleansed, saving Naaman the Syrian.

They in the synagogue, when they heard these things, were filled with wrath, and rose up, and thrust Jesus out, and led him unto the brow of the hill wheron their city was built, that they might cast him down headlong.

Now Jesus had heard that John was cast into prison; and, passing through the midst of them, he went his way: and leaving Nazareth, he departed into Galilee: he came to Capernaum.

Jesus dwelt in Capernaum, preaching the gospel of the kingdom of God, and saying, The time is fulfilled, and the kingdom of heaven is at hand: repent ye, and believe the gospel. Repent: for the kingdom of God is at hand.

From that time Jesus began to preach; and he taught them on the sabbath days.

Footnotes

^17:* This passage from Luke (4, 18-19) paraphrases verses 1-2 of Isaiah 61, which Jesus "stood up for to read."

XIII

BY THE SEA--CHRIST CHOOSES THE FOUR--THE CURE IN THE SYNAGOGUE--SOLITARY PRAYER--IN "THE NEXT TOWNS" ROUND ABOUT GALILEE

A.D. 28. Age 31. Galilee: Capernaum.

Mark 1, 16-26; Luke 4, 31 . . . 38 . . . 44; Matthew 4, 17 . . . 25.

NOW as Jesus walked by the sea of Galilee, he saw Simon Peter and Andrew his brother casting a net into the sea: for they were fishers. He said unto them, Come ye after me, and I will make you to become fishers of men. Follow me.

Straightway they forsook their nets, and followed him.

When he had gone a little further thence, he saw James the son of Zebedee, and John his brother, who were in a ship with their father, mending their nets. He called them: and they left their father in the ship with the hired servants, and followed Jesus.

They went into Capernaum; and on the sabbath day Jesus entered into the synagogue, and taught. They were astonished: for his word was with power: he taught them as one that had authority, and not as the scribes.

There was in their synagogue a man with an unclean spirit; and he cried out, Let us alone, thou Jesus of Nazareth. Art thou come to destroy us? I know who thou art: the Holy One of God.

Jesus rebuked him, saying, Hold thy peace, and come out of him.

When the unclean spirit had thrown the man in the midst, he came out of him, and hurt him not.

Jesus arose, and, when they were come out of the synagogue, entered the house of Peter and Andrew, with James and John.

In the morning, rising up a great while before day, Jesus went out into a solitary place, and there prayed.

The people sought him, and came unto him, and stayed him, that he should not depart. He said, I must preach the kingdom of God to other cities also: for therefore am I sent.

Simon and they that were with him followed after Jesus, and when they had found him, they said unto him, [**]All men seek for thee. He answered, Let us go into the next towns, that I may preach there also: for therefore came I forth.

And Jesus went about all Galilee, teaching in their synagogues, and preaching the gospel of the kingdom. His fame went throughout Syria. And there followed him multitudes from Galilee, and Decapolis; [**] from Jerusalem, and Judea; and from beyond Jordan.

Footnotes

^19:* Decapolis: The region bordering the Sea of Galilee eastward, and embracing the adjacent lands in which lay the ten (allied) cities then known collectively as Decapolis.

XIV

THE SERMON ON THE MOUNT: THE BEATITUDES, ADMONITIONS, PRECEPTS

A.D. 28, Age 31 Near Capernaum.

Matthew 5, 1-48.

SEEING the multitudes, Jesus went up into a mountain: and when he was set, his disciples came unto him: and he opened his mouth, and taught them, saying, Blessed are the poor in spirit: for theirs is the kingdom of heaven.

Blessed are they that mourn: for they shall be comforted.

Blessed are the meek: for they shall inherit the earth.

Blessed are they which do hunger and thirst after righteousness: for they shall be filled.

Blessed are the merciful: for they shall obtain mercy.

Blessed are the pure in heart: for they shall see God.

Blessed are the peacemakers: for they shall be called the children of God.

Blessed are they which are persecuted for righteousness' sake: for theirs is the kingdom of heaven.

Blessed are ye, when men shall revile you, and persecute you, and shall say all manner of evil against you falsely, for my sake.

Rejoice, and be exceeding glad: for great is your reward in heaven: for so persecuted they the prophets which were before you.

Ye are the salt of the earth; but if the salt have lost his savor, wherewith shall it be salted? it is thenceforth good for nothing, but to be cast out, and to be trodden under foot of men.

Ye are the light of the world. A city that is set on a hill cannot be hid. Neither do men light a candle, and put it under a bushel, but on a candlestick; and it giveth light unto all that are in the house. Let your light so shine before men, that they may see your good works, and glorify your Father which is in heaven.

Think not that I am come to destroy the law, or the prophets: I am not come to destroy, but to fulfil. For verily I say unto you, Till heaven and earth pass, one jot or one tittle shall in no wise pass from the law, till all be fulfilled.

Whosoever therefore shall break one of these least commandments, and shall teach men so, he shall be called the least in the kingdom of heaven: but whosoever shall do and teach them, the same shall be called great in the kingdom of heaven. For I say unto you, That except your righteousness shall exceed the righteousness of the scribes and Pharisees, ye shall in no case enter into the kingdom of heaven.

Ye have heard that it was said by them of old time, Thou shalt not kill; and whosoever shall kill shall be in danger of the judgment: but I say unto you, That whosoever is angry with his brother without a cause shall be in danger of the judgment: and whosoever shall say to his brother, Raca, shall be in danger of the council: but whosoever shall say, Thou fool, shall be in danger of hell fire.

Therefore if thou bring thy gift to the altar, and there rememberest that thy brother hath aught against thee; leave there thy gift before the altar, and go thy way; first be reconciled to thy brother, and then come and offer thy gift.

Agree with thine adversary quickly, while thou art in the way with him; lest at any time the adversary deliver thee to the judge, and the judge deliver thee to the officer, and thou be cast into prison. Verily I say unto thee, Thou shalt by no means come out thence, till thou hast paid the uttermost farthing.

Ye have heard that it was said by them of old time, Thou shalt not commit adultery: but I say unto you, That whosoever looketh on a woman to lust after her hath committed adultery with her already in his heart.

And if thy right eye offend thee, pluck it out, and cast it from thee: for it is profitable for thee that one of thy members should perish, and not that thy whole body should be cast into hell.

And if thy right hand offend thee, cut it off, and cast it from thee, for it is profitable for thee that one of thy members should perish, and not that thy whole body should be cast into hell.

It hath been said, Whosoever shall put away his wife, let him give her a writing of divorcement: but I say unto you, That whosoever shall put away his wife, saving for the cause of fornication, causeth her to commit adultery: and whosoever shall marry her that is divorced cornmitteth adultery. [**]

Again, ye have heard that it hath been said by them of old time, Thou shalt not forswear thyself, but shalt perform unto the Lord thine oaths: but I say unto you, Swear not at all; neither by heaven; for it is God's throne: nor by the earth; for it is his footstool: neither by Jerusalem; for it is the city of the great King. Neither shalt thou swear by thy head, because thou canst not make one hair white or black. But let your communication be, Yea, yea; Nay, nay: for whatsoever is more than these cometh of evil.

Ye have heard that it hath been said, An eye for an eye, and a tooth for a tooth: but I say unto you, That ye resist not evil: but whosoever shall smite thee on thy right cheek, turn to him the other also. And if any man will sue thee at the law, and take away thy coat, let him have thy cloak also. And whosoever shall compel thee to go a mile, go with him twain. Give to him that asketh thee, and from him that would borrow of thee turn not thou away.

Ye have heard that it hath been said, Thou shalt love thy neighbor, and hate thine enemy: but I say unto you,

[*+]Love your enemies, bless them that curse you, do good to them that hate you, and pray for them which despitefully use you, and persecute you; that ye may be the children of your Father which is in heaven: for he maketh his sun to rise on the evil and on the good, and sendeth rain on the just and on the unjust.

For if ye love them which love you, what reward have ye? do not even the publicans the same? And if ye salute your brethren only, what do ye more than others? do not even the publicans so? Be ye therefore perfect, even as your Father, which is in heaven is perfect.

Footnotes

^21:* Thus Matthew (5, 31-32).

^21:+ The spirit of the Golden Rule.

XV

THE SERMON ON THE MOUNT (CONTINUED): ALMSGIVING, THE LORD'S PRAYER, FORGIVING, TREASURES, GOD OR MAMMON, SUFFICIENT UNTO THE DAY

A.D. 28, Age 31 Near Capernaum.

Matthew 6, 1-34.

TAKE heed that ye do not your alms before men, to be seen of them; otherwise ye have no reward of your Father which is in heaven. Therefore when thou doest thine alms, do not sound a trumpet before thee, as the hypocrites do in the synagogues and in the streets, that they may have glory of men. Verily I say unto you, They have their reward. But when thou doest alms, let not thy left hand know what thy right hand doeth: that thine alms may be in secret: and thy Father which seeth in secret himself shall reward thee openly.

And when thou prayest, thou shalt not be as the hyprocites are: for they love to pray standing in the synagogues and in the corners of the streets, that they may be seen of men. Verily I say unto you, They have their reward. But thou, when thou prayest, enter into thy closet, and when thou hast shut thy door, pray to thy Father which is in secret; and thy Father which seeth in secret shall reward thee openly.

But when ye pray, use not vain repetitions, as the heathen do: for they think that they shall be heard for their much speaking. Be not ye therefore like unto them: for your Father knoweth what things ye have need of, before ye ask him.

After this manner therefore pray ye: Our Father which art in heaven, Hallowed be thy name. Thy kingdom come. Thy will be done in earth, as it is in heaven.

Give us this day our daily bread. And forgive us our debts, as we forgive our debtors.

And lead us not into temptation, but deliver us from evil: For thine is the kingdom, and the power, and the glory, for ever. Amen.

For if ye forgive men their trespasses, your heavenly Father will also forgive you: but if ye forgive not men their , neither will your Father forgive your trespasses.

Moreover when ye fast, be not, as the hypocrites, of a sad countenance: for they disfigure their faces, that they may appear unto men to fast. Verily I say unto you, They have their reward. But thou, when thou fastest, anoint thy head, and wash thy face; that thou appear not unto men to fast, but unto thy Father which is in secret: and thy Father, which seeth in secret, shall reward thee openly.

Lay not up for yourselves treasures upon earth, where moth and rust doth corrupt, and where thieves break through and steal: but lay up for yourselves treasures in heaven, where neither moth nor rust doth corrupt, and where thieves do not break through nor steal. For where your treasure is, there will your heart be also.

The light of the body is the eye: if therefore thine eye be single, thy whole body shall be full of light. But if thine eye be evil, thy whole body shall be full of darkness. If therefore the light that is in thee be darkness, how great is that darkness!

No man can serve two masters: for either he will hate the one, and love the other: or else he will hold to the one, and despise the other. Ye cannot serve God and mammon.

Therefore I say unto you, Take no thought for your life, what ye shall eat, or what ye shall drink; nor yet for your body, what ye shall put on. Is not the life more than meat, and the body than raiment? Behold the fowls of the air: for they sow not, neither do they reap, nor gather into barns; yet your heavenly Father feedeth them. Are ye not much better than they?

Which of you by taking thought can add one cubic unto his stature? And why take ye thought for raiment? Consider the lilies of the field, how they grow; they toil not, neither do they spin; and yet I say unto you, That even Solomon in all his glory was not arrayed like one of these. Wherefore, if God so clothe the grass of the field, which to day is, and to morrow is cast into the oven, shall he not much more clothe you, O ye of little faith?

Therefore take no thought, saying, What shall we eat? or, What shall we drink? or, Wherewithal shall we be clothed? (for after all these

278

things do the Gentiles seek) for your heavenly Father knoweth that ye have need of all these things.

But seek ye first the kingdom of God, and his righteousness; and all these things shall be added unto you. Take therefore no thought for the morrow: for the morrow shall take thought for the things of itself. Sufficient unto the day is the evil thereof.

XVI

THE SERMON ON THE MOUNT (CONCLUDED): JUDGE NOT, PEARLS BEFORE SWINE, PRAYER, THE GOLDEN RULE, THE STRAIT GATE, "I NEVER KNEW YOU," ROCK FOUNDATION

A.D. 28, Age 31 Near Capernaum.

Matthew 7, 1-29.

JUDGE not, that ye be not judged. For with what judgment ye judge, ye shall be judged: and with what measure ye mete, it shall be measured to you again.

And why beholdest thou the mote that is in thy brother's eye, but considerest not the beam that is in thine own eye? Or how wilt thou say to thy brother, Let me pull out the mote out of thine eye; and, behold, a beam is in thine own eye? Thou hypocrite, first cast out the beam out of thine own eye; and then shalt thou see clearly to cast out the mote out of thy brother's eye.

Give not that which is holy unto the dogs, neither cast ye your pearls before swine, lest they trample them under their feet, and turn again and rend you.

Ask, and it shall be given you; seek, and ye shall find; knock, and it shall be opened unto you: for every one that asketh receiveth; and he that seeketh findeth; and to him that knocketh it shall be opened.

Or what man is there of you, whom if his son ask bread, will he give him a stone? Or if he asks a fish, will he give him a serpent? If ye then, being evil, know how to give good gifts unto your children, how much more shall your Father which is in heaven give good things to them that ask him?

[**]Therefore all things whatsoever ye would that men should do to you, do ye even so to them: for this is the law and the prophets.

Enter ye in at the strait gate: for wide is the gate, and broad is the way, that leadeth to destruction, and many there be which go in thereat: because strait is the gate, and narrow is the way, which leadeth unto life, and few there be that find it.

Beware of false prophets, which come to you in sheep's clothing, but inwardly they are ravening wolves. Ye shall know them by their fruits. Do men gather grapes of thorns, or figs of thistles? Even so every good tree bringeth forth good fruit; but a corrupt tree bringeth forth evil fruit. A good tree cannot bring forth evil fruit, neither can a corrupt tree bring forth good fruit. Every tree that bringeth not forth good fruit is hewn down, and cast into the fire. Wherefore by their fruits ye shall know them.

Not every one that saith unto me, Lord, Lord, shall enter into the kingdom of heaven; but he that doeth the will of my Father which is in heaven. Many will say to me in that day, Lord, Lord, have we not prophesied in thy name? and in thy name have cast out devils? and in thy name done many wonderful works? And then will I profess unto them, I never knew you: depart from me, ye that work iniquity.

Therefore whosoever heareth these sayings of mine, and doeth them, I will liken him unto a wise man, which built his house upon a rock: and the rain descended, and the floods came, and the winds blew, and beat upon that house: and it fell not: for it was founded upon a rock.

And every one that heareth these sayings of mine, and doeth them not, shall be likened unto a foolish man, which built his house upon the sand: and the rain descended, and the floods came, and the winds blew, and beat upon that house; and it fell: and great was the fall of it.

When Jesus had ended these sayings, [*+] the people were astonished at his doctrine: for he taught them as one having authority, and not as the scribes.

Footnotes

^24:* The Golden Rule--the spirit of which pervades not only the Sermon on the Mount but Christ's life throughout. Luke's phrasing of the Golden Rule is in XX of this book.

^24:+ Matthew 7, 28-29. Mark also so declares (Mark 1, 22. See XIII in this book).

XVII

A LEPER CLEANSED--THE DRAUGHT OF FISH--PALSIED MAN CURED

A.D. 28. Age 31. By Lake Gennesaret. Capernaum.

Matthew 8, 1-4; 9, 2-7; Mark 1, 40-45; 2, 1-12; Luke 5, 1-15; and 18-25.

WHEN Jesus was come down from the mountain, multitudes followed him. And, behold, there came a leper, who, seeing Jesus, besought him, saying, Lord, if thou wilt, thou canst make me clean.

Jesus, moved with compassion, put forth his hand, and touched him, saying, I will; be thou clean.

And immediately his leprosy was cleansed. Jesus straitly charged him, See thou tell no man; but go thy way: say nothing to any man. Shew thyself to the priest, and offer the gift for thy cleansing, those things which Moses commanded, for a testimony unto them.

But he began to blaze abroad the matter; and so much the more went there a fame abroad of Jesus.

It came to pass, that, as the people pressed upon Jesus to hear the word of God, he stood by the lake of Gennesaret, and saw two ships. He entered into one, which was Simon's, and prayed him that he would thrust out a little from the land. And he sat down, and taught the people out of the ship.

Now when he had left speaking, he said unto Simon, Launch out into the deep, and let down your nets for a draught.

Simon answering said, Master we have toiled all the night, and have taken nothing: nevertheless at thy word I will let down the net.

When they had this done, they inclosed a multitude of fishes: and their net brake. They beckoned unto their partners, which were in the other ship, that they should come and help them. They came, and filled both the ships, so that they began to sink.

When Simon Peter saw it, he fell down at Jesus' knees, saying, Depart from me; for I am a sinful man, O Lord.

For he was astonished at the draught of the fishes: and so was also James, and John, which were partners with Simon.

Jesus said unto Simon, Fear not; from henceforth thou shalt catch men.

They brought their ships to land, forsook all, and followed Jesus.

Again Jesus entered into Capernaum after some days; and it was noised that he was in the house. Straightway many were gathered together, insomuch that there was no room to receive them, no, not so much as about the door: and he preached the word unto them.

And, behold, men brought one sick of the palsy, lying on a bed borne by four. They could not come nigh unto Jesus for the press: and when they could not find by what way they might bring him in, they went upon the housetop, and uncovered the roof, and let him down through the tiling with his couch into the midst before Jesus.

Jesus seeing their faith said unto the sick of the palsy, Son, be of good cheer; thy sins be forgiven thee. [**]

Certain of the scribes sitting there, and reasoning in their hearts, said within themselves, This man blasphemeth: who can forgive sins, but God alone? Jesus knowing their thoughts said, What reason ye in your hearts? Why reason ye these things? Wherefore think ye evil? Whether is it easier to say to the sick of the palsy, Thy sins be forgiven thee; or to say, Arise, and take up thy bed, and walk? But that ye may know that the Son of man hath power on earth to forgive sins, He saith to the sick of the palsy, I say unto thee, Arise, and take up thy couch, and go thy way into thine house. And he arose, took up his bed, and departed to his house.

Footnotes

^25:* Matthew, and Mark. Luke's narrative has it, "Man, thy sins are forgiven thee." (Luke 5, 20.)

XVIII

MATTHEW (LEVI) CALLED--HIS BANQUET--THE WHOLE NEED NOT A PHYSICIAN--JOHN'S DISCIPLES FAST: CHRIST'S FAST NOT--TWO PARABLES: OLD GARMENT, NEW WINE

A.D. 28, Age 31. Capernaum.

Luke 5, 27-39; Matthew 9, 9-17; Mark 2, 13-22.

JESUS went forth again by the sea side; and the multitudes resorted unto him, and he taught them.

As he passed forth from thence, he saw a man, named Matthew (Levi, a publican [**]), sitting at the receipt of custom: he said unto him, Follow me.
And he rose up, left all, and followed Jesus.

Levi made him a great feast [*+] in his own house: and, behold, many publicans and others sat at meat with Jesus and his disciples.

But their scribes and Pharisees murmured against his disciples, saying, Why do ye eat with publicans and sinners? Why eateth your master with publicans and sinners?

When Jesus heard that, he saith unto them, They that be whole need not a physician, but they that are sick. But go ye and learn what that meaneth. I will have mercy, and not sacrifice: [*++] for I am not come to call the righteous, but sinners to repentance.

The disciples of John used to fast often: and they come and say unto Jesus, Why do thy disciples fast not? Jesus said unto them, Can ye make the children of the bridechamber fast, while the bridegroom is with them? as long as they have the bridegroom with them, they cannot fast. But the days will come, when the bridegroom shall be taken away from them, and then shall they fast in those days.

And he spake also a parable unto them, No man also seweth a piece of new cloth upon an old garment; else the new piece that filleth it up agreeth not with the old: it taketh away from the old, and the rent is made worse.

Another parable put he forth.

And no man putteth new wine into old bottles: else the bottles will be marred: the new wine will burst the bottles, and be spilled, and the bottles shall perish. But new wine must be put into new bottles; and both are preserved.

No man also having drunk old wine straightway desireth new; for he saith, The old is better.

Footnotes

^26:* publican: a taxgatherer.

^26:+ The three accounts of Levi's feast (particularly of the bridechamber parable) exhibit interesting variations of text: Luke 5, 29-39; Mark 2, 15-22; Matthew 9, 10-17.

^26:++ Hosea 6. 6.

XIX

IN THE CORNFIELD ON THE SABBATH--"THE SABBATH WAS MADE FOR MAN"--THE WITHERED HAND--THE PHARISEES CONSPIRE--THE TWELVE ORDAINED--PARABLES

A.D. 28. Age 31. Capernaum.

Matthew 12, 1-16: Mark 2, 23-28; 3, 1-15; 22-29: Luke 6, 1-13; 11, 24-26.

AT that time Jesus went on the sabbath day through the cornfields; and his disciples were a hungered, and began, as they went, to pluck the ears of corn, and to eat, rubbing them with their hands.

But certain of the Pharisees said unto Jesus, Behold, why do thy disciples on the sabbath day that which is not lawful? Jesus said unto them, Have ye never read so much as this: what David did, when himself was a hungered, and had need, he, and they which were with him: how he went into the house of God in the days of Abiathar the high priest, and did take and eat the shewbread, and gave also to them which were with him, which was not lawful for him to eat, neither for them which were with him, but for the priests alone?

Or have ye not read in the law, how that on the sabbath days the priests in the temple profane the sabbath, and are blameless?

But I say unto you, That in this place is one greater than the temple. But if ye had known what this meaneth, I will have mercy, and not sacrifice, ye would not have condemned the guiltless.

The sabbath was made for man, and not man for the sabbath: therefore the Son of man is Lord even of the sabbath day.

On another sabbath, Jesus entered into the synagogue and taught.

There was a man there whose right hand was withered. The scribes and Pharisees watched Jesus, whether he would heal on the sabbath day. But he knew their thoughts, and he said to the man, Rise up, and stand forth in the midst.

He arose and stood forth. Then said Jesus unto them, I will ask you one thing: Is it lawful on the sabbath days to do good, or to do evil? to save life, or to kill? to save life, or to destroy it?

But thy held their peace. And Jesus said, What man shall there be among you, that shall have one sheep, and if it fall into a pit on the sabbath day, will he not lay hold on it, and lift it out? How much then is a man better than a sheep? Wherefore it is lawful to do well on the sabbath days.

When Jesus had looked round about on them with anger, being grieved for the hardness of their hearts, he saith unto the man,

Stretch forth thine hand.

He did so: and his hand was restored whole, like as the other.

The Pharisees were filled with madness; they went forth, and straightaway took counsel with the Herodians what they might do to Jesus.

Jesus knew it: he withdrew himself with his disciples to the sea. And he straitly charged them that they should not make him known.

Jesus goeth up into a mountain, and calleth unto him whom he would: and they came. He ordained twelve, whom also he named apostles, that they should be with him, and that he might send them forth to preach, and to have power to heal sicknesses, and to cast out devils.

The scribes said, He hath Beelzebub, and by the prince of devils casteth he out devils. Jesus said unto them in parables, [**]

How can Satan cast out Satan?

And if a kingdom be divided against itself, that kingdom cannot stand. And if a house be divided against itself, that house cannot stand. And if Satan rise up against himself, and be divided, he cannot stand, but hath an end.

No man can enter into a strong man's house, and spoil his goods, except he will first bind the strong man; and then he will spoil his house.

Verily I say unto you, All sins shall be forgiven unto the sons of men, and blasphemies wherewith soever they shall blaspheme: but he that shall blaspheme against the Holy Ghost hath never forgiveness, but is in danger of eternal damnation. Because they said, he hath an unclean spirit.

[**]When the unclean spirit is gone out of a man, he walketh through dry places, seeking rest: and finding none, he saith, I will return unto my house whence I came out. And when he cometh, he findeth it swept and garnished. Then goeth he, and taketh to him seven other spirits more wicked than himself; and the last state of that man is worse than the first.

Footnotes

^27:* Wine-skins were the "bottles."

^28:* This record of Christ's reply to the scribes is Mark's (3, 22-29). In XXVI of this book Christ's similar reply to certain Pharisees is from Matthew and Luke.

^29:* Thus Luke (11, 24-26). In XXVII of this book the same saying is phrased somewhat differently in the narrative from Matthew (12, 43-45).

XX

THE TWELVE BY NAME--THE SERMON IN THE PLAIN: BENISONS AND ADMONITIONS, PRECEPTS, THE GOLDEN RULE AGAIN), JUDGE NOT, GIVE

A.D. 28. Age 31. Near Capernaum.

Matthew 10, 2-4: Mark 3, 16-19: Luke 6, 14-38.

IN those days Jesus went out into a mountain, and continued all night in prayer to God. When it was day, he called unto him his twelve disciples.

Now the names of the twelve apostles are these: [*+]Simon [whom he also surnamed Peter], and Andrew his brother; James the son of Zebedee, and John his brother; James the son of Alpheus, and Thomas; and Lebbeus whose surname was Thaddeus [Jude]; Philip, Bartholomew [Nathanael]; and Matthew the publican [Levi]; and Simon called Zelotes, the Canaanite; and Judas Iscariot, who also was the traitor, and betrayed Jesus.

Jesus came down with them, and stood in the plain; and the company of the disciples stood with them. A multitude of people out of all Judea and Jerusalem, and from the sea coast of Tyre and Sidon came to hear him, and to be healed.

Jesus lifted up his eyes on his disciples, and said,
Blessed be ye poor: for yours is the kingdom of God.
Blessed are ye that hunger now: for ye shall be filled.
Blessed are ye that weep now: for ye shall laugh.
Blessed are ye, when men shall have you, and when they shall separate you from their company, and shall reproach you, and cast out your name as evil, for the Son of man's sake.

Before ye in that day, and leap for joy: for, behold, your reward is great in heaven: for in the like manner did their fathers unto the prophets.

But woe unto you that are rich! for ye have received your consolation.

Woe unto you that are full! for ye shall hunger.

Woe unto you that laugh now! for ye shall mourn and weep.

Woe unto you, when all men shall speak well of you! for so did their fathers to the false prophets.

But I say unto you which hear, Love your enemies, do good to them which hate you, bless them that curse you, and pray for them which despitefully use you.

And unto him that smiteth thee on the one cheek offer also the other; and him that taketh away by cloak forbid not to take thy coat also.

Give to every man that asketh of thee; and of him that taketh away thy goods ask them not again.

[**]And as ye would that men should do to you, do ye also to them likewise.

For if ye love them which love you, what thank have ye? for sinners also love those that love them. And if ye do good to them which do good to you, what thank have ye? for sinners also do even the same. And if ye lend to them of whom ye hope to receive, what thank have ye? for sinners also lend to sinners, to receive as much again.

But love ye your enemies, and do good, and lend, hoping for nothing again; and your reward shall be great, and ye shall be the children of the Highest: for he is kind unto the unthankful and to the evil. Be ye therefore merciful, as your Father also is merciful.

Judge not, and ye shall not be judged: condemn not, and ye shall not be condemned: forgive, and ye shall be forgiven: Give, and it shall be given unto you; good measure, pressed down, and shaken together, and running over, shall men give into your bosom. For with the same measure that ye mete withal it shall be measured to you again.

Footnotes

^29:+ As to the names of "the twelve," a comparison of the texts is interesting: Matthew 10, 2-4; Mark 3, 14-19; Luke 6, 13-16; and ("the eleven") Acts 1, 13.

^30:* The Golden Rule (Luke 6, 31). Compare with the paraphrase (Matthew 7, 12) in XVI of this book.

XXI

THE SERMON IN THE PLAIN (CONCLUDED)--MORE PARABLES--"WHY CALL YE ME, LORD, LORD?"--ROCK FOUNDATION

A.D. 28. Age 31. Near Capernaum.

Luke 6, 39-49.

AND he spake a parable unto them, Can the blind lead the blind? shall they not both fall into the ditch? The disciple is not above his master: but every one that is perfect shall be as his master.

And why beholdest thou the mote that is in thy brother's eye, but perceivest not the beam that is in thine own eye? Either how canst thou say to thy brother, Brother, let me pull out the mote that is in thine eye, when thou thyself beholdest not the beam that is in thine own eye? Thou hypocrite, cast out first the beam out of thine own eye, and then shalt thou see clearly to pull out the mote that is in thy brother's eye.

For a good tree bringeth not forth corrupt fruit; neither doth a corrupt tree bring forth good fruit. For every tree is known by his own fruit. For of thorns men do not gather figs, nor of a bramble bush gather they grapes.

A good man out of the good treasure of his heart bringeth forth that which is good; and an evil man out of the evil treasure of his heart bringeth forth that which is evil: for of the abundance of the heart his mouth speaketh.

And why call ye me, Lord, Lord, and do not the things which I say? Whosoever cometh to me, and heareth my sayings, and doeth them, I will shew you to whom he is like:
He is like a man which built a house, and digged deep, and laid the foundation on a rock: and when the flood arose, the stream beat

vehemently upon that house, and could not shake it: for it was founded upon a rock. But he that heareth, and doeth not, is like a man that without a foundation built a house upon the earth; against which the stream did beat vehemently, and immediately it fell; and the ruin of that house was great.

XXII

THE CENTURION'S SERVANT HEALED--THE WIDOW'S SON RESTORED

A.D. 28. Age 31. Capernaum. Nain.

Matthew 8, 5-13: Luke 7, 11-18.

WHEN Jesus was entered into Capernaum, there came unto him a centurion beseeching him, saying, Lord, my servant lieth at home sick of the palsy, grievously tormented.

The elders of the Jews came, saying, That he was worthy: for he loveth our nation, and hath built us a synagogue.

And Jesus saith unto the centurion, I will come and heal him.

The centurion answered, Lord, I am not worthy that thou shouldest come under my roof: but speak the word only, and my servant shall be healed. Jesus marvelled, and turned and said to the people that followed him, Verily I say unto you, I have not found so great faith, no, not in Israel. And I say unto you, That many shall come from the east and west, and shall sit down with Abraham, and Isaac, and Jacob, in the kingdom of heaven: but the children of the kingdom shall be cast out into outer darkness: there shall be weeping and gnashing of teeth.

And Jesus said unto the centurion, Go thy way; and as thou hast believed, so be it done unto thee.

His servant was healed in the selfsame hour. [**]

The day after, Jesus went into a city called Nain: many of his disciples, and much people went with him.

Now when he came nigh to the gate of the city, behold, there was a dead man carried out, the only son of a widow: much people of the city was with her. The Lord had compassion on her, and said, Weep not.

He touched the bier, and they that bare him stood still. Jesus said, Young man, I say unto thee, Arise.

And he that was dead sat up, and began to speak.

There came a fear on all: they glorified God, saying, A great prophet is risen among us.

This rumor of Jesus went forth throughout all Judea and the region round about. And the disciples of John shewed him [John the Baptist] of all these things.

Footnotes

^32:* Luke (7, 2-10) goes further into details regarding the centurion than does Matthew (above), but does not quote Jesus so fully.

XXIII

JOHN, FROM PRISON, SENDS MESSENGERS--JESUS REPLIES--EXTOLS JOHN: A SERMON WITH PARABLES--"FRIEND OF SINNERS"

A.D. 28 . Age 31. Galilee, near Cana.

Matthew 11, 2-15; 16-19: Luke 7, 24-35.

NOW when John had heard in the prison the works of Christ, he sent two of his disciples to Jesus. Unto him they said, John Baptist hath sent us unto thee, saying, Art thou he that should come? or do we look for another?

And in that same hour Jesus cured many of their infirmities; and unto many that were blind he gave sight.

Then said Jesus unto the two disciples [of John], Go your way, and tell John again what things ye have seen and heard: how that the blind receive their sight, and the lane walk, the lepers are cleansed, and the deaf hear, the dead are raised up, and the poor have the gospel preached to them. And blessed is he, whosoever shall not be offended [*+] in me.

When the messengers of John were departed, Jesus began to speak unto the people concerning John, [*++]
What went ye out into the wilderness for to see? A reed shaken with the wind? But what went ye out for to see? A man clothed in soft raiment? Behold, they that wear soft clothing, they which are gorgeously apparelled, and live delicately, are in kings' courts, in kings' houses.

But what went ye out for to see? A prophet? Yea, I say unto you, and much more than a prophet. For this is he of whom it is written, Behold, I send my messenger before thy face, which shall prepare thy way before thee.

Verily, I say unto you, Among them that are born of women there hath not risen a greater prophet than John the Baptist: notwithstanding, he that is least in the kingdom of God is greater than he.

And from the days of John the Baptist until now the kingdom of heaven suffereth violence, and the violent take it by force. For all the prophets and the law prophesied until John. And if ye will receive it, this is Elias, which was for to come.

He that hath ears to hear, let him hear.

The people that heard him, and the publicans, justified God, being baptized with the baptism of John. But the Pharisees and lawyers rejected the counsel of God against themselves, being not baptized of him. Jesus said, But whereunto then shall I liken the men of this generation? and to what are they like? They are like unto children sitting in the marketplace, and calling unto their fellows, one to another, and saying, We have piped unto you, and ye have not danced; we have mourned unto you, and ye have not lamented: ye have not wept.

For John the Baptist came neither eating bread nor drinking wine; and they say, He hath a devil. The Son of man is come eating and drinking; and they say, Behold a man gluttonous and a winebibber, a friend of publicans and sinners!

But wisdom is justified of all her children.

Footnotes

^32:+ ". . . be offended in me: find in me nothing to his hurt.

^32:++ The reader interested in comparing the two texts of Christ's address "to the people concerning John" will note that Luke's (7, 24-35) is briefer than Matthew's (11, 7-30).

XXIV

WOE UNTO CHORAZIN, BETHSAIDA, CAPERNAUM--"COME UNTO ME . . . MY YOKE IS EASY"

A.D. 28. Age 31. Capernaum?

Matthew 11, 20-30: Luke 10, 13-15.

THEN began he to upbraid the cities wherein most of his mighty works were done, because they repented not: [**]

Woe unto thee, Chorazin! woe unto thee, Bethsaida! for if the mighty works, which were done in you, had been done in Tyre and Sidon, they would have repented long ago in sackcloth and ashes. But I say unto you, It shall be more tolerable for Tyre and Sidon at the day of judgment, than for you.

And thou, Capernaum, which are exalted unto heaven, shall be brought down to hell: for if the mighty works, which have been done in thee, had been done in Sodom, it would have remained until this day. But I say unto you, That it shall be more tolerable for the land of Sodom in the day of judgment, than for thee.

At that time Jesus said, I thank thee, O Father, Lord of heaven and earth, because thou hast hid these things from the wise and prudent, and hast revealed them unto babes. Even so, Father: for so it seemed good in thy sight.

All things are delivered unto me of my Father, and no man knoweth the Son, but the Father; neither knoweth any man the Father, save the Son, and he to whomsoever the Son will reveal him.

Come unto me, all ye that labor and are heavy laden, and I will give you rest.

Take my yoke upon you, and learn of me; for I am meek and lowly in heart: and ye shall find rest unto your souls. For my yoke is easy, and my burden is light.

Footnotes

^33:* This censure of "the cities," and the homage, "I thank thee, O Father," are from Matthew (11, 20-27). In Luke (10, 13-15 and 21;22) is a paraphrase, being a part of Christ's admonition of the "other seventy . . . sent two and two into every city." Turn to XLVIII in this book.

XXV

THE WOMAN WITH THE ALABASTER BOX OF OINTMENT, AND SIMON THE PHARISEE: PARABLE OF THE TWO DEBTORS

A.D. 28. Age 31 Galilee (Capernaum?).

Luke 7, 36-50.

ONE of the Pharisees [Simon] desired him that he would eat with him. And Jesus went into the Pharisee's house, and sat down to meat.

And, behold, a woman in the city, which was a sinner, brought an alabaster box of ointment, and stood weeping; and began to wash Jesus' feet, and did wipe them with the hairs of her head, and kissed his feet, and anointed them with the ointment. [**]

Now the Pharisee [Simon, the leper] spake within himself, saying, This man, if he were a prophet, would have known what manner of woman this is; for she is a sinner. Jesus said unto him, Simon, I have somewhat to say unto thee:
There was a certain creditor which had two debtors; the one owed five hundred pence, and the other fifty. And when they had nothing to pay, he frankly forgave them both.

Tell me therefore, which of them will love him most?

Simon answered, I suppose that he to whom he forgave most. Jesus said, Thou hast rightly judged.

He turned to the woman, and said unto Simon, Seest thou this woman?

I entered into thine house, thou gavest me no water for my feet: but she hath washed my feet with tears, and wiped them with the hairs of her head.

Thou gavest me no kiss: but this woman, since the time I came in, hath not ceased to kiss my feet.

My head with oil thou didst not anoint: but this woman hath anointed my feet with ointment.

Wherefore I say unto thee, Her sins, which are many, are forgiven; for she loveth much: but to whom little is forgiven, the same loveth little.

And he said unto her, Thy sins are forgiven.

They that sat at meat with him began to say within themselves, Who is this that forgiveth sins also? Jesus said to the woman, Thy faith hath saved thee; go in peace.

Footnotes

^34:* Read in LXXIV of this book the account of a similar service done by Mary the sister of Martha and Lazarus.

XXVI

THE MAN BLIND, MUTE, AND BEDEVILED--DOUBTING PHARISEES ADMONISHED--PARABLES--"EVERY IDLE WORD"

A.D. 28. Age 31. Capernaum.

Matthew 12, 22-37: Luke 11, 17-23: Mark 3, 22-29.

UNTO Jesus was brought one possessed with a devil, blind, and dumb; and he healed him, insomuch that the blind and dumb both spake and saw.

The people were amazed, and said, Is not this the son of David? But the Pharisees said, This fellow doth not cast out devils, but by Beelzebub the prince of the devils.

Jesus knew their thoughts, and said unto them,

[**]Every kingdom divided against itself is brought to desolation; and every city or house divided against itself falleth: it shall not stand: and if Satan cast out Satan, he is divided against himself; how shall then his kingdom stand? because ye say that I cast out devils through Beelzebub.

And if I by Beelzebub cast out devils, by whom do your children cast them out? therefore they shall be your judges.

But if I with the finger of God cast out devils by the Spirit of God, no doubt then the kingdom of God is come unto you.

Or else, how can one enter into a strong man's house, and spoil his goods, except he first bind the strong man? and then he will spoil his house.

When a strong man armed keepeth his palace, his goods are in peace: but when a stronger than he shall come upon him, and overcome him, he taketh from him all his armor wherein he trusted, and divideth the spoils.

He that is not with me is against me; and he that gathereth not with me scattereth abroad.

Wherefore I say unto you, All manner of sin and blasphemy shall be forgiven unto the sons of men: but the blasphemy against the Holy Ghost shall not be forgiven unto men.

And whosoever speaketh a word against the Son of man, it shall be forgiven him: but whosoever speaketh against the Holy Ghost is in danger of eternal damnation: it shall not be forgiven him, neither in this world, neither in the world to come.

Either make the tree good, and his fruit good; or else make the tree corrupt: for the tree is known by his fruit.

O generation of vipers, how can ye, being evil, speak good things? for out of the abundance of the heart the mouth speaketh. A good man out of the good treasure of the heart bringeth forth good things: and an evil man out of the evil treasure bringeth forth evil things.

But I say unto you, That every idle word that men shall speak, they shall give account thereof in the day of judgment.

For by thy words thou shalt be justified, and by thy words thou shalt be condemned.

Footnotes

^35:* From Matthew, and Luke. In XIX of this book a rebuke similar to the following, but addressed to certain scribes, is a part of Mark's narrative.

XXVII

DOUBTERS SEEK A SIGN--"A GREATER THAN SOLOMON IS HERE"--PARABLE: THE BACKSLIDER

A.D. 28. Age 31. Capernaum.

Matthew 12, 38-45.

CERTAIN of the scribes and of the Pharisees answered Jesus, saying, Master, we would see a sign from thee. But he said unto them, An evil and adulterous generation seeketh after a sign; and there shall no sign be given to it, but the sign of the prophet Jonas: for as Jonas was three days and three nights in the whale's belly; so shall the Son of man be three days and three nights in the heart of the earth.

The men of Nineveh shall rise in judgment with this generation, and shall condemn it: because they repented at the preaching of Jonas; and, behold, a greater than Jonas is here.

The queen of the south shall rise up in the judgment with this generation, and shall condemn it: for she came from the uttermost parts of the earth to hear the wisdom of Solomon; and, behold, a greater than Solomon is here.

When the unclean spirit is gone out of a man, he walketh through dry places, seeking rest, and findeth none. Then he saith, I will return into my house from whence I came out; and when he is come, he findeth it empty, swept, and garnished. Then goeth he, and taketh with himself seven other spirits more wicked than himself, and they enter in and dwell there: and the last state of that man is worse than the first. Even so shall it be also unto this wicked generation. [**]

Footnotes

^37:* Thus Matthew (12, 43-45). In XIX of this book the same saying is phrased somewhat differently in the narrative by Luke (11, 24-26).

XXVIII

HIS MOTHER AND BRETHREN WOULD SPEAK WITH JESUS-- FROM SHIP TALKS TO HEARERS ON THE SHORE: THREE PARABLES ON SEEDS, ONE ON THE CANDLE

A.D. 28, Age 31, Capernaum: Sea of Galilee.

Matt. 12, 46-50; 13, 1-30; Mark 3, 31-35; 4, 1-29: Luke 8, 4-18; 19-21.

WHILE Jesus yet talked, behold, there came his mother and his brethren, desiring to speak with him, and could not come at him for the press. Then one said unto him, Thy mother and thy brethren without seek for thee. But Jesus answered him that told him,

Who is my mother? and who are my brethren?
He looked on them which sat about him, stretched forth his hand toward his disciples, and said, Behold my mother and my brethren! My mother and my brethren are these which hear the word of God, and do it. For whosoever shall do the will of God my Father which is in heaven, the same is my brother, and my sister, and mother.

The same day went Jesus out of the house, and sat by the sea side. Much people were come to him out of every city; so that he entered into a ship, and sat. The multitude stood on the shore. And Jesus spake many things unto them in parables, saying, [*+]

Hearken: Behold, a sower went forth to sow his seed: and it came to pass, as he sowed, some fell by the way side, and it was trodden down, and the fowls of the air came and devoured it up.

Some seed fell on stony ground where it had not much earth: and immediately it sprang up, because it had not much deepness of earth: but when the sun was up, because it had no depth of earth, it was scorched; and because it had no root, it withered away.

And some fell upon a rock: as soon as it was sprung up, it withered away, because it lacked moisture.

And some fell among thorns, and the thorns grew up with it, and choked it, and it yielded no fruit.

But other fell into good ground, and did yield fruit that sprang up, and increased; and bare fruit, some a hundredfold, some sixtyfold, and some thirtyfold.

He that hath ears to hear, let him hear.

When he was alone, his disciples came and said unto Jesus, Why speakest thou in parables? He answered, Because it is given unto you to know the mysteries of the kingdom of heaven, but to them it is not given but in parables: unto them that are without, all these things are done in parables.

[**]For whosoever hath, to him shall be given, and he shall have more abundance: but whosoever hath not, from him shall be taken away even that he hath.

Therefore speak I to them in parables: because they seeing see not; and hearing they hear not, neither do they understand.

And in them is fulfilled the prophecy of Esaias, [*+] which saith, By hearing ye shall hear, and shall not understand; and seeing ye shall see, and shall not perceive: for this people's heart is waxed gross, and their ears are dull of hearing, and their eyes they have closed; lest at any time they should see with their eyes, and hear with their ears, and should understand with their heart, and should be converted, and I should heal them, and their sins should be forgiven them.

[*++]But blessed are your eyes, for they see: and your ears, for they hear. For verily I say unto you, That many prophets and righteous men have desired to see those things which ye see, and have not seen them; and to hear those things which ye hear, and have not heard them.

And he said unto them, Know ye not this parable? And how then will ye know all parables?

Hear ye therefore the parable of the sower. Now the parable is this: The seed is the word of God. The sower soweth the word. When any one heareth the word of the kingdom, and understandeth it not, then cometh immediately Satan the wicked one, and catcheth away that word, which was sown in his heart: the devil taketh away the word out of their hearts, lest they should believe and be saved. This is he which received seed by the way side, where the word is sown.

They on the rock received seed into stony places: these are they who when they have heard the word, anon with joy receive it, and for a while believe; yet have no root in themselves, and so endure but for a time; and in time of temptation fall away: for afterward, when affliction or tribulation or persecution ariseth for the word's sake, immediately they are offended. [**]

And they which received the seed among thorns, are they, which, when they have heard the word, go forth, and are choked with the cares of this world and the deceitfulness of riches and the pleasures of this life; and bring no fruit to perfection: the lusts of other things entering in, choke the word, and it becometh unfruitful.

But he that received the seed into the good ground is he that in an honest and good heart, having heard the word, understandeth it, and keepeth it, and beareth fruit with patience, and bringeth forth, some a hundredfold, some sixty, some thirty.

Another parable put he forth unto them, saying, The kingdom of heaven is likened unto a man which sowed good seed in his field: but while men slept, his enemy came and sowed tares among the wheat, and went his way. But when the blade was sprung up, and brought forth fruit, then appeared the tares also.

So the servants of the householder came and said unto him, Sir, didst not thou sow good seed in thy field? from whence then hath it tares?

He said unto them, An enemy hath done this.

The servants said unto him, Wilt thou then that we go and gather them up?

But he said, Nay; lest while ye gather up the tares, ye root up also the wheat with them. Let both grow together until the harvest: and in the time of harvest I will say to the reapers, Gather ye together first the tares, and bind them in bundles to burn them: but gather the wheat into my barn.

And he said unto them, Is a candle brought to be put under a bushel, or under a bed? and not to be set on a candlestick?

No man, when he hath lighted a candle, covereth it with a vessel, or putteth it under a bed; but setteth it on a candlestick, that they which enter in may see the light.

For there is nothing hid, neither was anything kept secret, which shall not be manifested; but that it should be known and come abroad. If any man have ears to hear, let him hear.

Take heed what ye hear. With what measure ye mete, it shall be measured to you; and unto you that hear shall more be given: for he that hath, to him shall be given; and he that hath not, from him shall be taken even that which he hath. [**]

And he said, So is the kingdom of God, as if a man should cast seed into the ground; and should sleep, and rise night and day, and the seed should spring and grow up, he knoweth not how. For the earth bringeth forth fruit of herself; first the blade, then the ear, after that the full corn in the ear. But when the fruit is brought forth, immediately he putteth in the sickle, because the harvest is come.

Footnotes

^37:+ The interested reader will be repaid who compares the three texts of these parables and those following in XXIX, and contrasts paragraph by paragraph the phrasing of each text with that of the other two: Matthew 13, 3-52; Mark 4, 3-34; Luke 8, 5-18.

^38:* Thus Matthew (13, 12). Turn to the last footnote in this XXVIII, and compare.

^38:+ Isaiah 6, 9-10.

^38:++ Thus Matthew (13, 16-17); compare with last paragraph of XLVIII in this book (Luke 10, 23-24).

^39:* The Revised Version, instead of "they are offended," has "they stumble." Discouraged? Disheartened? Moffatt has it, "repelled."

^40:* Thus Mark (4, 25). Luke's phrasing of this reads (8, 18): Take heed therefore how ye hear: for whosoever hath, to him shall be given; and whosoever hath not, from him shall be taken even that which he seemeth to have. (For Matthew's, turn back to the second footnote of this XXVIII.)

XXIX

PARABLES: THE MUSTARD SEED, THE LEAVEN, THE MERCHANTMAN, THE NET--PARABLE OF THE TARES EXPLAINED--THE TEMPEST QUELLED

A.D. 28. Age 31. Capernaum: Sea of Galilee.

Mk. 4, 30-34; 35-41: Matt. 13, 31-34; 36-52: Lk. 13, 18-21; 8, 22-25.

ANOTHER parable put he forth unto them, saying,
[*+]Whereunto shall we liken the kingdom of God? or with what comparison shall we compare it? A grain of mustard seed is the least of all seeds: is indeed less than all the seeds that be in the earth; but when it is sown in the earth, it groweth up: it becometh greater than all herbs; it shooteth out great branches, and becometh a tree, so that the fowls of the air come and lodge in the branches thereof.

Then said he, Unto what is the kingdom of God like? and whereunto shall I resemble it? The kingdom of heaven is like unto a grain of mustard seed, which a man took and cast into a garden in his field; and it grew, and waxed a great tree, and the birds of the air lodged in the branches thereof, in the shadow of it.

Again Jesus said, Whereunto shall I liken the kingdom of God?

And another parable spake he unto them, The kingdom of heaven is like unto leaven, which a woman took, and hid in three measures of meal, till the whole was leavened.

All these things spake Jesus unto the multitude in parables.

Then he sent the multitude away, and went into the house: and his disciples came, saying, Declare unto us the parable of the tares of the field. He answered, He that soweth the good seed is the Son of man; the field is the world; the good seed are the children of the kingdom; but the tares are the children of the wicked one; the enemy that sowed them is the devil; the harvest is the end of the world; and the reapers are the angels.

As therefore the tares are gathered and burned in the fire; so shall it be in the end of this world. The Son of man shall send forth his angels, and they shall gather out of his kingdom all things that offend, and them which do iniquity; and shall cast them into a furnace of fire: there shall be wailing and gnashing of teeth.

Then shall the righteous shine forth as the sun in the kingdom of their Father.

Who hath ears to hear, let him hear.

Again, the kingdom of heaven is like unto a treasure hid in a field; the which when a man hath found, he hideth, and for joy thereof goeth and selleth all that he hath, and buyeth that field.

Again, the kingdom of heaven is like unto a merchantman, seeking goodly pearls: who, when he had found one pearl of great price, went and sold all that he had, and bought it.

Again, the kingdom of heaven is like unto a net, that was cast into the sea, and gathered of every kind: which, when it was full, they drew to shore, and sat down, and gathered the good into vessels, but cast the bad away.

So shall it be at the end of the world: the angels shall come forth, and sever the wicked from the just, and shall cast them into the furnace of fire: there shall be wailing and gnashing of teeth.

Jesus saith unto them, Have ye understood all these things?

They say, Yea, Lord. Then said he unto them, Therefore every scribe which is instructed until the kingdom of heaven, is like unto a man that is a householder, which bringeth forth out of his treasure things new and old.

And with many such parables spake Jesus the word unto them, as they were able to hear it. But without a parable spake he not unto them: and when they were alone, he expounded all things to his disciples.

The same day, when even was come, Jesus entered into a ship. His disciples followed, and he said unto them, Let us pass over unto the other side of the lake.

They took him even as he was in the ship. And they launched forth.

As they sailed, behold, there came down a storm of wind: the waves beat into the ship, insomuch that the ship was covered with the waves.

Jesus was in the hinder part of the ship, asleep on a pillow: and his disciples awoke him, saying, Lord, save us: we perish. He said unto them, Why are ye fearful, O ye of little faith?

Then he arose and rebuked the winds, and the raging of the water: he said unto the sea, Peace, be still.

The wind ceased: there was a great calm, and Jesus said unto his disciples, Why are ye fearful? where is your faith? how is it that ye have no faith?

But the men marvelled, saying, What manner of man is this, that even the winds and the sea obey him?

Footnotes

^40:+ This parable and the one following may profitably be compared with the similar ones from Luke (13, 18-21) at the end of LIII in this book.

.

XXX

THE MADMAN AND THE SWINE

A.D. 28. Age 31. Sea of Galilee. Decapolis.

Mark 5, 1-20: Luke 8, 26-40: Matthew 8, 28-34.

THEY came over unto the other side of the sea, and arrived at the country of the Gadarenes, over against Galilee.

And when Jesus was come out of the ship, immediately there met him out of the tombs a man [**] with an unclean spirit, who ware no clothes, neither abode in any house, but among the tombs: he had devils long time, and no man could bind him, no not with chains.

Jesus said, Come out of the man, thou unclean spirit.

He fell down before Jesus, and cried out, What have I to do with thee, Jesus, thou Son of God most high? I beseech thee, torment me not. And Jesus asked him, What is thy name?

He answered, Legion: for we are many.

Now there was a good way off from them a herd of swine feeding. And the devils besought Jesus, saying, If thou cast us out, suffer us to go away into the herd of swine.

Jesus gave them leave: he said, Go.

The unclean spirits went out, and entered into the swine; and the herd ran violently down a steep place into the sea, and perished in the waters. They were about two thousand.

They that fed the swine went and told it in the city. And, behold, the whole city came out: they come to Jesus, and see him that had the legion, sitting at the feet of Jesus, clothed, and in his right mind: they were afraid. And the Gadarenes round about besought Jesus to depart out of their coasts.

Jesus went up into the ship.

Now the man, out of whom the devils were departed, besought Jesus that he might be with him: but Jesus sent him away, saying, Return to thine own house. Go home to thy friends; tell them how the Lord had compassion on thee, and shew them how great things God hath done unto thee.

Jesus passed over by ship unto the other side, and came into his own city. Much people gladly received him.

Footnotes

^42:* The narratives of Mark and Luke say one man; Matthew's, two.

XXXI

JAIRUS' DAUGHTER HEALED--THE WOMAN WHO HAD SPENT HER ALL ON PHYSICIANS--THE TWO BLIND MEN

A.D. 28. Age 31. Capernaum.

Luke 9, 41-42; 49-56; 43-48: Mark 5, 22-24; 35-43; 25-34: Matthew 9, 18-19; 23-26; 27-30.

AND, behold, there came one of the rulers of the synagogue, a man named Jairus. He fell at Jesus' feet: and he besought Jesus that he would come to his house, saying, My little daughter lieth at the point of death: I pray thee, come and lay thy hands on her: and she shall live.

He had one only daughter; she was of the age of twelve years.

Jesus arose and followed him, and so did his disciples: much people thronged him.

There cometh one from the ruler's house, saying to Jairus, Thy daughter is dead: why troublest thou the Master further? Jesus heard. He said, Be not afraid, only believe. Fear not, believe only, and she shall be made whole.

Jesus came to Jairus' house, and saw the tumult: the minstrels making a noise, and them that wept.

He suffered no man to go in, save Peter, and James, and John, and the father and the mother of the maiden. All wept, and bewailed her. When Jesus was come in, he saith unto them, Why make ye this ado, and weep? Weep not. Give place. The damsel is not dead, but sleepeth.

They laughed him to scorn, knowing that she was dead. He put them all out.

Jesus, and the father and mother of the damsel, and they that were with them, entered in where the maiden was lying. He took her by the hand, saying, Maid, arise.

She arose straightway, and walked. Jesus commanded that something be given her to eat.

Behold, a certain woman, which was diseased twelve years, and had suffered many things from many physicians, and had spent all that she had, and was nothing bettered, but rather grew worse: she came in the press behind, and touched the hem of Jesus' garment: for she said within herself, If I may but touch his clothes, I shall be whole.

Straightway she felt in her body that she was healed.

Jesus, knowing that virtue had gone out of him, turned him about in the press, and said, Who touched me?

When all denied, Peter said, Master, the multitude throng thee and press thee, and sayest thou, Who touched me? Jesus said, Somebody hath touched me: for I perceive that virtue is gone out of me. Who touched my clothes?

He looked about to see her that had done this thing. The woman fearing and trembling, knowing what was done in her, came and told him the truth, before all the people: for what cause she had touched him, and how she was healed immediately. Jesus said unto her, Daughter, be of good comfort; thy faith hath made thee whole. Go in peace, and be whole of thy plague.

When Jesus departed thence, two blind men followed him, crying Thou Son of David, have mercy on us.

When he was come into the house, the blind men came to him: and Jesus saith unto them, Believe ye that I am able to do this?

They said, Yea, Lord. Then touched he their eyes, saying, According to your faith be it unto you.

And their eyes were opened. Jesus straitly charged them, See that no man know it.

But they spread abroad his fame in all that country.

XXXII

HOME AGAIN: A PROPHET WITHOUT HONOR--MISSION OF THE TWELVE: INSTRUCTIONS, ADMONITIONS, SPARROWS, HAIRS NUMBERED--THEY SET OUT

A.D. 29. Age 32. Nazareth. Capernaum.

Mark 6, 1-6, 7-13: Matthew 13, 54-58; 9, 35-38; 10, 5-42: Luke 9, 1-6.

JESUS went out from thence, and came into his own country. When the sabbath day was come, he began to teach in the synagogue: and many hearing him were astonished, saying, What wisdom is this which is given unto him? Is not this the carpenter, the son of Joseph? Is not his mother called Mary? and his brethren, James, and Joses, and Simon, and Judas? and his sisters, are they not all here? Whence then has this man all these things and they were offended in him. But Jesus said unto them,

A prophet is not without honor, save in his own country, and among his own kin, and in his own house.

And he did not many works, there, because of their unbelief.

Jesus went about the cities and villages, teaching in synagogues, and preaching the gospel of the kingdom, and healing sickness among the people.

But when he saw the multitudes, he was moved with compassion, because they fainted and were scattered abroad, as sheep having no shepherd. Then saith he to his disciples, The harvest truly is plenteous, but the laborers are few; pray ye therefore the Lord of the harvest, that he will send forth laborers into his harvest.

Jesus called unto him the twelve, [**] and began to send them forth by two and two; and gave them power over unclean spirits, and to cure diseases.

These twelve Jesus sent forth to preach the gospel of the kingdom; and he commanded them: Go not into the way of the Gentiles, and into any city of the Samaritans enter ye not: but go rather to the lost sheep of the house of Israel. And as ye go, preach, saying, The kingdom of heaven is at hand.

Heal the sick, cleanse the lepers, raise the dead, cast out devils: freely ye have received, freely give.

Take nothing for your journey, neither staves [**] nor bread; provide neither gold, nor silver, nor brass in your purses, nor scrip for your journey, neither two coats apiece; nor yet shoes, but be shod with sandals; for the workman is worthy of his meat.

And into whatsoever city or town ye shall enter, in what place soever ye enter into a house, inquire who in it is worthy; and there abide till ye go, and thence depart. And when ye come into a house, salute it. [*+] And if the house be worthy, let your peace come upon it: but if it be not worthy, let your peace return to you. And whosoever shall not receive you, nor hear your words, when ye depart out of that house or city, shake off the very dust from your feet for a testimony against them. Verily I say unto you, It shall be more tolerable for the land of Sodom and Gomorrah in the day of judgment, than for that city.

Behold, I send you forth as sheep in the midst of wolves: be ye therefore wise as serpents, and harmless as doves.

But beware of men: for they will deliver you up to the councils, and they will scourge you in their synagogues; and ye shall be brought before governors and kings for my sake, for a testimony against them and the Gentiles.

But when they deliver you up, take no thought how or what ye shall speak: for it shall be given you in that same hour what ye shall speak. For it is not ye that speak, but the Spirit of your Father which speaketh in you.

And the brother shall deliver up the brother to death, and the father the child: and the children shall rise up against their parents, and cause them to be put to death.

And ye shall be hated of all men for my name's sake: but he that endureth to the end shall be saved. But when they persecute you in this city, flee ye into another: for verily I say unto you, Ye shall not have gone over the cities of Israel, till the Son of man be come.

The disciple is not above his master, nor the servant above his lord. It is enough for the disciple that he be as his master, and the servant as his lord. If they have called the master of the house Beelzebub, how much more shall they call them of his household?

Fear them not therefore: for there is nothing covered that shall not be revealed; and hid that shall not be known. What I tell you in darkness that speak ye in light: and what ye hear in the ear, that preach ye upon the housetops. And fear not them which kill the body, but are not able to kill the soul: but rather fear him which is able to destroy both soul and body in hell.

Are not two sparrows sold for a farthing? and one of them shall not fall on the ground without your Father. But the very hairs of your head are all numbered. Fear ye not therefore, ye are of more value than many sparrows.

Whosoever therefore shall confess me before men, him will I confess also before my Father which is in heaven. But whosoever shall deny me before men, him will I also deny before my Father which is in heaven.

Think not that I am come to send peace on earth: I came not to send peace, but a sword. For I am come to set a man at variance against his father, and the daughter against her mother, and the daughter in law against her mother in law. And a man's foes shall be they of his own household. He that loveth father or mother more than me is not worthy of me: and he that loveth son or daughter more than me is not worthy of me. And he that taketh not his cross, and followeth after me, is not worthy of me. He that findeth his life shall lose it; and he that loseth his life for my sake shall find it.

He that receiveth you receiveth me, and he that receiveth me receiveth him that sent me. He that receiveth a prophet in the name of a prophet shall receive a prophet's reward; and he that receiveth a righteous man in the name of a righteous man shall receive a righteous man's reward.

And whosoever shall give to drink unto one of these little ones a cup of cold water only in the name of a disciple, verily I say unto you, he shall in no wise lose his reward.

They went out through the towns, and preached that men should repent. Healing every where, they anointed with oil many that were sick, and cast out many unclean spirits.

Footnotes

^45:* Listed by name in XX of this book (page <page 29>). The reader interested in the personnel of "the twelve," and in the Master's instructions to them, will profit by a comparison of the three texts: Matthew 10, 1-42: Mark 3, 13-19; 6, 7-11: Luke 6, 13-16; 9, 1-5.

^46:* . . . save a staff only. Mark 6, 8.

^46:+ Say, Peace be to this house. And if the son of peace be there, your peace shall rest upon it: if not, it shall turn to you again (Luke 10, 5-6).

XXXIII

HEROD THE TETRARCH DESIRES TO SEE CHRIST--CHRIST WITHDRAWS

A D. 29. Age 32. Decapolis: Bethsaida.

Matthew 14, 1-4; 13-14: Luke 9, 7-11: Mark 6, 17-18; 30-33: John 6, 1-3.

NOW Herod the tetrarch heard of the fame of Jesus: and he was perplexed, because it was said of some, that John was risen from the dead. Herod himself had laid hold upon John, and bound him in prison for Herodias' sake, his brother Philip's wife: for John had said unto Herod, It is not lawful for thee to have thy brother's wife.

And Herod had married her: and sent an executioner, and beheaded John in the prison. Herod said, John have I beheaded; but who is this of whom I hear such things?

And he desired to see Jesus. Jesus' disciples went and told him [Jesus]. And he went over the sea of Galilee, by ship.

When the apostles were returned, and were gathered unto Jesus, they told all things, both what they had done, and what they had taught. Jesus said unto them. Come ye yourselves apart into a desert place, and rest a while.

He took his disciples, and went privately into a desert place belonging to the city called Bethsaida. He went up into a mountain, and there he sat with his disciples.

The people saw them departing, and many knew him, and ran afoot and outwent them, and came together unto him.

XXXIV

FIVE LOAVES AND TWO FISHES SUFFICE FIVE THOUSAND PERSONS

A.D. 29. Age 32. Bethsaida.

John 6, 5-13: Matthew 14, 15-21: Mark 6, 35-44: Luke 9, 12-17.

WHEN Jesus saw a great company come unto him, he saith unto Philip, Whence shall we buy bread, that these may eat?

This he said to prove Philip, for he himself knew what he would do. Jesus' disciples said, Shall we go and buy two hundred pennyworth of bread, and give them to eat?

Philip answered, Two hundred pennyworth of bread is not sufficient.

When the day began to wear away, then came the twelve and said, This is a desert place: send the multitude away, that they may go into the towns and villages round about, and lodge, and buy themselves victuals: for they have nothing to eat. Jesus answered, They need not depart; give ye them to eat. How many loaves have ye? Go and see.

Andrew, Simon Peter's brother, saith, A lad here hath five barley loaves, and two small fishes: but what are they among so many? Jesus said, Bring them hither to me. Make the men sit down by fifties in a company.

Now there was much green grass in the place. So the men sat down, in ranks, by hundreds, and by fifties.

Jesus took the loaves, and when, looking up to heaven, he had given thanks, he blessed and brake, and distributed to the disciples, and the disciples to them that were set down; and likewise of the fishes.

They did all eat. And when they were filled, Jesus said unto his disciples, Gather up the fragments that remain, that nothing be lost.

They filled twelve baskets. They that had eaten were about five thousand men, beside women and children.

XXXV

JESUS WOULD NOT BE MADE KING--WALKS ON THE SEA-- DOUBTING PETER'S ADVENTURE--JESUS EXALTS FAITH

A.D. 29. Age 32. Sea of Galilee. Gennesaret.

Matthew 14, 22-32: Mark 6, 45-53: John 6, 15-21.

WHEN Jesus perceived that they would take him by force, to make him a king, he constrained his disciples to get into a ship, and to go before him unto the other side, while he sent the multitude away.

If He went up into a mountain apart, to pray: when the evening was come, he was there alone.

His disciples went over the sea toward Capernaum. The sea arose by reason of a great wind that blew. It was now dark, and the ship in the midst of the sea, tossed with the waves, and Jesus on the land, alone.

He saw them toiling in rowing; and about the fourth watch of the night, they see Jesus walking on the sea, and drawing nigh unto the ship. They cried out for fear, saying, It is a spirit.

But straightway Jesus spake, Be of good cheer; it is I: be not afraid.

Peter answered, Lord, if it be thou, bid me come unto thee on the water. Jesus said, Come.

And Peter walked on the water, to go to Jesus. But he was afraid; and beginning to sink, he cried, Lord, save me.

Jesus stretched forth his hand, and caught him, and said, O thou of little faith, wherefore didst thou doubt?

When they were come into the ship, the wind ceased. They came into the land of Gennesaret.

XXXVI

"I AM THE BREAD OF LIFE"--IN THE SYNAGOGUE: TO THE PEOPLE, TO THE DISCIPLES, TO THE TWELVE: "ONE OF YOU IS A DEVIL"--MANY DISCIPLES FALL AWAY

A.D. 29. Age 32. Capernaum.

John 6, 22-71.

THE day following, the people which stood on the other side of the sea, where they did eat bread, when they saw that Jesus was not there, neither his disciples, took shipping, and came to Capernaum, seeking him. And When they had found him, they said unto him, Master when camest thou hither? Jesus answered,

Verily, verily, I say unto you, ye seek me, not because ye saw the miracles, but because ye did eat of the loaves, and were filled. Labor not for the meat which perisheth, but for the meat which endureth unto everlasting life, which the Son of man shall give unto you: for him hath God the Father sealed.

Then said they, What shall we do, that we might work the works of God? Jesus answered, This is the work of God, that ye believe on him whom he hath sent.

They said, What sign shewest thou then, that we may see and believe thee? Our fathers did eat manna in the desert; as it is written, He gave them bread from heaven. Then said Jesus,
Verily, verily, I say unto you, Moses gave you not that bread from heaven; but my Father giveth you the true bread from heaven. For the bread of God is he which cometh down from heaven, and giveth life unto the world.

Then said they, Lord, evermore give us this bread. And Jesus said, I am the bread of life: he that cometh to me shall never hunger; and he that believeth on me shall never thirst. But I said unto you, That ye also have seen me, and believe not.

All that the Father giveth me shall come to me; and him that cometh to me I will in no wise cast out.

For I came down from heaven, not to do mine own will, but the will of him that sent me. And this is the Father's will which hath sent me, that of all which he hath given me I should lose nothing, but should raise it up again at the last day. And this is the will of him that sent me, that every one which seeth the Son, and believeth on him, may have everlasting life: and I will raise him up at the last day.

The Jews then murmured because he said, I am the bread which came down from heaven. And they said, Is not this Jesus, the son of Joseph, whose father and mother we know? How is it then that he saith, I came down from heaven? Jesus answered,

Murmur not among yourselves. No man can come to me, except the Father which hath sent me draw him: and I will raise him up at the last day. It is written in the prophets, And they shall be all taught of God.

Every man therefore that hath heard, and hath learned of the Father, cometh unto me. Not that any man hath seen the Father, save he which is of God, he hath seen the Father.

Verily, verily, I say unto you, He that believeth on me hath everlasting life.

I am that bread of life.

Your fathers did eat manna in the , and are dead. This is the bread which cometh down from heaven, that a man may eat thereof, and not die. I am the living bread which came down from heaven: if any man eat of this bread, he shall live forever: and the bread that I will give is my flesh, which I will give for the life of the world.

The Jews therefore strove among themselves saying, How can this man give us his flesh to eat? Then said Jesus, [**]
Verily, verily, I say unto you, Except ye eat the flesh of the Son of man, and drink his blood, ye have no life in you. Whoso eateth my flesh, and drinketh my blood, hath eternal life; and I will raise him up at the last day. For my flesh is meat indeed, and my blood is drink indeed. He that eateth my flesh, and drinketh my blood, dwelleth in me, and I in him. As the living Father hath sent me, and I live by the Father, so he that eateth me, even he shall live by me. This is that bread which came down from heaven: not as your fathers did eat manna, and are dead: he that eateth of this bread shall live for ever. [**]

These things said Jesus in the synagogue in Capernaum. Many of his disciples said, This is a hard saying; who can hear it?

When Jesus knew in himself that his disciples murmured, he said unto them, Doth this offend you?

What and if ye shall see the Son of man ascend up where he was before?

It is the Spirit that quickeneth; the flesh profiteth nothing: the words that I speak unto you, they are spirit, and they are life.

But there are some of you that believe not.

For Jesus knew from the beginning who they were that believed not, and who should betray him. And he said, Therefore said I unto you, that no man can come unto me, except it were given unto him of my Father.

From that time many of his disciples walked not with him. Then said Jesus unto the twelve, Will ye also go away?

Simon Peter answered, Lord, to whom shall we go? thou hast the words of eternal life. And we are sure that thou art that Christ, the Son of the living God. Jesus answered, Have I not chosen you twelve, and one of you is a devil?

He spake of Judas Iscariot; for he it was that should betray Jesus, being one of the twelve.

Footnotes

^51:* Symbolism: Turn to the paragraph in parenthesis in XLV of this book being from verse 39 of John 7).

XXXVII

PHARISEES QUERULOUS--TRADITION OF THE ELDERS: UNWASHEN HANDS--WASHING OF POTS NOT THE WHOLE OF GODLINESS--BLIND LEADERS OF THE BLIND

A.D. 29. Age 32. Capernaum.

Mark 7, 1-23: Matthew 15, 1-20.

[**]CERTAIN of the scribes saw some of Jesus' disciples eat bread with unwashen hands. They found fault: for the Pharisees, and all the Jews, except they wash their hands oft, eat not, holding the tradition of the elders. And many other things there be, which they

have received to hold, as the washing of cups, and pots, brazen vessels, and of tables.

The Pharisees and scribes asked Jesus, Why walk not thy disciples according to the tradition of the elders, but eat bread with unwashen hands? Why do thy disciples transgress?

But Jesus answered, Why do ye also transgress the commandment of God by your tradition? Full well ye reject the commandment of God, that ye may keep your tradition. For God commanded, saying (Moses said), Honor thy father and thy mother: and, Whoso curseth father or mother, let him die the death.

But ye say, If a man shall say (Whosoever shall say) to his father or his mother, It is Corban, that is to say, a gift, by whatsoever thou mightest be profited by me; and honor not his father or his mother: he shall be free. And ye suffer him no more to do aught for his father or his mother; making the word of God of none effect through your tradition, which ye have delivered; and many such like things do ye. Thus have ye made the commandment of God of none effect by your tradition.

Well hath Elias prophesied of you hypocrites, as it is written, This people draweth night unto me with their mouth, this people honoreth me with their lips; but their heart is far from me. Howbeit in vain do they worship me, teaching for doctrines the commandments of men.

Ye hypocrites! For, laying aside the commandment of God, ye hold the tradition of men, as the washing of pots and cups: and many other like things ye do.

And he called the multitude, and said unto them, Hearken unto me every one of you. Hear, and understand. Not that which goeth into the mouth defileth a man. There is nothing from without a man, that entering into him can defile him; but the things which come out of him, those are they that defile the man.

If any man have ears to hear, let him hear.

His disciples, when he was entered into the house from the people, asked Jesus concerning the parable. Jesus said, Are ye also yet so without understanding? Do not ye yet perceive that whatsoever thing from without entereth into a man, entereth in at the mouth, goeth into the belly, and is cast out into the draught, purging all meats? It entereth not into his heart; it cannot defile him.

But those things which proceed out of the mouth come forth from the heart; and they defile the man: for from within, out of the heart of men, proceed evil thoughts, adulteries, fornications, murders, thefts, covetousness, wickedness, false witness, deceit, lasciviousness, an evil eye, blasphemies, pride, foolishness: all these evil things come from within, and these are the things which defile the man; but to eat with unwashen hands defileth not a man.

Then his disciples said unto Jesus, Knowest thou that the Pharisees were offended, after they heard this saying? But he answered, Every plant which my heavenly Father hath not planted, shall be rooted up. Let them alone: they be blind leaders of the blind. And if the blind lead the blind, both shall fall into the ditch.

Footnotes

^52:* The two accounts of this episode (Matthew's and Mark's) abound in interesting likenesses and contrasts.

XXXVIII

SYROPHENICIAN'S DAUGHTER HEALED--A DEAF MUTE HEARS AND TALKS

A.D. 29. Age 32. Phenicia. Decapolis.

Matthew 15, 21-28: Mark 7, 24-36.

FROM thence Jesus went into the borders of Tyre and Sidon.

And, behold, a woman of Canaan came out of the same coasts, and cried unto him, saying, Have mercy on me, O Lord, thou Son of David: my daughter is grievously vexed with an unclean spirit.

The woman was a Greek, a Syrophenician by nation.

Jesus answered her not a word. And his disciples came, saying, Send her away. Jesus said, I am not sent but unto the lost sheep of the house of Israel.

He entered into a house, and would have no man know it: but he could not be hid. For then came she whose young daughter had an unclean spirit, saying, Lord, help me.

But Jesus said unto her, Let the children first be filled: for it is not meet to take the children's bread, and to cast it unto the dogs.

She said, Yes, Lord: yet the dogs under the table eat of the children's crumbs which fall from their masters' table. Jesus answered,
O woman, great is thy faith: be it unto thee even as thou wilt. For this saying go thy way; the devil is gone out of thy daughter.

Her daughter was made whole from that very hour.

Departing from the coasts of Tyre and Sidon, Jesus came unto the sea of Galilee, through the midst of the coasts of Decapolis.

They bring unto him one that was deaf, and had an impediment in his speech. Jesus took him aside, and put his fingers into his ears, and touched his tongue; and looking up to heaven, he sighed, and saith, Be opened.

Straightway his ears were opened, and the string of his tongue was loosed, and he spake plain.

Jesus charged them that they should tell no man: but the more he charged them, so much the more a great deal they published it.

XXXIX

SEVEN LOAVES, A FEW FISHES--TEST OF FAITH--LEAVEN OF THE PHARISEES--THE BETHSAIDAN'S SIGHT RESTORED

A.D. 29. Age 32. Decapolis. Dalmanutha. Bethsaida.

Mark 8, 1-26: Matthew 15, 32-39; John 6, 1-12.

IN those days the multitude being great, and having nothing to eat, Jesus called his disciples, and saith, I have compassion on the multitude, because they have now been with me three days, and have nothing to eat: and if I send them away fasting to their own houses, they will faint by the way.

For divers of them came from far.

His disciples say, From whence can a man satisfy these men with bread here in the wilderness? Jesus saith,
I will not send them away fasting, lest they faint in the way. How many loaves have ye?

They said, Seven, and a few little fishes.

He commanded the people to sit on the ground: and he took the seven loaves, and gave thanks, and brake, and gave to his disciples to set before the people. The few small fishes he blessed, and commanded to set them also before them.

So they did all eat, and were filled. They took up of the broken meat that was left seven baskets full. And they that had eaten were about four thousand, beside women and children. He sent them away.

Straightway Jesus entered into a ship with his disciples, and came into the coasts of Magdala, into the parts of Dalmanutha.

The Pharisees with the Sadducees came forth to question with him, seeking of him a sign from heaven, tempting him. He sighed deeply in his spirit, and saith, Why doth this generation seek after a sign? verily I say unto you, There shall no sign be given unto this generation.

When it is evening, ye say, It will be fair weather: for the sky is red.

And in the morning, It will be foul weather to day: for the sky is red and lowering.

O ye hypocrites, ye can discern the face of the sky; but can ye not discern the signs of the times? A wicked and adulterous generation seeketh after a sign; and there shall no sign be given unto it, but the sign of the prophet Jonas.

Entering into the ship again, Jesus departed to the other side.

Now the disciples had forgotten to take bread; neither had they in the ship with them more than one loaf. Then Jesus charged them, Take heed and beware of the leaven of the Pharisees and of the Sadducees, and of the leaven of Herod.

They reasoned among themselves, saying, It is because we have taken no bread. Which when Jesus perceived, he said unto them, O ye of little faith, why reason ye among yourselves, because ye have brought no bread? Perceive ye not yet, neither understand? Have ye your heart yet hardened? Having eyes, see ye not? and having ears, hear ye not? and do ye not remember?

Do ye not understand, neither remember the five loaves of the five thousand, and how many baskets ye took up? Neither the seven loaves of the four thousand, and how many baskets ye took up?

When I brake the five loaves among the five thousand, how many baskets full of fragments took ye up?

They answer, Twelve.

And when the seven among four thousand, how many baskets full of fragments took ye up?

They said, seven. And Jesus said, How is it that ye do not understand that I spake it not to you concerning bread, that ye should beware of the leaven of the Pharisees and of the Sadducees?

Then understood they how that he bade them not beware of the leaven of bread, but of the doctrine of the Pharisees and of the Sadducees. [**]

Jesus cometh to Bethsaida; and they bring a blind man unto him.
He took the man by the hand, and led him out of the town; and when Jesus had put his hands upon his eyes, he asked him if he saw aught. The man looked up, and said, I see men as trees, walking.

Jesus again put his hands upon his eyes, and made him look up: and he was restored, and saw every man clearly. Jesus sent him away, saying, Neither go into the town, nor tell it to any in the town.

Footnotes

^55:* For two of the other examples of symbolism turn to the footnotes in XXXVI and in XLV in this book.

XL

CHRIST DISCLOSES HIS SONSHIP--ADVANCES PETER--FORETELLS HIS OWN FATE--"WHAT SHALL IT PROFIT A MAN"

A.D. 29. Age 32. Cesarea Philippi.

Matthew 16, 13-28: Mark 8, 27-38; 9, 1: Luke 9, 18-27. [**]

JESUS, and his disciples, came into the towns of Cesarea Philippi. And by the way he asked them, [**]

Whom do men say that I, the Son of man, am? Whom say the people that I am?
They answering said, John the Baptist; but some say, Elias; and others, Jeremias, or, that one of the old prophets is risen again. Jesus said, But whom say ye that I am?

Simon Peter answering said, The Christ of God. [*+] Jesus saith unto Peter, Blessed art thou, Simon Bar-jona: for flesh and blood hath not revealed it unto thee, but my Father which is in heaven.

And I say unto thee, That thou art Peter, [*++] and upon this rock I will build my church; and the gates of hell shall not prevail against it.

And I will give unto thee the keys of the kingdom of heaven: and whatsoever thou shalt bind on earth, shall be bound in heaven; and whatsoever thou shalt loose on earth shall be loosed in heaven.

And he straitly charged them that they should tell no man of him: that he was Jesus the Christ.

From that time forth began Jesus to shew unto his disciples, how that he, the Son of man, must go unto Jerusalem, and be killed, saying, The Son of man must suffer many things, and be rejected of the elders and chief priests and scribes, and be slain, and be raised the third day.

He spake that saying openly. Then Peter began to rebuke him, saying, Be it far from thee, Lord: this shall not be unto thee.

When Jesus had turned and looked on his disciples, he rebuked Peter, saying, Get thee behind me, Satan: thou are an offence [**]

unto me: for thou savorest not the things that be of God, but the things that be of men.

When he had called the people unto him, with his disciples also, he said unto them, If any man will come after me, whosoever will, let him deny himself, and take up his cross daily, and follow me.

For whosoever will save his life shall lose it: but whosoever will lose his life for my sake and the gospel's, the same shall save it. For what shall it profit a man, what is a man advantaged, if he gain the whole world, and lose himself, lose his own soul? or be cast away? Or what shall a man give in exchange for his soul? For the Son of man shall come in the glory of his Father with his angels; and then he shall reward every man according to his works.

Whosoever therefore shall be ashamed of me and of my words, in this adulterous and sinful generation, of him also shall the Son of man be ashamed, when he shall come in his own glory: and cometh in the glory of his Father with his holy angels.

And he said, But I tell you of a truth, there be some standing here which shall not taste of death, till they have seen the kingdom of God come with power, the Son of man coming in his kingdom.

Footnotes

^56:* The interested reader will enjoy paralleling these three indicated texts.

^56:+ Thus Luke. Mark has it, "Thou art the Christ." Matthew has it: "Thou art the Christ, the Son of the living God."

^56:++ Turn back to footnote in VI of this book.

^57:* ". . . offence: stumbling-block.

XLI

JESUS TRANSFIGURED--MOSES AND ELIAS APPEAR--A LUNATIC CURED: "HELP THOU MINE UNBELIEF"

A.D. 29 Age 32. On, and near, Mt. Hermon.

Luke 9, 28-42: Matthew 17, 1-21: Mark 9, 2-29.

IT came to pass, about an eight [*+] days after these sayings, Jesus taketh Peter, John, and James his brother, and went up into a high mountain apart to pray: and Jesus was transfigured before them.

As he prayed, the fashion of his countenance was altered: his face did shine as the sun, and his raiment was white as the light, and glistering, shining as snow, exceeding white, so as no fuller on earth can white them. And, behold, two men, Moses and Elias: who appeared in glory: talking with Jesus [they] spake of his decease which he should accomplish at Jerusalem.

Peter and they that were with Jesus saw his glory, and the two men with Jesus.

There came a bright cloud, and overshadowed them: and a voice out of the cloud, saying, This is my beloved Son, in whom I am well pleased; hear ye him.

The disciples fell on their face, and were sore afraid. Jesus came and touched them, and said, Arise, and be not afraid.

Suddenly, when they had lifted up their eyes, they saw no man any more, save Jesus only. And he charged them, Tell the vision to no man, until the Son of man be risen again from the dead.

Questioning with one another what the rising from the dead should mean, his disciples asked Jesus, Why say the scribes that Elias must first come? Jesus told them, Elias verily cometh first, and restoreth all things; and how it is written of the Son of man, that he must suffer many things, and be set at nought.

But I say unto you, That Elias is indeed come already, and they knew him not; and they have done unto him whatsoever they listed, as it is written of him.

Likewise shall also the Son of man suffer of them.

The disciples understood that he spake of John the Baptist. They kept it close, and told no man in those days any of the things which they had seen.

When Jesus saw a multitude about his disciples, and the scribes questioning with them, he asked the scribes, What question ye with them?

One of the multitude answered, Master, I have brought unto thee my son: Lord, have mercy; for he is lunatic, and sore vexed: ofttimes he falleth into the fire, and oft into the water. A spirit teareth him that he foameth again, and gnasheth his teeth, and pineth away. I brought him to thy disciples, and they could not cure him. He is mine only child.

Then Jesus said, O faithless and perverse generation, how long shall I be with you? How long shall I suffer you?

Bring thy son hither to me. They brought him: and as he was yet a coming, the spirit tare him; and he fell, and wallowed foaming. Jesus asked his father, How long is it ago since this came unto him?

He said, Of a child. Have compassion on us. Jesus said, If thou canst believe, all things are possible to him that believeth.

Straightway the father said with tears, Lord, I believe; help thou my unbelief.

Jesus rebuked the foul spirit, saying, Thou dumb and deaf spirit, I charge thee, come out of him, and enter no more into him.

The child was cured from that very hour.

When Jesus was come into the house, his disciples asked him privately, Why could not we cast him out? Jesus answered,
Because of your unbelief: for verily I say unto you, If ye have faith as a grain of mustard seed, ye shall say unto this mountain, Remove hence; and it shall remove; and nothing shall be impossible unto you. Howbeit this kind goeth not out, can come forth, by nothing, but by prayer and fasting.

Footnotes

^57:+ Thus Luke. Matthew and Mark have it, "after six days."

Joseph Lumpkin

XLII

JESUS FORETELLS HIS DEATH AND RESURRECTION--
EXHORTS TO HUMILITY--TRIBUTE: THE FISH AND THE COIN

A.D. 29. Age 32. Galilee. Capernaum.

Mark 9, 30-37: Luke 9, 44-48: Matthew 17, 22-27.

JESUS departed thence, and passed through Galilee. While in
Galilee, all wondered at the things which Jesus did. But while they
wondered, Jesus said unto his disciples, Let these sayings sink
down into your ears: for the Son of man shall be betrayed, and
delivered into the hands of men: and they shall kill him; and the
third day after that he is killed, he shall be raised again.

But they understood not.

There arose a reasoning among the disciples: for by the way [to
Capernaum] they had disputed amongst themselves which of them
should be the greatest. In the house Jesus asked,

What was it that ye disputed among yourselves by the way?

357

But they held their peace: and Jesus, perceiving the thought of their heart, saith, If any man desire to be first, the same shall be last of all.

He took a child in his arms, and said, Whosoever shall receive this child in my name, receiveth me; whosoever shall receive one of such children in my name, receiveth me: and whosoever shall receive me, receiveth me not, but him that sent me: for he that is least among you all, the same shall be great.

When they were come to Capernaum, they that received tribute money came to Peter, and said, Doth not your master pay tribute?

Peter saith, Yes. And when he was come into the house, Jesus prevented [**] him, saying, What thinkest thou, Simon? Of whom do the kings of the earth take custom or tribute? of their own children, or of strangers?

Peter saith, of strangers. Jesus answered, Then are the children free.

Notwithstanding, lest we should offend them, go thou to the sea, and cast a hook, and take up the fish that first cometh up; and when thou has opened his mouth, thou shalt find a piece of money: that take, and give unto them for me and thee. [*+]

Footnotes

^60:* . . . prevented him: anticipated him, in the sense of spoke first.

^60:+ For "Render unto Cesar the things which be Cesar's," turn forward to LXVII in this book.

XLIII

JOHN ANSWERED: "FORBID HIM NOT"--SALT--"HAVE PEACE WITH ONE ANOTHER"

A.D. 29. Age 32 Capernaum.

Mark 9, 38-50: Luke 9, 49-50.

JOHN [*++] said, Master, we saw one casting out devils in thy name: and we forbade him, because he followeth not with us. But Jesus said, Forbid him not: for there is no man which shall do a miracle in my name, that can lightly speak evil of me. For he that is not against us is for us, is on our part.

For whosoever shall give you a cup of water to drink in my name, because ye belong to Christ, verily I say unto you, he shall not lose his reward.

And whosoever shall offend one of these little ones that believe in me, it is better for him that a millstone were hanged about his neck, and he were cast into the sea.

And if thy hand offend thee, cut it off: it is better for thee to enter into life maimed, than having two hands to go into hell, into the fire that never shall be quenched: where their worm dieth not, and the fire is not quenched.

And if thy foot offend thee, cut it off: it is better for thee to enter halt into life, than having two feet to be cast into hell, into the fire that never shall be quenched: where their worm dieth not, and the fire is not quenched.

And if thine eye offend thee, pluck it out: it is better for thee to enter into the kingdom of God with one eye, than having two eyes to be cast into hell fire: where their worm dieth not, and the fire is not quenched.

For every one shall be salted with fire, and every sacrifice shall be salted with salt. Salt is good: but if the salt have lost his saltness, wherewith will ye season it? Have salt in yourselves, and have peace one with another.

Footnotes

^60:++ John: brother of James, and son of Zebedee.

XLIV

"EXCEPT YE BECOME AS LITTLE CHILDREN"--HUMILITY AND FORGIVENESS--PARABLES: THE NINETY AND NINE, THE WICKED SERVANT--"WHERE TWO OR THREE ARE GATHERED TOGETHER"

A.D. 29. Age 32. Capernaum.

Matthew 18, 1-35.

AT the same time came the disciples unto Jesus, saying, Who is the greatest in the kingdom of heaven? And Jesus called a little child unto him, set him in the midst of them, and said, [**]

Verily I say unto you, Except ye be converted, and become as little children, ye shall not enter into the kingdom of heaven.

Whosoever therefore shall humble himself as this little child, the same is greatest in the kingdom of heaven. And whoso shall receive one such little child in my name receiveth me.

But whoso shall offend one of these little ones which believe in me, it were better for him that a millstone were hanged about his neck, and that he were drowned in the depth of the sea.

Woe unto the world because of offences! for it must needs be that offences come; but woe to that man by whom the offence cometh!

Wherefore, if thy hand or thy foot offend thee, cut them off, and cast them from thee: it is better for thee to enter into life halt or maimed, rather than having' two hands or two feet to be cast into everlasting fire.

And if thine eye offend thee, pluck it out, and cast it from thee: it is better for thee to enter into life with one eye, rather than having two eyes to be cast into hell fire.

Take heed that ye despise not one of these little ones; for I say unto you, That in heaven their angels do always behold the face of my Father which is in heaven. For the Son of man is come to save that which was lost.

[**] How think ye? if a man have a hundred sheep, and one of them be gone astray, doth he not leave the ninety and nine, and goeth into the mountains, and seeketh that which is gone astray? And if so be that he find it, verily I say unto you, he rejoiceth more of that sheep, than of the ninety and nine which went not astray. Even so it

is not the will of your Father which is in heaven, that one of these little ones should perish.

Moreover if thy brother shall trespass against thee, go and tell him his fault between thee and him alone: if he shall hear thee, thou hast gained thy brother. But if he will not hear thee, then take with thee one or two more, that in the mouth of two or three witnesses every word may be established. And if he shall neglect to hear them, tell it unto the church: but if he neglect to hear the church, let him be unto thee as a heathen man and a publican.

Verily I say unto you, Whatsoever ye shall bind on earth shall be bound in heaven: and whatsoever ye shall loose on earth shall be loosed in heaven. [*+]

Again I say unto you, That if two of you shall agree on earth as touching any thing that they shall ask, it shall be done for them of my Father which is in heaven. For where two or three are gathered together in my name, there am I in the midst of them.

Then Peter said, Lord, how oft shall my brother sin against me, and I forgive him? till seven times? Jesus saith, I say not unto thee, Until seven times: but, Until seventy times seven. Therefore is the kingdom of heaven likened unto a certain king, which would take account of his servants. And when he had begun to reckon, one was brought unto him, which owed him ten thousand talents. But forasmuch as he had not to pay, his lord commanded him to be sold, and his wife, and children, and all that he had, and payment to be made. The servant therefore fell down, and worshipped him, saying, Lord, have patience with me, and I will pay thee all. Then the lord of that servant was moved with compassion and loosed him, and forgave him the debt.

But the same servant went out, and found one of his fellow servants, which owed him a hundred pence: and he laid hands on him, and took him by the throat, saying, Pay me that thou owest. And his fellow servant fell down at his feet, and besought him, saying, Have patience with me, and I will pay thee all. And he would not: but went and cast him into prison, till he should pay the debt.

So when his fellow servants saw what was done, they were very sorry, and came and told unto their lord all that was done. Then his lord, after that he had called him, said unto him, O thou wicked servant, I forgave thee all that debt, because thou desiredst me; shouldest not thou also have had compassion on thy fellow servant, even as I had pity on thee?

And his lord was wroth, and delivered him to the tormentors, till he should pay all that was due unto him. So likewise shall my heavenly Father do also unto you, if ye from your hearts forgive not every one his brother their trespasses.

Footnotes

^61:* It is of interest to note that some of these sayings (from Matthew) addressed by Jesus to the disciples are like some of his sayings addressed to John (as reported by Mark in XLIII just preceding).

^62:* Compare with similar parable from Luke (15, 4-7) in LVI in this book.

^62:+ Thus Jesus to the disciples (from Matthew). Turn back to XL in this book, and note the same promise, to Peter (also from Matthew).

XLV

AT THE FEAST OF THE TABERNACLE--OPINIONS DIVIDED

A.D. 29. Age 32. Jerusalem. Galilee.

John 7, 1-46, 53; 8, 1.

AFTER these things, Jesus [**] walked in Galilee: for he would not walk in Jewry, because the Jews sought to kill him.

Now the Jews' feast of the tabernacles was at hand. Jesus' brethren therefore said unto him, Go into Judea, that thy disciples also may see the works that thou doest. For there is no man that doeth anything in secret, and he himself seeketh to be known openly. If thou do these things, shew thyself to the world.

For neither did his brethren believe in him.

Then Jesus said, My time is not yet come: but your time is always ready. The world cannot hate you; but me it hateth, because I testify of it, that the works thereof are evil. Go ye up unto this feast: for my time is not yet full come.

Jesus abode still in Galilee.

But when his brethren were gone up, then went he also up unto the feast, not openly, but as it were in secret.

There was much murmuring among the people concerning him: for some said, He is a good man: others said, Nay; but he deceiveth the people. Howbeit no man spake openly of him for fear of the Jews. The Jews sought him at the feast.

Now about the midst of the feast Jesus went up into the temple and taught. The Jews marvelled, saying, How knoweth this man letters, having never learned? Jesus answered, My doctrine is not mine, but his that sent me. If any man will do his will, he shall know of the doctrine, whether it be of God, or whether I speak of myself. He that speaketh of himself seeketh his own glory: but he that seeketh his glory that sent him, the same is true, and no unrighteousness is in him.

Did not Moses give you the law, and yet none of you keepeth the law? Why go ye about to kill me?
The people answered, Who goeth about to kill thee? Thou hast a devil. Jesus answered,

I have done one work, and ye all marvel.

Moses therefore gave unto you circumcision (not because it is of Moses, but of the fathers); and ye on the sabbath day circumcise a man. If a man on the sabbath day receive circumcision, that the law of Moses should not be broken; are ye angry at me, because I have made a man every whit whole on the sabbath day?

Judge not according to the appearance, but judge righteous judgment.

Then said some of them of Jerusalem, Is not this he, whom they seek to kill? But, lo, he speaketh boldly, and they say nothing unto him. Do the rulers know indeed that this is the very Christ? Howbeit we know this man whence he is, but when Christ cometh, no man knoweth whence he is.

Then cried Jesus in the temple as he taught, saying,

Ye both know me, and ye know whence I am: and I am not come of myself, but he that sent me is true, whom ye know not. But I know him; for I am from him, and he hath sent me.

Then they sought to take him: but his hour was not yet come.

Many believed on Jesus, and said, When Christ cometh, will he do more miracles than those which this man hath done?

The Pharisees and chief priests heard that the people murmured such things concerning Jesus, and sent officers to take him. Then said Jesus, Yet a little while am I with you, and then I go unto him that sent me. Ye shall seek me, and shall not find me: and where I am, thither ye cannot come.

Then said the Jews among themselves, What manner of saying is this that he said, Ye shall seek me, and shall not find me: and where I am, thither ye cannot come?

In the last day, that great day of the feast, Jesus stood and cried, If any man thirst, let him come unto me, and drink. He that believeth on me, as the Scripture hath said, out of his belly shall flow rivers of living water.

[**] (But this spake he of the Spirit, which they that believe on him should receive.)

Many of the people, when they heard this saying, said, Of a truth this is the Prophet. Others said, This is the Christ. But some said, Shall Christ come out of Galilee?

So there was a division among the people because of him. And some of them would have taken him; but no man laid hands upon him.

Then came the officers to the chief priests and Pharisees. They said, Why have ye not brought him? The officers answered, Never man spake like this man.

And every man went unto his own home. Jesus went unto the mount of Olives.

Footnotes

^63:* Turn back, and reread XXXVI in this book.

^64:*

For other examples of symbolism turn back to the footnotes in VII and XXXVI in this book.

XLVI

A WOMAN'S ACCUSERS SHAMED--CHRIST CONFUTES THE JEWS--"I AM THE LIGHT OF THE WORLD"--"THE TRUTH SHALL MAKE YOU FREE"--"I SEEK NOT MINE OWN GLORY"-- "BEFORE ABRAHAM WAS, I AM"--HE ELUDES THE MOB

A.D. 29. Age 32. Jerusalem.

John 8, 2-59.

EARLY in the morning Jesus came again into the temple. The people came; and he sat down, and taught them.

The scribes and Pharisees brought a woman taken in adultery. [*+] They say unto Jesus, Master, Moses in the law commanded us, that such should be stoned: but what sayest thou?

This they said, tempting him, that they might have to accuse him.

But Jesus stooped, and with his finger wrote on the ground, as though he heard them not. So when they continued asking him, he lifted up himself, and said unto them, He that is without sin among you, let him first cast a stone at her.

370

Again Jesus stooped, and wrote on the ground. And they, being convicted by their own conscience, went out one by one, beginning at the eldest: Jesus was left alone, and the woman standing in the midst.

When he had lifited up himself, and saw none but the woman, he said, Woman, where are those thine accusers? hath no man condemned thee?

She said, No man, Lord. And Jesus said unto her, Neither do I condemn thee: go, and sin no more.

Jesus spake again unto the people, saying, I am the light of the world: he that followeth me shall not walk in darkness, but shall have the light of life.

The Pharisees therefore said, Thou bearest record of thyself; thy record is not true. Jesus answered, Though I bear record of myself, yet my record is true: for I know whence I came, and whither I go; but ye cannot tell whence I come, and whither I go.

Ye judge after the flesh; I judge no man. And yet if I judge, my judgment is true: for I am not alone, but I and the Father that sent me.

It is also written in your law, that the testimony of two men is true. I am one that bear witness of myself, and the Father that sent me beareth witness of me.

Then said they, Where is thy father? Jesus answered, Ye neither know me, nor my Father: if ye had known me, ye should have known my Father also.

These words spake Jesus in the treasury, as he taught in the temple: and no man laid hands on him; for his hour was not yet come. Then said Jesus again, I go my way, and ye shall seek me, and shall die in your sins: whither I go, ye cannot come.

Then said the Jews, Will he kill himself? because he saith, Whither I go, ye cannot come. And he said, Ye are from beneath; I am from above: ye are of this world; I am not of this world. I said therefore unto you that ye shall die in your sins: for if ye believe not that I am he, ye shall die in your sins.

Then said they, Who art thou? And Jesus answered,
Even the same that I said unto you from the beginning.

I have many things to say and to judge of you: but he that sent me is true; and I speak to the world those things which I have heard of him.

They understood not that he spake to them of the Father. Then said Jesus, When ye have lifted up the Son of man, then shall ye know that I am he, and that I do nothing of myself; but as my Father hath taught me, I speak these things. And he that sent me is with me: the Father hath not left me alone; for I do always those things that please him.

As he spake these words, many believed. Then said Jesus to those Jews which believed on him, If ye continue in my word, then are ye my disciples indeed; and ye shall know the truth, and the truth shall make you free.

They answered, We be Abraham's seed, and were never in bondage to any man: how sayest thou, Ye shall be made free? Jesus answered, Verily, verily, I say unto you, Whosoever committeth sin is the servant of sin. And the servant abideth not in the house for ever: but the Son abideth ever. If the Son therefore shall make you free, ye shall be free indeed.

I know that ye are Abraham's seed; but ye seek to kill me, because my word hath no place in you. I speak that which I have seen with my Father: and ye do that which ye have seen with your father.

They answered, Abraham is our father. Jesus saith, If ye were Abraham's children, ye would do the works of Abraham. But now ye seek to kill me, a man that hath told you the truth, which I have heard of God: this did not Abraham. Ye do the deeds of your father.

Then they said, We be not born of fornication; we have one Father, even God. Jesus answered, If God were your Father, ye would love me: for I proceeded forth and came from God; neither came I of myself, but he sent me.

Why do ye not understand my speech? even because ye cannot hear my word. Ye are of your father the devil, and the lusts of your father ye will do: he was a murderer from the beginning, and abode not in the truth, because there is no truth in him. When he speaketh a lie, he speaketh of his own: for he is a liar, and the father of it.

And because I tell you the truth, ye believe me not. Which of you convinceth me of sin? And if I say the truth, why do ye not believe me? He that is of God heareth God's words: ye therefore hear them not, because ye are not of God.

Then answered the Jews, Say we not well that thou art a Samaritan, and hast a devil? Jesus answered, I have not a devil; but I honor my Father, and ye do dishonor me. And I seek not mine own glory: there is one that seeketh and judgeth.

Verily, verily, I say unto you, if a man keep my saying, he shall never see death.

Then said the Jews, Now we know that thou hast a devil. Abraham is dead, and the prophets, and thou sayest, If a man keep my saying, he shall never taste of death. Art thou greater than our father Abraham, which is dead? and the prophets are dead: who makest thou thyself? Jesus answered, If I honor myself, my honor is nothing: it is my Father that honoreth me; of whom ye say, that he is your God: yet ye have not known him: but I know him: and if I should say, I know him not, I shall be a liar like unto you; but I know him, and keep his saying. Your father Abraham rejoiced to see my day; and he saw it, and was glad.

Then said the Jews, Thou art not yet fifty years old, and hast thou seen Abraham? Jesus answered, Verily, verily I say unto you, Before Abraham was, I am.

They took up stones to cast at him: but Jesus hid himself, and went out of the temple, going through the midst of them, and so passed by.

Footnotes

^65:+ In the Revised Version the account of this episode is enclosed in brackets. In the margin is this: "Most of the ancient authorities omit John vii, 63-viii, 11. Those which contain it vary much from each other."

XLVII

JESUS HEALS MAN BORN BLIND--THE JEWS CROSSEXAMINE THE MAN--AGAIN: "I AM THE LIGHT OF THE WORLD"-- PARABLE: "I AM THE DOOR. I AM THE GOOD SHEPHERD"-- WINTER FEAST OF THE DEDICATION--AGAIN HE ELUDES THE JEWS

A.D. 29. Age 32. Jerusalem.

John 9, 1-41; 10, 1-18; 22-40.

AS JESUS passed by, he saw a man which was blind from his birth. His disciples asked, Master, who did sin, this man, or his parents, that he was born blind? Jesus answered, Neither hath this man sinned, nor his parents: but that the works of God should be made manifest in him.

I must work the works of him that sent me, while it is day: the night cometh, when no man can work. As long as I am in the world, I am the light of the world.

When he had thus spoken, he anointed the eyes of the blind man with clay, and said unto him, Go, wash in the pool of Siloam.

He went, and washed, and came seeing.

The neighbors said, Is not this he that sat and begged? He answered, I am he.

Therefore, said they, how were thine eyes opened?

He said, A man called Jesus made clay, and anointed mine eyes, and said unto me, Go to the pool of Siloam, and wash: and I went and washed, and I received sight.

It was the sabbath day when Jesus opened his eyes. Therefore said some of the Pharisees, This man [Jesus] is not of God, because he keepeth not the sabbath day. Others said, How can a man that is a sinner do such miracles? And there was a division among them.

The Jews called the parents, and asked them, Is this your son, who ye say was born blind? how then doth he now see?

His parents answered, We know that this is our son, and that he was born blind: but by what means he now seeth, we know not; he is of age; ask him.

His parents feared the Jews: for the Jews had agreed already, that if any man did confess that Jesus was Christ, he should be put out of the synagogue.

Again the Jews called the man that was blind, and said unto him, Give God the praise: we know that this man [Jesus] is a sinner: we know not from whence he is.

The man answered, Why herein is a marvellous thing, that ye know not from whence he is, and yet he hath opened mine eyes. Now we know that God heareth not sinners: but if any man be a worshipper of God, and doeth his will, him he heareth. If this man were not of God, he could do nothing.

They answered, Thou wast altogether born in sins, and dost thou teach us? And they cast him out.

Jesus heard that they had cast him out; and when he had found him, he said unto him,

Dost thou believe on the Son of God?

He answered, Who is he, Lord, that I might believe on him? Jesus said, Thou hast both seen him, and it is he that talketh with thee.

And he said, Lord, I believe.

Jesus said, For judgment I am come into this world, that they which see not might see; and that they which see might be made blind.

Some of the Pharisees heard these words, and said, Are we blind also? Jesus answered, If ye were blind, ye should have no sin: but now ye say, We see; therefore your sin remaineth.

This parable spake Jesus unto them, Verily, verily, I say unto you, He that entereth not by the door into the sheepfold, but climbeth up some other way, the same is a thief and a robber. But he that entereth in by the door is the shepherd of the sheep. To him the porter openeth; and the sheep hear his voice: and he calleth his own sheep by name, and leadeth them out.

And when he putteth forth his own sheep, he goeth before them, and the sheep follow him: for they know his voice. And a stranger will they not follow, but will flee from him: for they know not the voice of strangers.

But they understood not. Then said Jesus, Verily, verily, I say unto you, I am the door of the sheep. All that ever came before me are thieves and robbers: but the sheep did not hear them.

I am the door: by me if any man enter in, he shall be saved, and shall go in and out, and find pasture.

The thief cometh not, but for to steal, and to kill, and to destroy: I am come that they might have life, and that they might have it more abundantly.

I am the good shepherd: the good shepherd giveth his life for the sheep. But he that is a hireling, and not the shepherd, whose own the sheep are not, seeth the wolf coming, and leaveth the sheep, and fleeth: and the wolf catcheth them, and scattereth the sheep. The hireling fleeth, because he is a hireling, and careth not for the sheep.

I am the good shepherd, and know my sheep, and am known of mine. As the Father knoweth me, even so know I the Father: and I lay down my life for the sheep.

And other sheep I have, which are not of this fold: them also I must bring, and they shall hear my voice; and there shall be one fold, and one shepherd.

Therefore doth my Father love me, because I lay down my life, that I might take it again. No man taketh it from me, but I lay it down of myself. I have power to lay it down, and I have power to take it again. This commandment have I received of my Father.

At Jerusalem it was the feast of the dedication. It was winter. Jesus walked in the temple in Solomon's porch.

Then came the Jews round about him, and said, How long dost thou make us to doubt? If thou be the Christ, tell us plainly. Jesus answered, I told you, and ye believed not: the works that I do in my Father's name, they bear witness of me. But ye believe not, because ye are not of my sheep, as I said unto you. My sheep hear my voice, and I know them, and they follow me: and I give unto them eternal life; and they shall never perish, neither shall any man pluck them out of my hand.

My Father, which gave them me, is greater than all; and no man is able to pluck them out of my Father's hand.

I and my Father are one.

The Jews took up stones again to stone him, Jesus answered,
Many good works have I shewed you from my Father; for which of those works do ye stone me?

The Jews answered, For a good work we stone thee not; but for blasphemy; and because that thou, being a man, makest thyself God. Jesus answered, Is it not written in your law, I said, Ye are gods?

If he called them gods, unto whom the word of God came, and the Scripture cannot be broken; say ye of him, whom the Father hath sanctified and sent into the world, Thou blasphemest; because I said, I am the Son of God?

If I do not the works of my Father, believe me not. But if I do, though ye believe not me, believe the works; that ye may know, and believe, that the Father is in me, and I in him.

Therefore they sought again to take him: but he escaped out of their hand, and went away again beyond Jordan into the place where John at first baptized; and there he abode.

XLVIII

JAMES AND JOHN REBUKED--"HATH NOT WHERE TO LAY HIS HEAD"--THE SEVENTY SENT TWO AND TWO: RETURN REJOICING--EXPLICIT INSTRUCTIONS--A PRAYER

A.D. 29, Age 32. Leaving Galilee. Samaria. Perea.

Luke 9, 51-62; 10, 1-24

WHEN the time was come that Jesus should be received up, he steadfastly set his face to go to Jerusalem, and sent messengers before: they entered into a village of the Samaritans.

They did not receive him; and his disciples James and John said, Lord wilt thou that we command fire to come down and consume them, as Elias did? But he rebuked them, saying, Ye know not what manner of spirit ye are of. For the Son of man is not come to destroy men's lives, but to save them.

They went to another village. In the way, a certain man said unto Jesus, Lord, I will follow thee whithersoever thou goest. Jesus said unto him, Foxes have holes, and birds of the air have nests; but the Son of man hath not where to lay his head.

And he said unto another, Follow me.

But he said, Lord, suffer me first to go and bury my father. Jesus said unto him, Let the dead bury their dead: but go thou and preach the kingdom of God.

Another said, Lord, I will follow thee; but let me first go bid them farewell, which are at home at my house. Jesus said unto him, No man, having put his hand to the plough, and looking back, is fit for the kingdom of God.

After these things the Lord appointed other seventy also, and sent them two and two before his face into every city and place, whither he himself would come. Therefore said he unto them, The harvest truly is great, but the laborers are few: pray ye therefore the Lord of the harvest, that he would send forth laborers into his harvest.

[**]Go your ways: behold, I send you forth as lambs among wolves. Carry neither purse, nor scrip, nor shoes: and salute no man by the way.

And into whatsoever house ye enter, first say, Peace be to this house. And if the son of peace be there, your peace shall rest upon it: if not, it shall turn to you again.

And in the same house remain, eating and drinking such things as they give: for the laborer is worthy of his hire. Go not from house to house.

And into whatsoever city ye enter, and they receive you, eat such things as are set before you: and heal the sick that are therein, and say unto them, The kingdom of God is come nigh unto you.

But into whatsoever city ye enter, and they receive you not, go your ways out into the streets of the same, and say, Even the very dust of your city, which cleaveth on us, we do wipe off against you: notwithstanding, be ye sure of this, that the kingdom of God is come nigh unto you.

But I say unto you, that it shall be more tolerable in that day for Sodom, than for that city.

[*+]Woe unto thee, Chorazin! woe unto thee, Bethsaida! for if the mighty works had been done in Tyre and Sidon, which have been done in you, they had a great while ago repented, sitting in sackcloth and ashes. But it shall be more tolerable for Tyre and Sidon at the judgment, than for you.

And thou, Capernaum, which art exalted to heaven, shalt be thrust down to hell.

He that heareth you heareth me; and he that despiseth you despiseth me; and he that despiseth me despiseth him that sent me.

The seventy returned with joy, saying, Lord, even the devils are subject unto us through thy name. Jesus said unto them, I beheld Satan as lightning fall from heaven. Behold, I give unto you power to tread on serpents and scorpions, and over all the power of the enemy; and nothing shall by any means hurt you. Notwithstanding, in this rejoice not, that the spirits are subject unto you; but rather rejoice, because your names are written in heaven.

In that hour Jesus rejoiced in spirit, and said, I thank thee, O Father, Lord of heaven and earth, that thou hast hid these things from the wise and prudent, and has revealed them unto babes: even so, Father; for so it seemed good in thy sight.

All things are delivered to me of my Father: and no man knoweth who the Son is, but the Father; and who the Father is, but the Son, and he to whom the Son will reveal him.

He turned him unto his disciples, and said privately,
[**]Blessed are the eyes which see the things that ye see: for I tell you, that many prophets and kings have desired to see those things which ye see, and have not seen them; and to hear those things which ye hear, and have not heard them.

Footnotes

^72:* Beginning here, compare these instructions to the "other seventy" with the similar instructions to "the twelve" in XXXII of this book.

^72:+ This censure of the cities, and the following homage, "I thank thee," are from Luke (10, 13-15, and 21-22). See footnote in XXIV of this book.

^73:* Thus Luke (10, 23-24). Turn back to the fourth footnote in XXVIII in this book.

XLIX

THE GOOD SAMARITAN: A LAWYER ANSWERED

A.D. 29, Age 32. Perea.

Luke 10, 25-37.

A CERTAIN lawyer stood up, and tempted Jesus, saying, Master, what shall I do to inherit eternal life? Jesus said, What is written in the law? how readest thou?

He answering said, Thou shalt love the Lord thy God with all thy heart, and with all thy soul, and with all thy strength, and with all thy mind; and thy neighbor as thyself. Jesus said unto him, Thou hast answered right: this do, and thou shalt live.

But he, willing to himself, said, And who is my neighbor? Jesus answering said, A certain man went down from Jerusalem to Jericho, and fell among thieves, which stripped him of his raiment, and wounded him, and departed, leaving him half dead. And by chance there came down a certain priest that way: and when he saw him, he passed by on the other side. And like wise a Levite, when he was at the place, came and looked on him, and passed by on the other side.

But a certain Samaritan, as he journeyed, came where he was: and when he saw him, he had compassion on him, and went to him, and bound up his wounds, pouring in oil and wine, and set him on his own beast, and brought him to an inn, and took care of him. And on the morrow when he departed, he took out two pence, and gave them to the host, and said unto him, Take care of him: and whatsoever thou spendest more, when I come again, I will repay thee. Which now of these three, thinkest thou, was neighbor unto him that fell among the thieves?

He said, He that shewed mercy on him. Then said Jesus unto him, Go, and do thou likewise.

L

"WHEN YE PRAY, SAY" (LUKE 11, 2)--PARABLES AND PRECEPTS--"BLESSED IS THE WOMB THAT BARE THEE"--"A GREATER THAN SOLOMON IS HERE"--JESUS DINES WITH PHARISEE: CHIDES PHARISEES AND LAWYERS

A.D. 29. Age 32. Perea.

Luke 11, 1-13; 27-54.

AS Jesus was praying in a certain place, when he ceased, one of his disciples said unto him, Lord, teach us to pray, as John also taught his disciples. Jesus said unto them,

[**]When ye pray, say, Our Father which art in heaven, Hallowed be thy name. Thy kingdom come. Thy will be done, as in heaven, so in earth.

Give us day by day our daily bread.

And forgive us our sins; for we also forgive every one that is indebted to us.

And lead us not into temptation; but deliver us from evil.

And he said unto them, Which of you shall have a friend, and shall go unto him at midnight, and say unto him, Friend, lend me three loaves; for a friend of mine in his journey is come to me, and I have nothing to set before him?

And he from within shall answer and say, Trouble me not: the door is now shut, and my children are with me in bed; I cannot rise and give thee.

I say unto you, Though he will not rise and give him, because he is his friend, yet because of his importunity he will rise and give him as many as he needeth.

And I say unto you, Ask, and it shall be given you: seek, and ye shall find; knock, and it shall be opened unto you. For every one that asketh receiveth; and he that seeketh findeth; and to him that knocketh it shall be opened.

If a son shall ask bread of any of you that is a father, will he give him a stone? or if he ask a fish, will he for a fish give him a serpent? Or, if he shall ask an egg, will he offer him a scorpion?

If ye then, being evil, know how to give good gifts unto your children; how much more shall your heavenly Father give the Holy Spirit to them that ask him?

And it came to pass, as he spake these things, a certain woman of the company lifted up her voice, and said, Blessed is the womb that bare thee, and the paps which thou hast sucked. But Jesus said,

Yea rather, blessed are they that hear the word of God, and keep it.

When the people were gathered thick together, he began to say, [**]This is an evil generation: they seek a sign; and there shall no sign be given it, but the sign of Jonas the prophet. For as Jonas was a sign unto the Ninevites, so shall also the Son of man be to this generation.

The queen of the south shall rise up in the judgment with the men of this generation, and condemn them: for she came from the utmost parts of the earth to hear the wisdom of Solomon; and, behold, a greater than Solomon is here.

The men of Nineveh shall rise up in the judgment with this generation, and shall condemn it: for they repented at the preaching of Jonas; and, behold, a greater than Jonas is here.

No man, when he hath lighted a candle, putteth it in a secret place, neither under a bushel, but on a candlestick, that they which come in may see the light. The light of the body is the eye: therefore when thine eye is single, thy whole body also is full of light; but when thine eye is evil, thy body also is full of darkness. Take heed therefore that the light which is in thee be not darkness. If thy whole body therefore be full of light, having no part dark, the whole shall be full of light, as when the bright shining of a candle doth give thee light.

As Jesus spake, a certain Pharisee besought him to dine with him: he went in, and sat down to meat. The Pharisee marvelled that Jesus had not washed before dinner. The Lord said unto him,
Now do ye Pharisees make clean the outside of the cup and the platter; but your inward part is full of ravening and wickedness. Ye fools, did not he that made that which is without, make that which is within also? But rather give alms of such things as ye have; and, behold, all things are clean unto you.

But woe unto you, Pharisees! for ye tithe mint and rue and all manner of herbs, and pass over judgment and the love of God: these ought ye to have done, and not to leave the other undone.

Woe unto you, Pharisees! for ye love the uppermost seats in the synagogues, and greetings in the markets.

Woe unto you, scribes and Pharisees, hypocrites! for ye are as graves which appear not, and the men that walk over them are not aware of them.

Then answered one of the lawyers, Master, thus saying thou reproachest us also. Jesus said, Woe unto you also, ye lawyers! for ye lade men with burdens grievous to be borne, and ye yourselves touch not the burdens with one of your fingers.

Woe unto you! for we build the sepulchres of the prophets, and your fathers killed them. Truly ye bear witness that ye allow the deeds of your fathers: for they indeed killed them, and ye build their sepulchres.

Therefore also said the wisdom of God, I will send them prophets and apostles, and some of them they shall slay and persecute: that the blood of all the prophets, which was shed from the foundation of the world, may be required of this generation; from the blood of Abel unto the blood of Zacharias, which perished between the altar and the temple: verily I say unto you, It shall be required of this generation.

Woe unto you, lawyers! for ye have taken away the key of knowledge: ye entered not in yourselves, and them that were entering in ye hindered.

As he said these things, the scribes and the Pharisees began to provoke him to speak of many things: laying wait for him, to catch something out of his mouth, that they might accuse him.

Footnotes

^74:* Thus Luke (11, 2-4). Turn back to XV in this book, and compare with the Lord's Prayer in the Sermon On The Mount (Matthew 6, 9-13).

^75:* Thus Luke (11, 29-32). Compare with similar saying in XXVII of this book (being Matthew 12, 39-42).

LI

SERMON TO THE INNUMERABLE MULTITUDE: PRECEPTS, PARABLES: THE SPARROWS, THE SELF-CENTERED RICH MAN, THE RAVENS, THE LILIES--"THE HAIRS OF YOUR HEAD ARE NUMBERED"--"LET YOUR LIGHTS BE BURNING"

A.D. 29. Age 32. Perea.

Luke 12, 1-40.

IN the mean time, when there were gathered together an innumerable multitude of people, insomuch that they trode one upon another, Jesus began to say unto his disciples first of all,
Beware ye of the leaven of the Pharisees, which is hypocrisy. For there is nothing covered, that shall not be revealed; neither hid, that shall not be known. Therefore, whatsoever ye have spoken in darkness shall be heard in the light; and that which ye have spoken in the ear in closets shall be proclaimed upon the housetops.

And I say unto you my friend, Be not afraid of them that kill the body, and after that have no more that they can do. But I will forewarn you whom ye shall fear: Fear him, which after he hath killed hath power to cast into hell; yea, I say unto you, Fear him.

Are not five sparrows sold for two farthings, and not one of them is forgotten before God? But even the very hairs on your head are all numbered. Fear not therefore; ye are of more value than many sparrows.

Also I say unto you, Whosoever shall confess me before men, him shall the Son of man also confess before the angels of God: but he that denieth me before men shall be denied before the angels of

God. And whosoever shall speak a word against the Son of man, it shall be forgiven him: but unto him that blasphemeth against the Holy Ghost it shall not be forgiven.

And when they bring you unto the synagogues, and unto magistrates, and powers, take ye no thought how or what thing ye shall answer, or what ye shall say: for the Holy Ghost shall teach you in the same hour what ye ought to say.

One of the company said, Master, speak to my brother, that he divide the inheritance with me. Jesus answered, Man, who made me a judge or a divider over you?

And he said unto them, Take heed, and beware of covetousness: for a man's life consisteth not in the abundance of the things which he possesseth.

And he spake a parable:
The ground of a certain rich man brought forth plentifully: and he thought within himself, saying, What shall I do, because I have no room where to bestow my fruits.

And he said, This will I do: I will pull down my barns, and build greater and there will I bestow all my fruits and my goods. And I will say to my soul, Soul, thou hast much goods laid up for many years; take thine ease, eat, drink, and be merry.

But God said unto him, Thou fool, this night thy soul shall be required of thee: then whose shall those things be, which thou hast provided?

So is he that layeth up treasure for himself, and is not rich toward God.

Jesus said unto his disciples, Therefore I say unto you, Take no thought for your life, what ye shall eat, neither for the body, what ye shall put on. The life is more than meat, and the body is more than raiment.

Consider the ravens: for they neither sow nor reap; which neither have storehouse nor barn; and God feedeth them: how much more are ye better than the fowls?

And which of you with taking thought can add to his stature one cubit? If ye then be not able to do that thing which is least, why take ye thought for the rest?

Consider the lilies how they grow: they toil not, they spin not; and yet I say unto you, that Solomon in all his glory was not arrayed like one of these. If then God so clothe the grass, which is to day in the field, and to morrow is cast into the oven; how much more will he clothe you, O ye of little faith?

And seek not ye what ye shall eat, or what ye shall drink, neither be ye of doubtful mind. For all these things do the nations of the world seek after; and your Father knoweth that ye have need of these things.

But rather seek ye the kingdom of God; and all these things shall be added unto you.

Fear not, little flock; for it is your Father's good pleasure to give you the kingdom. Sell that ye have, and give alms; provide yourselves bags which wax not old, a treasure in the heavens that faileth not, where no thief approacheth, neither moth corrupteth. For where your treasure is, there will your heart be also.

Let your loins be girded about, and your lights burning; and ye yourselves like unto men that wait for their lord, when he will return from the wedding; that when he cometh and knocketh, they may open unto him immediately.

Blessed are those servants, whom the lord when he cometh shall find watching: verily I say unto you, that he shall gird himself, and make them to sit down to meat, and will come forth and serve them. And if he shall come in the second watch, or come in the third watch, and find them so, blessed are those servants. [**]And this know, that if the goodman of the house had known what hour the thief would come, he would have watched, and not have suffered his house to be broken through. Be ye therefore ready also; for the Son of man cometh at an hour when ye think not.

Footnotes

^78:* This paragraph and the first four paragraphs of LII furnish an interesting comparison with a similar passage near the end of LXXII in this book (being Matthew 24, 43-51).

LII

SERMON CONTINUED: "SPEAKEST THOU THIS PARABLE TO ALL?"--"I AM COME TO SEND FIRE"--THE FACE OF THE SKY--"UNLESS YE REPENT"--THE FIG TREE SPARED

A.D. 29. Age 32. Perea.

Luke 12, 41-59; 13, 1-9.

THEN Peter said, Lord, speakest thou this parable unto us, or even to all? and the Lord said,
[**]Who then is that faithful and wise steward, whom his lord shall make ruler over his household, to give them their portion of meat in due season?

Blessed is that servant, whom his lord when he cometh shall find so doing. Of a truth I say unto you, that he will make him ruler over all that he hath.

But if that servant say in his heart, My lord delayeth his coming; and shall begin to beat the menservants and maidens, and to eat and drink, and to be drunken; the lord of that servant will come in a day when he looketh not for him, and at an hour when he is not aware, and will cut him in sunder, and will appoint him his portion with the unbelievers.

And that servant, which knew his lord's will, and prepared not himself, neither did according to his will, shall be beaten with many stripes. But he that knew not, and did commit things worthy of stripes, shall be beaten with few stripes. For unto whomsoever much is given, of him shall be much required; and to whom men have committeth much, of him they will ask more.

I am come to send fire on the earth; and what will I, if it be already kindled? But I have a baptism to be baptized with; and how am I straitened till it be accomplished!

Suppose ye that I am come to give peace on earth? I tell you, Nay; but rather division: for from henceforth there shall be five in one house divided, three against two, and two against three. The father shall be divided against the son, and the son against the father; the mother against the daughter, and the daughter against the mother;

the mother in law against her daughter in law, and the daughter in law against her mother in law.

He said also to the people, When ye see a cloud rise out of the west, straightway ye say, There cometh a shower; and so it is. And when ye see the south wind blow, ye say, There will be heat; and it cometh to pass. Ye hypocrites, ye can discern the face of the sky and of the earth: but how is it that ye do not discern this time? Yea, and why even of yourselves judge ye not what is right?

When thou goest with thine adversary to the magistrate, as thou art in the way, give diligence that thou mayest be delivered from him; lest he hale thee to the judge, and the judge deliver thee to the officer, and the officer cast thee into prison. I tell thee, thou shalt not depart thence, till thou hast paid the very last mite.

There were present at that season some that told him of the Galileans, whose blood Pilate had mingled with their sacrifices. Jesus said unto them, Suppose ye that these Galileans were sinners above all Galileans, because they suffered such things? I tell you, Nay: but, except ye repent, ye shall all likewise perish.

Or those eighteen, upon whom the tower in Siloam fell, and slew them, think ye that they were sinners above all men that dwelt in Jerusalem? I tell you, Nay: but, except ye repent, ye shall all likewise perish.

He spake also this parable:

A certain man had a fig tree planted in his vineyard; and he came and sought fruit thereon, and found none. Then said he unto the dresser of his vineyard, Behold, these three years I come seeking fruit on this fig tree, and find none: cut it down; why cumbereth it the ground?

And he answering said unto him, Lord, let it alone this year also, till I shall dig about it, and dung it: and if it bear fruit, well: and if not, then after that thou shalt cut it down.

Footnotes

^79:* See footnote at end of LI just preceding.

LIII

SABBATH CURE OF CRIPPLED WOMAN: HYPOCRITES SHAMED--PARABLES AND PRECEPTS: THE MUSTARD SEED, LEAVEN

A.D. 29. Age 32. Perea.

Luke 13, 10-21.

JESUS was teaching in one of the synagogues on the sabbath. And, behold, there was a woman which had a spirit of infirmity eighteen years, and was bowed together, and could in no wise lift up herself. Jesus saw her, and said unto her, Woman, thou are loosed from thine infirmity.

He laid his hands on her: and immediately she was made straight.

The ruler of the synagogue, because that Jesus had healed on the sabbath day, said with indignation unto the people, There are six days in which men ought to work: in them therefore come and be healed, and not on the Sabbath day.

The Lord answered, Thou hypocrite, doth not each one of you on the sabbath loose his ox or his ass from the stall, and lead him away to watering? And ought not this woman, being a daughter of Abraham, who Satan hath bound, lo, these eighteen years, be loosed from this bond on the sabbath day?

His adversaries were ashamed: and the people rejoiced for the glorious things that were done by him. Then said he,
 [**]Unto what is the kingdom of God like? and whereunto shall I resemble it? It is like a grain of mustard seed, which a man took, and cast into his garden; and it grew, and waxed a great tree; and the fowls of the air lodged in the branches of it.

And again he said, Whereunto shall I liken the kingdom of God? It is like leaven, which a woman took and hid in three measures of meal, till the whole was leavened.

Footnotes

^81:* This parable, and the one following, may with interest be compared with the similar ones from Matthew (13, 31-33) at the beginning of XXIX in this book.

LIV

JOURNEYING TOWARD JERUSALEM--PARABLE: THE SHUT DOOR--WARNED OF HEROD--"O JERUSALEM, JERUSALEM!"-- MARTHA AND MARY

A.D. 29. Age 32. Perea. Bethany.

Luke 13, 22-35; 10, 38-42: John 10, 39-40.

JESUS went through the cities and villages, teaching, and journeying toward Jerusalem.

One said unto him, Lord, are there few that be saved? And he said,

Strive to enter in at the strait gate: for many, I say unto you, will seek to enter in, and shall not be able.

When once the master of the house is risen up, and hath shut the door, and ye being to stand without, and to knock at the door, saying, Lord, Lord, open unto us: and he shall answer and say unto you, I know you not whence ye are: Then shall ye begin to say, We have eaten and drunk in thy presence, and thou hast taught in our streets.

But he shall say, I tell you, I know you not whence ye are; depart from me, all ye workers of iniquity.

There shall be weeping and gnashing of teeth, when ye shall see Abraham, and Isaac, and Jacob, and all the prophets, in the kingdom of God, and you yourselves thrust out.

And they shall come from the east, and from the west, and from the north, and from the south, and shall sit down in the kingdom of God.

And, behold, there are last which shall be first; and there are first which shall be last.

The same day there came Pharisees saying unto Jesus, Depart hence; for Herod will kill thee. And he said unto them, Go ye, and tell that fox, Behold, I cast out devils, and I do cures to day and to morrow, and the third day I shall be perfected. Nevertheless I must walk to day, and to morrow, and the day following: for it cannot be that a prophet perish out of Jerusalem.

O Jerusalem, Jerusalem, which killest the prophets, and stonest them that are sent unto thee; how often would I have gathered thy children together, as a hen doth gather her brood under her wings, and ye would not! Behold, your house is left unto you desolate: and verily I say unto you, Ye shall not see me, until the time come when ye shall say, Blessed is he that cometh in the name of the Lord.

Now it came to pass, as they went, that Jesus entered into a certain village: [**] and a woman named Martha received him into her house. She had a sister, Mary, which sat at Jesus' feet, and heard his word.

But Martha, cumbered about much serving, said, Lord, dost thou not care that my sister hath left me to serve alone? Bid her that she help me.

Jesus answered, Martha, Martha, thou are careful and troubled about many things: but one thing is needful; and Mary hath chosen that good part, which shall not be taken away from her.

The Jews sought again to take Jesus: but he went away beyond Jordan into the place where John at first baptized; and he abode there.

Footnotes

^82:* Bethany.

LV

SABBATH HEALING OF DROPSY--A SERMON IN PARABLES: HUMBLE GUEST, GREAT SUPPER, COUNTING THE COST, THE WARRING KING--EXCUSE-MAKING--SALT

A.D. 29. Age 32. Perea.

Luke 14, 1-35.

ON a sabbath day, as Jesus went into the house of one of the chief Pharisees to eat bread, they watched him. And, behold, there was a man which had the dropsy. And Jesus spake unto the lawyers and Pharisees, saying, Is it lawful to heal on the sabbath day?

They held their peace. Jesus healed the man, and let him go, saying unto them, Which of you shall have an ass or an ox fallen into a pit, and will not straightway pull him out on the sabbath day?
They could not answer him.

To those which were bidden, when he marked how they chose out the chief rooms, he put forth a parable, saying, When thou are bidden of any man to a wedding, sit not down in the highest room; lest a more honorable man than thou be bidden of him; and he that bade thee and him come and say to thee, Give this man place; and thou begin with shame to take the lowest room.

But when thou are bidden, go and sit down in the lowest room; that when he that bade thee cometh, he may say unto thee, Friend, go up higher: then shalt thou have worship in the presence of them that sit at meat with thee.

For whosoever exalteth himself shall be abased; and he that humbleth himself shall be exalted.

Then said he to the Pharisee that bade him, When thou makest a dinner or a supper, call not thy friends, nor thy brethren, neither thy kinsmen, nor thy rich neighbors; lest they also bid thee again, and a recompense be made thee. But when thou makest a feast, call the poor, the maimed, the lame, the blind; and thou shalt be blessed; for they cannot recompense thee: for thou shalt be recompensed at the resurrection of the just.

One of them that sat at meat with Jesus said unto him, Blessed is he that shall eat bread in the kingdom of God. Then said Jesus, A certain man made a great supper, and bade many: and sent his servant at supper time to say to them that were bidden, Come; for all things are now ready. And they all with one consent began to make excuse.

The first said unto him, I have bought a piece of ground, and I must needs go and see it: I pray thee have me excused. And another said, I have bought five yoke of oxen, and I go to prove them: I pray thee have me excused. And another said, I have married a wife, and therefore I cannot come.

So that servant came and shewed his lord these things. Then the master of the house being angry said to his servant, Go out quickly into the streets and lanes of the city, and bring in hither the poor, and the maimed, and the halt, and the blind.

And the servant said, Lord, it is done as thou hast commanded, and yet there is room.

And the lord said unto the servant, Go out into the highways and hedges, and compel them to come in, that my house may be filled. For I say unto you, That none of those men which were bidden shall taste of my supper.

There went multitudes with Jesus: and he turned, and said unto them, If any man come to me, and hate not his father, and mother, and wife, and children, and brethren, and sisters, yea, and his own life also, he cannot be my disciple. And whosoever doth not bear his cross, and come after me, cannot be my disciple.

For which of you, intending to build a tower, sitteth not down first, and counteth the cost, whether he have sufficient to finish it? Lest haply, after he hath laid the foundation, and is not able to finish it, all that behold it begin to mock him, saying, This man began to build, and was not able to finish.

Or what king, going to make war against another king, sitteth not down first, and consulteth whether he be able with ten thousand to meet him that cometh against him with twenty thousand? Or else, while the other is yet a great way off, he sendeth an ambassage, and desireth conditions of peace. So likewise, whosoever he be of you that forsaketh not all that he hath, he cannot be my disciple.

Salt is good: but if the salt have lost his savor, wherewith shall it be seasoned? It is neither fit for the land, nor yet for the dunghill; but men cast it out. He that hath ears to hear, let him hear.

LVI

SERMON IN PARABLES (CONTINUED): THE NINETY AND NINE, THE LOST COIN, THE PRODIGAL SON

A.D. 30. Age 33. Perea.

Luke 15, 1-32.

THEN drew near unto Jesus the publicans and sinners for to hear him. The Pharisees and scribes murmured, This man receiveth sinners, and eateth with them.

Jesus spake this parable unto them,

[**]What man of you, having a hundred sheep, if he lose one of them, doth not leave the ninety and nine in the wilderness, and go after that which is lost, until he find it? And when he hath found it, he layeth it on his shoulders, rejoicing. And when he cometh home, he calleth together his friends and neighbors, saying unto them, Rejoice with me, for I have found my sheep which was lost.

I say unto you, that likewise joy shall be in heaven over one sinner that repenteth, more than over ninety and nine just persons, which need no repentance.

Either what woman having ten pieces of silver, if she lose one piece, doth not light a candle, and sweep the house, and seek diligently till she find it? And when she hath found it, she calleth her friends and her neighbors together, saying, Rejoice with me: for I have found the piece which I had lost.

Likewise, I say unto you, there is joy in the presence of the angels of God over one sinner that repenteth.

A certain man had two sons: and the younger of them said to his father, Father, give me the portion of goods that falleth to me. And he divided unto them his living.

And not many days after, the younger son gathered all together, and took his journey into a far country, and there wasted his substance with riotous living. And when he had spent all, there arose a mighty famine in that land; and he began to be in want.

And he went and joined himself to a citizen of that country; and he sent him into his fields to feed swine. And he would fain have filled his belly with the husks that the swine did eat; and no man gave unto him.

And when he came to himself, he said, How many hired servants of my father's have bread enough and to spare, and I perish with hunger! I will arise and go to my father, and will say unto him, Father, I have sinned against heaven, and before thee, and am no more worthy to be called thy son: make me as one of thy hired servants.

And he arose, and came to his father. But when he was yet a great way off, his father saw him, and had compassion, and ran, and fell on his neck, and kissed him.

And the son said unto him, Father, I have sinned against heaven, and in thy sight, and am no more worthy to be called thy son.

But the father said to his servants, Bring forth the best robe, and put it on him; and put a ring on his hand, and shoes on his feet: and bring hither the fatted calf, and kill it; and let us eat, and be merry: for this my son was dead, and is alive again; he was lost, and is found. And they began to be merry.

Now his elder son was in the field: and as he came and drew nigh to the house, he heard music and dancing. And he called one of the servants, and asked what these things meant. And he said unto him, Thy brother is come; and thy father hath killed the fatted calf, because he hath received him safe and sound. And he was angry, and would not go in: therefore came his father out, and entreated him.

And he answering said to his father, Lo, these many years do I serve thee, neither transgressed I at any time thy commandment; and yet thou never gavest me a kid, that I might make merry with my friends: but as soon as this thy son was come, which hath devoured thy living with harlots, thou hast killed for him the fatted calf.

And he said unto him, Son, thou art ever with me, and all that I have is thine. It was meet that we should make merry, and be glad: for this thy brother was dead, and is alive again; and was lost, and is found.

Footnotes

^84:* This furnishes an interesting likeness to the one from Matthew (18, 12-14) in XLIV of this book.

LVII

SERMON IN PARABLES (CONTINUED): THE UNJUST STEWARD, THE RICH MAN AND LAZARUS--"YE CANNOT SERVE GOD AND MAMMON"

A.D. 30. Age 33. Perea.

Luke 16, 1-31.

JESUS said also to his disciples, There was a certain rich man, which had a steward; and the same was accused unto him that he had wasted his goods. And he called him, and said unto him, How is it that I hear this of thee? give an account of thy stewardship; for thou mayest be no longer steward.

Then the steward said within himself, What shall I do? for my lord taketh away from me the stewardship: I cannot dig: to beg I am ashamed. I am resolved what to do, that, when I am put out of the stewardship, they may receive me into their houses.

So he called every one of his lord's debtors unto him, and said unto the first, How much owest thou unto my lord? And he said, A hundred measures of oil. And he said unto him, Take thy bill, and sit down quickly, and write fifty.

Then said he to another, And how much owest thou? And he said, A hundred measures of wheat. And he said unto him, Take thy bill, and write four-score.

And the lord commended the unjust steward, because he had done wisely: for the children of this world are in their generation wiser than the children of light.

And I say unto you, Make to yourselves friends of the mammon of unrighteousness; that, when ye fail, they may receive you into everlasting habitations.

He that is faithful in that which is least is faithful also in much: and he that is unjust in the least is unjust also in much.

If herefore ye have not been faithful in the unrighteous mammon, who will commit to your trust the true riches? And if ye have not been faithful in that which is another man's who, shall give you that which is your own?

No servant can serve two masters: for either he will hate the one, and love the other, or else he will hold to the one and despise the other. Ye cannot serve God and mammon.

The Pharisees also, who were covetous, heard all these things: and they derided Jesus. He said unto them, Ye are they which justify yourselves before men; but God knoweth your hearts: for that which is highly esteemed among men is abomination in the sight of God. The law and the prophets were unto John: since that time the kingdom of God is preached, and every man presseth into it. And it is easier for heaven and earth to pass, than one tittle of the law to fail.

Whosoever putteth away his wife, and married another, committeth adultery: and whosoever marrieth her that is put away from her husband committeth adultery.

There was a certain rich man, which was clothed in purple and fine linen, and fared sumptuously every day: and there was a certain beggar named Lazarus, which was laid at his gate, full of sores, and desiring to be fed with the crumbs which fell from the rich man's table: moreover the dogs came and licked his sores.

And it came to pass, that the beggar died, and it was carried by the angels into Abraham's bosom: the rich man also died and was buried; and in hell he lifted up his eyes, being in torments, and seeth Abraham afar off, and Lazarus in his bosom. And he cried and said, Father Abraham, have mercy on me, and send Lazarus, that he may dip the tip of his finger in water, and cool my tongue: for I am tormented in this flame.

But Abraham said, Son, remember that thou in thy lifetime receivedst thy good things, and likewise Lazarus evil things: but now he is comforted, and thou art tormented. And beside all this, between us and you there is a great gulf fixed: so that they which would pass from hence to you cannot; neither can they pass to us, that would come from thence.

Then he said, I pray thee therefore, father, that thou wouldest send him to my father's house: for I have five brethren; that he may testify unto them, lest they also come into this place of torment.

Abraham saith unto him, They have Moses and the prophets; let them hear them.

And he said, Nay, father Abraham: but if one went unto them from the dead, they will repent.

And he said unto him, If they hear not Moses and the prophets, neither will they be persuaded, though one rose from the dead.

LVIII

SERMON IN PARABLES (CONCLUDED): OFFENCES, FORGIVENESS, FAITH, MASTER AND SERVANT, MARTHA, MARY, LAZARUS: "LAZARUS, COME FORTH"--"I AM THE RESURRECTION"--JEWS TAKE COUNSEL TO KILL JESUS

A.D. 30. Age 33. Perea. Bethany. Perea.

Luke 17, 1-10: John 11, 1-54.

THEN said Jesus unto the disciples, It is impossible but that offences will come: but woe unto him, through whom they come! It were better for him that a millstone were hanged about his neck, and he cast into the sea, than that he should offend [**] one of these little ones.

Take heed to yourselves: If thy brother trespass against thee, rebuke him; and if he repent, forgive him. And if he trespass against thee seven times in a day, and seven times in a day turn again to thee, saying, I repent; thou shalt forgive him.

The apostles said unto the Lord, Increase our faith. And the Lord said, If ye had faith as a grain of mustard seed, ye might say unto this sycamine tree, Be thou plucked up by the root, and be thou planted in the sea; and it should obey you.

But which of you, having a servant ploughing or feeding cattle, will say unto him by and by, when he is come from the field, Go and sit down to meat? and will not rather say unto him, Make ready wherewith I may sup, and gird thyself, and serve me, till I have eaten and drunken; and afterward thou shalt eat and drink?

Doth he thank that servant because he did the things that were commanded him? I trow not.

So likewise ye, when ye shall have done all those things which are commanded you, say, We are unprofitable servants: we have done that which was our duty to do.

Lazarus, of Bethany, the brother of Mary and Martha, was sick. (It was that Mary which anointed the Lord with ointment, and wiped his feet with her hair. [*+]) The sisters sent unto Jesus, saying, Lord, behold, he whom thou lovest is sick. Jesus said, This sickness is not unto death, but for the glory of God, that the Son of God might be glorified thereby.

Now Jesus loved Martha, and her sister, and Lazarus. He abode two days in the place where he was; then saith he to his disciples, Let us go into Judea again.

His disciples say, Master, the Jews of late sought to stone thee; and goest thou thither again? Jesus answered, Are there not twelve hours in the day? If any man walk in the day, he stumbleth not, because he seeth the light of this world. But if a man walk in the night, he stumbleth, because there is no light in him.

Our friend Lazarus sleepeth; but I go, that I may awake him out of his sleep. Howbeit Jesus spake of Lazarus' death; but they thought that he had spoken of rest in sleep. Then said Jesus plainly, Lazarus is dead. And I am glad for your sakes that I was not there, to the intent ye may believe; nevertheless let us go unto him.

And when Jesus came, he found that Lazarus had lain in the grave four days.

Martha, as soon as she heard that Jesus was coming, went and met him; but Mary was still in the house. Then said Martha unto Jesus, Lord, if thou hadst been here, my brother had not died. But I know, that even now, whatsoever thou wilt ask of God, God will give it thee. Jesus saith unto her, Thy brother shall rise again.

Martha answered, I know that he shall rise again in the resurrection at the last day. Jesus said unto her, I am the resurrection, and the life; he that believeth in me, though he were dead, yet shall he live: and whosoever liveth and believeth in me shall never die. Believest thou this?

Martha saith, Yea, Lord: I believe that thou art the Christ, the Son of God, which should come into the world.

When she had so said, she went her way, and called Mary her sister secretly, saying, The Master is come.

Mary arose quickly, and came unto him in that place where Martha met him. The Jews which were with Mary in the house followed her. She fell at Jesus' feet, saying, Lord, if thou hadst been here, my brother had not died.

Jesus saw her weeping: he groaned in the spirit, and was troubled, and said, Where have ye laid him?

They say, Lord, come and see.

Jesus wept.

Then said the Jews, Behold how he loved him!

Jesus cometh to the grave. It was a cave, and a stone lay upon it. Jesus said, Take ye away the stone.

Martha, the sister, saith, Lord, he hath been dead four days. Jesus saith, Said I not unto thee, that, if thou wouldst believe, thou shouldst see the glory of God?

Then they took away the stone. And Jesus lifted up his eyes, and said, Father, I thank thee that thou hast heard me. And I knew that thou hearest me always: but because of the people which stand by I said it, that they may believe that thou hast sent me.

When he had thus spoken, he cried, Lazarus, come forth.

He that was dead came forth, bound with graveclothes. Jesus saith unto them, Loose him, and let him go.

Then gathered the chief priests, and the Pharisees a council, and said, What do we? for this man doeth many miracles. If we let him alone, all men will believe on him: and the Romans shall come and take away both our place and nation.

Then from that day forth they took counsel together for to put Jesus to death.

Jesus therefore walked no more openly among the Jews; but went thence unto a country near to the wilderness, into a city called Ephraim, and there continued with his disciples.

Footnotes

^87:* Thus Luke (16, 18). See also in XIV of this book (from Matthew 5, 31-32), and in LXI of this book (from Matthew 19, 9; and Mark 10, 11).

^88:* Offend: be a hindrance to, or cause to stumble.

^88:+ Some weeks later, as told in LXXIV of this book (in part from John 12, 3-4).

LIX

ONE GRATEFUL SAMARITAN AMONG TEN LEPERS HEALED--"THE KINGDOM OF GOD IS WITHIN YOU"--"THE SON OF MAN MUST SUFFER"--"REMEMBER LOT'S WIFE"--PARABLE: THE UNJUST JUDGE WAVERS--"SHALL THE SON OF MAN FIND FAITH ON THE EARTH?"

A.D. 30. Age 33. Galilee. Samaria. Perea.

Luke 17, 11-37; 18, 1-8.

AS Jesus went to Jerusalem, he passed through Samaria and Galilee. In a certain village ten lepers, which stood far off, lifted up their voices, and said, Jesus, Master, have mercy on us. He said unto them, Go shew yourselves unto the priests.

As they went, they were cleansed. And one of them turned back, and fell at Jesus' feet, giving him thanks: he was a Samaritan. Jesus said, Were there not ten cleansed? but where are the nine? There are not found that returned to give glory to God, save this stranger.

And he said unto him, Arise, go thy way: thy faith hath made thee whole.

When Jesus was demanded of the Pharisees, when the kingdom of God should come, he answered, The kingdom of God cometh not with observation: neither shall they say, Lo here! or, lo there! for, behold, the kingdom of God is within you.

And he said unto his disciples, The days will come, when ye shall desire to see one of the days of the Son of man, and ye shall not see it. And they shall say to you, See here; or, see there: go not after them, nor follow them. For as the lightning, which lighteneth out of the one part under heaven, shineth unto the other part under heaven; so shall also the Son of man be in his day.

But first must he suffer many things, and be rejected of this generation.

And as it was in the days of Noe, so shall it be also in the days of the Son of man. They did eat, they drank, they married wives, they were given in marriage, until the day that Noe entered into the ark, and the flood came, and destroyed them all.

Likewise also as it was in the days of Lot; they did eat, they drank, they bought, they sold, they planted, they builded; but the same day that Lot went out of Sodom it rained fire and brimstone from heaven, and destroyed them all.

Even thus shall it be in the day when the Son of man is revealed. In that day, he which shall be upon the housetop, and his stuff in the house, let him not come down to take it away: and he that is in the field, let him likewise not return back.

Remember Lot's wife.

Whosoever shall seek to save his life shall lose it; and whosoever shall lose his life shall preserve it.

I tell you, in that night there shall be two men in one bed; the one shall be taken, and the other shall be left. Two women shall be grinding together; the one shall be taken, and the other left. Two men shall be in the field; the one shall be taken, and the other left. [**]

They said unto Jesus, Where, Lord? He answered, Wheresoever the body is, thither will the eagles be gathered together.

He spake a parable to this end, that men ought always to pray, and not to faint, saying, There was in a city a judge, which feared not

God, neither regarded man: and there was a widow in that city; and she came unto him, saying, Avenge me of mine adversary.

And he would not for a while: but afterward he said within himself, Though I fear not God, nor regard man; yet because this widow troubleth me, I will avenge her, lest by her continual coming she weary me.

And the Lord said, Hear what the unjust judge saith. And shall not God avenge his own elect, which cry day and night unto him, though he bear long with them? I tell you that he will avenge them speedily. Nevertheless, when the Son of man cometh, shall he find faith on the earth?

Footnotes

^91:* Thus Luke (17, 34-36). Compare with Matthew 24, 40-41, in LXXII of this book.

LX

PARABLE: PRESUMPTUOUS PHARISEE, PENITENT PUBLICAN--"SUFFER LITTLE CHILDREN"--THE POOR RICH YOUNG RULER--PARABLE: THE VINEYARD-MEN'S WAGES

A.D. 30. Age 33. Perea.

Luke 18, 9-30: Mark 10, 13-31: Matthew 19, 13-30; and 20, 1-16.

JESUS spake this parable unto certain which trusted in themselves that they were righteous, and despised others:
Two men went up into the temple to pray; the one a Pharisee, and the other a publican.

The Pharisee stood and prayed thus with himself: God, I thank thee, that I am not as other men are, extortioners, unjust, adulterers, or even as this publican. I fast twice in the week, I give tithes of all that I possess.

And the publican, standing afar off, would not lift up so much as his eyes unto heaven, but smote upon his breast, saying, God be merciful to me a sinner.

I tell you, this man went down to his house justified rather than the other: for every man that exalteth himself shall be abased; and he that humbleth himself shall be exalted.

Then were brought infants, that Jesus should touch them: but the disciples rebuked them that brought them. Jesus, much displeased, said unto the disciples, Suffer the little children, and forbid them not, to come unto me: for of such is the kingdom of heaven.

Verily I say unto you, Whosoever shall not receive the kingdom of God as a little child, he shall in no wise enter therein.

He took them up in his arms, put his hands upon them, and blessed them; and he departed thence.

When he was gone forth into the way there came one running, a ruler, and kneeled, and asked, Good Master, what good thing shall I do to inherit eternal life? [**] Jesus answered, Why callest thou me good? None is good, save one, that is, God: but if thou wilt enter into life, keep the commandments.

He saith, Which? Jesus said, Thou knowest the commandments, Do not commit adultery, Do not kill, Do not steal, Do not bear false witness, Defraud not, Honor thy father and thy mother: and, Thou shalt love thy neighbor as thyself.

The young man saith, All these things have I kept from my youth up: what lack I yet? Jesus beholding him loved him, and said, Yet lackest thou one thing; if thou wilt be perfect, go thy way, sell all that thou hast, and distribute unto the poor, and thou shalt have treasure in heaven: and come, take up the cross, and follow me.

The young man went away grieved, for he was rich, and had great possessions.

Jesus looked round about, and saith, How hardly shall they that have riches enter into the kingdom of God? It is easier for a camel to go through the eye of a needle, [*+] than for a rich man to enter into the kingdom of God.

The disciples were amazed at his words. But Jesus saith again, Children, how hard is it for them that trust in riches to enter into the kingdom of God! Verily I say unto you, That a rich man shall hardly enter into the kingdom of heaven! And again I say unto you, It is easier for a camel to go through a needle's eye, than for a rich man to enter into the kingdom of God.

The disciples were saying among themselves, Who then can be saved? And Jesus answered, With men this is impossible; but not with God. The things which are impossible with men are possible with God: for with God all things are possible.

Then Peter said, Lo, we have left all, and have followed thee. What shall we have therefore? Jesus saith, Ye which have followed me, in the regeneration when the Son of man shall sit in the throne of his glory, ye also shall sit upon twelve thrones, judging the twelve tribes of Israel.

There is not a man that hath forsaken houses, or father, or mother, or brethren, or sisters, or wife, or children, or lands, for the kingdom of God's sake, for my sake and the gospel's, but he shall receive a hundredfold, and shall inherit everlasting life.

Verily I say unto you, every one that hath left house, or father, or mother, or brethren, or sisters, or wife, or children, or lands, for my name's sake, and the gospel's, shall receive manifold more in this present time: houses, and brethren, and sisters, and mothers, and children, and lands, with persecutions; and shall inherit life everlasting in the world to come.

But many that are first shall be last; and the last shall be first.

For the kingdom of heaven is like unto a man that is a householder, which went out early in the morning to hire laborers into his vineyard. And when he had agreed with the laborers for a penny a day, he sent them into his vineyard.

And he went out about the third hour, and saw others standing idle in the marketplace, and said unto them, Go ye also into the vineyard, and whatsoever is right I will give you. And they went their way.

Again he went out about the sixth and ninth hour, and did likewise.

And about the eleventh hour he went out, and found others standing idle, and saith unto them, Why stand ye here all the day idle? They say unto him, Because no man hath hired us. He saith unto them, Go ye also into the vineyard; and whatsoever is right, that shall ye receive.

So when even was come, the lord of the vineyard saith unto his steward, Call the laborers, and give them their hire, beginning from the last unto the first.

And when they came that were hired about the eleventh hour, they received every man a penny.

But when the first came, they supposed that they should have received more; and they likewise received every man a penny. And when they had received it, they murmured against the goodman of the house, saying, These last have wrought but one hour, and thou hast made them equal unto us, which have borne the burden and heat of the day.

But he answered one of them, and said, Friend, I do thee no wrong: didst not thou agree with me for a penny? Take that thine is, and go thy way: I will give unto this last, even as unto thee. Is it not lawful for me to do what I will with mine own? Is thine eye evil, because I am good?

So the last shall be first, and the first last; for many be called, but few chosen.

Footnotes

^93:* The interested reader will be repaid who will compare closely, noting the likenesses and contrasts, all three accounts of this episode: Luke 18, 18-30: Mark 10, 17-31: Matthew 19, 16-30; and 20, 1-16.

^93:+ Needle's Eye: According to some commentators a certain gate, narrow and quite low, in Jerusalem's wall, was called Needle's Eye, or Eye of a Needle.

LXI

DIVORCE DENOUNCED: JESUS ANSWERS PHARISEES

A.D. 30. Age 33. Perea.

Mark 10, 1-12: Matthew 19, 1-12.

INTO the coasts of Judea by the farther side of Jordan, multitudes followed Jesus: and the people resort unto him; and, as he was wont, he taught them.

The Pharisees also came, and tempting him asked Jesus, Is it lawful for a man to put away his wife for every cause? [**] He answered, What did Moses command you?

They said, Moses suffered to write a bill of divorcement, and to put her away. Jesus answered, For the hardness of your heart he wrote you his precept. But from the beginning of creation God made them male and female. For this cause shall a man leave his father and mother, and cleave to his wife.

Have ye not read, that he which made them at the beginning made them male and female, and said, For this cause shall man leave father and mother, and shall cleave to his wife: and they twain shall be one flesh? So then they are no more twain, but one flesh. What therefore God hath joined together, let no man put asunder.

They say unto him, Why did Moses then command to give a writing of divorcement and to put her away? He saith, Moses because of the hardness of your hearts suffered you to put away your wives: but from the beginning it was not so. And I say unto you, Whosoever shall put away his wife, except it be for fornication, and shall marry another, committeth adultery: and whoso marrieth her which is put away doth commit adultery.

In the house his disciples asked Jesus again of the same matter. He saith, Whosoever shall put away his wife, and marry another, committeth adultery against her. And if a woman shall put away her husband, and be married to another, she committeth adultery.

The disciples say unto him, If the case of the man be so with his wife, it is not good to marry. But Jesus answered, All men cannot receive this saying, save they to whom it is given. For there are some eunuchs, which were so born from their mother's womb: and there are some eunuchs which were made eunuchs of men: and there be eunuchs, which have made themselves eunuchs for the kingdom of heaven's sake.

He that is able to receive it, let him receive it.

Footnotes

^95:* The account of this episode in Mark 10 gains interest by comparison with that in Matthew 19. See also Matthew 5, 31-32; and Luke 16, 18.

LXII

JESUS TELLS OF IMMINENT BETRAYAL, DEATH, RESURRECTION--THE MOTHER OF JAMES AND JOHN VOICES THEIR AMBITION--"THE CHIEFEST SHALL BE SERVANT"

A.D. 30. Age 33. Perea.

Matthew 20, 17-28: Mark 10, 32-45: Luke 18, 31-34.

JESUS going up to Jerusalem took again the disciples apart in the way, and began to tell them what things should happen unto him, saying, Behold, we go up to Jerusalem; and the Son of man shall be betrayed and delivered unto the chief priests, and unto the scribes; and he shall be spitefully entreated and spitted on; and they shall condemn him to death, and shall deliver him unto the Gentiles.

They shall mock him, and shall scourge him, and shall crucify and kill him: and the third day he shall rise again.

And all the things that are written by the prophets concerning the Son of man shall be accomplished.

They (the twelve) understood none of this saying; neither knew they the things which were spoken.

Then came unto Jesus the mother of James and John, the sons of Zebedee, desiring a certain thing of him. [**] He said unto her, What wilt thou?

And he said unto them, What would ye that I should do for you?

She saith, Grant that these my two sons may sit, the one on thy right hand, and the other on the left, in glory in thy kingdom. But Jesus said unto them, Ye know not what ye ask: are ye able to drink of the cup that I shall drink of, and to be baptized with the baptism that I am baptized with?

And they say, We can. Jesus answered, Ye shall drink indeed of my cup, the cup that I drink of: and with the baptism that I am baptized withal ye shall be baptized: but to sit on my right hand and on my left hand, is not mine to give, but it shall be given to them for whom it is prepared of my Father.

The ten were moved with indignation against the two brethren. But Jesus called them to him, and said, Ye know that the princes of the Gentiles exercise dominion over them; ye know that they which are accounted to rule over the Gentiles exercise lordship over them; and their great ones exercise authority upon them.

But so shall it not be among you: but whosoever will be great among you, shall be your minister: and whosoever of you will be the chiefest, shall be servant of all: let him be your servant, even as the Son of man: for even the Son of man came not to be ministered unto, but to minister, and to give his life a ransom for many.

Footnotes

^96:* Thus Matthew. Mark puts the plea into the mouths of the sons themselves. The two accounts are: Matthew 20, 20-28: Mark 10, 35-45.

LXIII

SIGHT RESTORED TO TWO BLIND BEGGARS--PARABLE: THE NOBLEMAN, THE SERVANTS, AND THE MONEY (POUNDS)

A.D. 30. Age 33. Jericho.

Luke 18, 35-43; 19, 1-27: Mark 10, 46-52.

A MULTITUDE followed Jesus. Nigh [**] unto Jericho, a certain blind man sat by the way side begging: and hearing the multitude, he asked what it meant. They told him, Jesus of Nazareth passeth by.

And he cried, Jesus, thou Son of David, have mercy on me.

Jesus commanded him to be brought; and asked him, What wilt thou that I shall do unto thee?

And he said, Lord, that I may receive my sight. Jesus said unto him, Receive thy sight: thy faith hath saved thee.

Immediately he received his sight. And Jesus entered and passed through Jericho.

As he went out [**] of Jericho with his disciples, blind Bartimeus sat by the highway side begging. When he heard that it was Jesus of Nazareth, he began to cry out, Jesus, Son of David, have mercy on me.

Many charged him that he should hold his peace: but he cried the more, Thou Son of David, have mercy on me.

Jesus commanded him to be called. And they call the blind man, saying, Be of good comfort; he calleth thee.

Casting away his garment, he came to Jesus. He said unto the man, What wilt thou that I shall do unto thee?

The blind man said, Lord, that I might receive my sight. And Jesus said, Go thy way; thy faith hath made thee whole.

Immediately his eyes received sight, and he followed Jesus in the way.

Jesus [had] entered and passed through Jericho. And a man named Zaccheus, which was the chief among the publicans, and rich, sought to see Jesus who he was, and could not for the press, because he was little of stature. He ran before, and climbed into a sycamore tree to see Jesus: for he was to pass that way.

When Jesus came to the place, he looked up, and saw Zaccheus, and said, Zaccheus, make haste, and come down: for to day I must abide at thy house.

He came down, and received Jesus joyfully. When they saw it, they murmured, He was gone to be guest with a man that is a sinner.

Zaccheus said unto the Lord: Behold, the half of my goods I give to the poor; and if I have taken any thing from any man by false accusation, I restore him fourfold. Jesus said, This day is salvation come to this house, forasmuch as he also is a son of Abraham.

For the Son of man is come to seek and to save that which was lost.

And he added a parable, because he was nigh to Jerusalem, and they thought that the kingdom of God should immediately appear. He said therefore,
[**]A certain nobleman went into a far country to receive for himself a kingdom, and to return. And he called his ten servants, and delivered them ten pounds, and said unto them, Occupy till I come.

But his citizens hated him, and sent a message after him, saying, We will not have this man to reign over us.

And it came to pass, that when he was returned, having received the kingdom, then he commanded these servants to be called unto him, to whom he had given the money, that he might know how much every man had gained by trading.

Then came the first saying, Lord, thy pound hath gained ten pounds. And he said unto him, Well, thou good servant: because thou hast been faithful in a very little, have thou authority over ten cities.

And the second came, saying, Lord, thy pound hath gained five pounds. And he said likewise to him, Be thou also over five cities.

And another came, saying, Lord, behold, here is thy pound, which I have kept laid up in a napkin; for I feared thee, because thou art an austere man: thou takest up that thou layest not down, and reapest that thou didst not sow.

And he saith unto him, Out of thine own mouth will I judge thee, thou wicked servant. Thou knewest that I was an austere man, taking up that I laid not down, and reaping that I did not sow: Wherefore then gavest not thou my money into the bank, that at my coming I might have required mine own with usury?

And he said unto them that stood by, Take from him the pound, and give it to him that hath ten pounds. (And they said unto him, Lord, he hath ten pounds.) But those mine enemies, which would not that I should reign over them, bring hither, and slay them before me.

For I say unto you, That unto every one which hath shall be given; and from him that hath not, even that he hath shall be taken away from him.

Footnotes

^97:* Luke 18, 35-42: "As Jesus was come nigh unto Jericho ." Mark 10, 46-52: "As Jesus went out of Jericho . . . " The two narratives are enough alike to imply but one blind beggar. Matthew, however, has two blind men, but sitting side by side; pleading at the same time, and cured at the same time, the dialogue being strikingly similar (Matthew 20, 30-34).

^98:* Compare this passage (Luke 19, 12-27) with the similar passage in LXXIII of this book (Matthew 25, 14-30).

LXIV

FARING TOWARD JERUSALEM AMIDST HOSANNAS--JESUS WEEPS FORETELLING JERUSALEM'S FATE

A.D. 30. Age 33. Bethphage. Jerusalem.

John 11, 55-57: Matthew 21, 1-6: Mark 77, 1-11: Luke 19, 28-44.

THE Jews' passover was nigh at hand; and many went out of the country up to Jerusalem, before the passover, to purify themselves. Jesus went before, ascending up to Jerusalem.

Now the chief priests and the Pharisees had given a commandment, that if any man knew where Jesus were, he should shew it, that they might take him. Then they sought for him.

When Jesus was come to Bethphage and Bethany, at the mount of Olives, nigh unto Jerusalem, he sendeth forth two disciples, saying, Go ye your way into the village over against you, in the which, as soon as ye be entered into it, straightway ye shall find an ass tied, and a colt with her, [**] whereon yet never man sat; loose them, and bring them hither unto me.

And if any man say aught unto you, and ask you, Why do ye this? why do ye loose them? ye shall say, Because the Lord hath need of them; and straightway he will send them hither.

The [two] disciples went, and did as Jesus had commanded. The owners said, Why loose ye them? They answered, The Lord hath need of them. And they let them go.

They brought the ass, and the colt, and put their garments on the colt; and they set Jesus thereon.

As he went, many spread their clothes in the way; and others cut branches off the trees, and strewed them in the way.

At the descent of the mount of Olives, the multitude began to praise God, saying, Blessed be the King that cometh in the name of he Lord. Hosanna in the highest: peace in heaven!

Some of the Pharisees said unto Jesus, Master, rebuke thy disciples. He answered, I tell you, that if these should hold their peace, the stones would immediately cry out.

When Jesus was come near, he beheld the city (Jerusalem), and wept over it, saying, If thou hadst known, even thou, at least in this thy day, the things which belong unto thy peace! but now they are hid from thine eyes.

For the days shall come upon thee, that thine enemies shall cast a trench about thee, and compass thee round, and keep thee in on every side. And shall lay thee even with the ground, and thy children within thee; and they shall not leave in thee one stone upon another; because thou knewest not the time of thy visitation.

When Jesus was come into Jerusalem, he taught daily in the temple. All the city was moved. The blind and the lame came to him, and he healed them.

The wonderful things that he did, and the children crying in the temple, Hosanna to the Son of David, displeased the chief priests and the scribes; and they said unto Jesus, Hearest thou what these say? He answered, Yea; have ye never read, Out of the mouth of babes and sucklings thou hast perfected praise?

And when he had looked round about upon all things, and now the eventide was come, he went out. With the twelve he went unto Bethany, and lodged there.

Footnotes

^99:* Thus Matthew. The other three narrators tell of the colt only. The interested reader will be repaid who will compare all four accounts, contrasting the characteristic Phrasings (book, chapter, and verse indicated above).

LXV

THE FIG TREE WITHERED--FAITH EXALTED--PRAYER WITH FAITH EXTOLLED

A.D. 30. Age 33. Near Bethany. Jerusalem.

Mark 11, 12-26: Matthew 21, 12-13; 18-22: Luke 19, 45-48.

NOW on the morrow in the morning, when they were come from Bethany, as Jesus returned into the city, he was hungry: and seeing afar off a fig tree having leaves, he came, if haply he might find any thing thereon. He found nothing but leaves, for the time of the figs was not yet. And he said, Let no fruit grow on thee henceforward. No man eat fruit of thee hereafter for ever.

Presently the fig tree withered away. The disciples saw it, saying, How soon is the fig tree withered away! Jesus answered, Verily I say unto you, If ye have faith, and doubt not, ye shall not only do this which is done to the fig tree, but also if ye shall say to this mountain, Be thou removed, and be thou cast into the sea; it shall be done. And all things, whatsoever ye shall ask in prayer, believing, ye shall receive.

[**]They came to Jerusalem, and Jesus went into the temple, and began to cast out them that sold and bought therein, and overthrew the tables of the money changers, and the seats of them that sold doves; and would not suffer that any man should carry any vessel through the temple. And he taught, saying, My house is the house of prayer. Is it not written, My house shall be called of all nations the house of prayer? but ye have made it a den of thieves.

The scribes and chief priests heard it, and sought how they might destroy Jesus: for they feared him, because all the people were attentive to hear him.

When even was come, he went out of the city. In the morning, as they came by, they saw the fig tree dried up from the roots. And

Peter calling to remembrance saith unto Jesus, Master, behold, the fig tree which thou cursedst is withered away. Jesus answering saith, Have faith in God. For verily I say unto you, That whosoever shall say unto this mountain, Be thou removed, and be thou cast into the sea; and shall not doubt in his heart, but shall believe that those things which he saith shall come to pass, he shall have whatsoever he saith.

Therefore I say unto you, What things soever ye desire, when ye pray, believe that ye receive them, and ye shall receive them.

And when ye stand praying, forgive, if ye have ought against any; that your Father also which is in heaven may forgive you your trespasses. But if ye do not forgive, neither will your Father which is in heaven forgive your trespasses.

Footnotes

^101:* There is in John, also (2, 14-16), a chiding by Jesus of the desecrators of the temple (turn back to VII of this book).

LXVI

CHRIST'S AUTHORITY CHALLENGED--PARABLES: THE SONS WHO WERE OF TWO MINDS; THE LORD OF THE VINEYARD, HIS SON, AND THE MURDEROUS HUSBANDMEN

A.D. 30. Age 33. Jerusalem, in the Temple.

Matthew 21, 23-46: Mark 11, 27-33; 12, 1-12: Luke 20, 1-19.

[**]ON one of those days, as Jesus was walking in the temple, and preached the gospel, the chief priests, and the scribes came with the elders, saying, By what authority doest thou these things? Jesus answered,

I also will ask of you one question, which if ye will tell me, and answer me, I in like wise will tell you by what authority I do these things: The baptism of John, whence was it? was it from heaven, or of men? Answer me.

They reasoned with themselves, saying, If we shall say, From heaven; he will say, Why then did ye not believe him? But and if we shall say, Of men; the people will stone us: for they be persuaded that John was indeed a prophet.

They feared the people. And they answered, We cannot tell.

Jesus saith unto them, Neither tell I you by what authority I do these things.

Then began he to speak by parables:

But what think ye? A certain man had two sons; and he came to the first, and said, Son, go work to day in my vineyard. He answered and said, I will not: but afterward he repented, and went.
And he came to the second, and said likewise. And he answered and said, I go, sir: and went not.

Whether of them twain did the will of his father?

They say, The first. Jesus saith, Verily I say unto you, That the publicans and the harlots go into the kingdom of God before you. For John came unto you in the way of righteousness, and ye believed him not: but the publicans and the harlots believed him: and ye, when ye had seen it, repented not afterward, that ye might believe him.

Hear another parable: There was a certain householder, which planted a vineyard, and set a hedge round about it, and digged a place in it for the winevat; and digged a winepress in it; and built a tower, and let it out to husbandmen, and went into a far country for a long time.

And at the season when the time of the fruit drew near, he sent a servant to the husbandmen, that he might receive from them of the fruit of the vineyard: but the husbandmen caught him, and beat him, and sent him away empty.

And again he sent unto them another servant; they beat him also, and at him they cast stones, and wounded him in the head, and handled him shamefully, and sent him away empty.

And again he sent a third: and him they wounded also, and killed, and they cast him out: and many others, more than the first: and they did unto them likewise, beating some, and killing some.

Having yet therefore one son, his well beloved, then said the lord of the vineyard, What shall I do? I will send my beloved son: last of all he sent unto them his son, saying, It may be they will reverence him, my son, when they see him.

But when those husbandmen saw the son, they reasoned among themselves, saying, This is the heir; come, let us kill him, and let us seize on his inheritance, and the inheritance shall be ours.

So they caught him, and slew him, and cast him out of the vineyard.

When the lord therefore of the vineyard cometh, what will he do unto those husbandmen? He will come and miserably destroy those wicked men, and will let out his vineyard unto other husbandmen, which shall render him the fruits in their seasons.

When they heard it, they said, God forbid. Jesus beheld them, and said, Did ye never read in the Scriptures?

What is this then that is written? Have ye not read this Scripture: The stone which the builders rejected, the same is become the head of the corner: this was the Lord's doing, and it is marvellous in our eyes? [**]

Therefore I say unto you, The kingdom of God shall be taken from you, and given to a nation bringing forth the fruits thereof. And whosoever shall fall on this stone shall be broken: but on whomsoever it shall fall, it will grind him to powder.

The chief priests and Pharisees heard Jesus' parables: they perceived that he had spoken the parables against them. And they sought to lay hold on him, but feared the people, because they took him for a prophet; and they left him, and went their way.

Footnotes

^102:* The text itself, as phrased by the three narrators of these episodes, furnishes interesting likenesses and contrasts (book, chapter, and verse indicated above.)

^103:* Psalms 118, 22-23.

LXVII

PARABLE: THE KING'S GUESTS FOR HIS SON'S WEDDING--
FUTILE WILES: CESAR'S TRIBUTE, THE SEVEN BROTHERS'
WIDOW

A.D. 30. Age 33. Jerusalem, in the Temple.

Matthew 22, 1-32: Mark 12, 13-27: Luke 20, 20-38.

JESUS spake unto them again by parables,

The kingdom of heaven is like unto a certain king which made a marriage for his son, and sent forth his servants to call them that were bidden to the wedding: and they would not come.

Again, he sent forth other servants, saying, Tell them which are bidden, Behold, I have prepared my dinner: my oxen and my fatlings are killed, and all things are ready: come unto the marriage. But they made light of it, and went their ways, one to his farm, another to his merchandise: and the remnant took his servants, and entreated them spitefully, and slew them. But when the king heard thereof, he was wroth: and sent forth his armies, and destroyed those murderers, and burned up their city.

Then saith he to his servants, The wedding is ready, but they which were bidden were not worthy. Go ye therefore into the highways, and as many as ye shall find, bid to the marriage. So those servants went out into the highways, and gathered all together as many as they found, both bad and good: and the wedding was furnished with guests.

And when the king came in to see the guests, he saw there a man which had not on a wedding garment: and he saith unto him, Friend, how earnest thou in hither not having a wedding garment? And he was speechless.

Then said the king to the servants, Bind him hand and foot, and take him away, and cast him into outer darkness; there shall be weeping and gnashing of teeth.

For many are called, but few are chosen.

Then the Pharisees took counsel how they might entangle Jesus in his talk. They sent spies, which should feign themselves just men, to catch him in his words, that so they might deliver him unto the authority of the governor.

When these were come, they say unto Jesus, Master, we know that thou teachest the way of God in truth, neither acceptest the person of men. Tell us, Is it lawful to give tribute to Cesar, or not?

Jesus perceived their craftiness, and said, Why tempt ye me, ye hypocrites? Shew me the tribute money; bring me a penny, that I may see it. Shew me a penny.

And they brought it. He said unto them, Whose image and superscription hath it? Whose is this image and superscription?

They answered, Cesar's. Then saith he, Render therefore unto Cesar the things which be Cesar's; and unto God the things which be God's.

They marvelled at his answers: they held their peace, and left him.

The same day came Sadducees, which say that there is no resurrection: and asked Jesus, saying, Moses wrote, If a man's brother die, and leave his wife behind him, and leave no children, the brother shall marry the wife, and raise up seed unto his brother. [**]

Now there were seven brethren: the first took a wife, and died without children: the second took her to wife, and he died : the third likewise; and in like manner the seven also: they died, and left no children. Last of all, the woman died. Therefore in the resurrection whose wife of them is she?

Jesus answering said, Do ye not therefore err, because ye know not the Scriptures? Ye do err, not knowing the Scriptures, neither the power of God.

The children of this world marry, and are given in marriage; but they which shall be accounted worthy to obtain that world, and the resurrection from the dead; when they shall rise from the dead, they neither marry, nor are given in marriage: for they are equal unto the angels of God which are in heaven; and are the children of God, being the children of the resurrection.

Now that the dead are raised, even Moses shewed at the bush, when he calleth the Lord the God of Abraham, and the God of Isaac, and the God of Jacob.

And as touching the resurrection of the dead, that they rise, have ye not read in the book of Moses that which was spoken unto you by God: how in the bush God spake unto Moses, saying, I am the God of Abraham, and the God of Isaac, and the God of Jacob?

God is not the God of the dead, but the God of the living; for all live unto him: ye therefore do greatly err.

Footnotes

^105:* Comparison of the three texts will disclose interesting differences in the phrasing (book, chapter, and verse indicated at the beginning of LXVII).

LXVIII

THE FIRST GREAT COMMANDMENT: AND THE SECOND--
"WHOSE SON IS CHRIST?"--WIDOW'S MITE

A.D. 30. Age 33. Jerusalem, in the Temple.

Matthew 22, 34-46: Mark 12, 28-44: Luke 20, 41-47; 21, 1-4.

THE Pharisees had heard that Jesus had put the Sadducees to silence; and one of them which was a lawyer, perceiving that Jesus had answered the Sadducees well, asked him, tempting him, Master, which is the great commandment in the law? Which is the first commandment of all? Jesus said unto him, The first of all the commandments is, Hear, O Israel; The Lord our God is one Lord: and thou shalt love the Lord thy God with all thy heart, and with all thy soul, and with all thy mind, and with all thy strength: this is the first and great commandment. And the second is like unto it, namely this, Thou shalt love thy neighbor as thyself. On these two commandments hang all the law and the prophets. There is none other commandment greater than these.

And the scribe (lawyer) said, Well, Master, thou hast said the truth: for there is one God; and there is none other: and to love him with all the heart, and with all the understanding, and with all the soul, and with all the strength; and to love his neighbor as himself, is more than all burnt offerings and sacrifices.

Jesus saw that he answered discreetly; and said unto him, Thou art not far from the kingdom of God.

While the Pharisees were gathered together, Jesus asked them, What think ye of Christ? whose son is he?

They say unto him, The son of David. He saith unto them, How then doth David in spirit call him Lord, saying, The Lord said unto my Lord, Sit thou on my right hand, till I make thine enemies thy footstool? If David then call him Lord, how is he his son?

And no man was able to answer him a word: neither durst any man from that day forth ask him questions. The common people heard him gladly.

While Jesus taught in the temple, he said, How say the scribes that Christ is David's son? For in the book of Psalms David himself saith by the Holy Ghost, The Lord said unto my Lord, Sit thou on my right hand, till I make thine enemies thy footstool. David therefore himself calleth him Lord; and how is he then his son?

Then in the audience of all the people he said unto his disciples, Beware of the scribes, which desire to walk in long robes, and love greetings in the marketplaces, and the highest seats in the synagogues, and the uppermost rooms at feasts; which devour widows' houses, and for a shew make long prayers: these same shall receive greater damnation.

Jesus sat over against the treasury. He beheld people cast money and gifts into the treasury. Many that were rich cast in much. He saw also a certain poor widow casting in thither two mites, which make a farthing. He called his disciples, and saith unto them, Of a truth I say unto you, that this poor widow doth cast in more than they all which have cast into the treasury: for all these have of their abundance cast in unto the offerings of God: but she of her penury did cast in all that she had, even all her living.

LXIX

"WOE UNTO YOU, SCRIBES AND PHARISEES!"--HYPOCRISY AND CANT CONDEMNED--"O JERUSALEM, JERUSALEM!"-- "BLESSED IS HE THAT COMETH IN THE NAME OF THE LORD"

A.D. 30. Age 33. Jerusalem, in the Temple.

Matthew 23, 1-39.

TO the multitude, and to his disciples spake Jesus, saying,

The scribes and the Pharisees sit in Moses' seat: all therefore whatsoever they bid you observe, that observe and do; but do not ye after their works: for they say, and do not. For they bind heavy burdens and grievous to be borne, and lay them on men's shoulders; but they themselves will not move them with one of their fingers.

But all their works they do for to be seen of men: they make broad their phylacteries, and enlarge the borders of their garments, and love the uppermost rooms at feasts, and the chief seats in the synagogues, and greetings in the markets, and to be called of men, Rabbi, Rabbi. But be not ye called Rabbi: for one is your Master, even Christ; and all ye are brethren.

And call no man your father upon the earth: for one is your Father which is in heaven. Neither be ye called masters: for one is your Master, even Christ.

But he that is greatest among you shall be your servant. And whosoever shall exalt himself shall be abased; and he that shall humble himself shall be exalted.

But woe unto you, scribes and pharisees, hypocrites! for ye shut up the kingdom of heaven against men: for ye neither go in yourselves, neither suffer ye them that are entering to go in.

Woe unto you, scribes and Pharisees, hypocrites! for ye pay tithe of mint and anise and cummin, and have omitted the weightier matters of the law, judgment, mercy and faith: these ought ye to have done, and not to leave the other undone. Ye blind guides, which strain at a gnat, and swallow a camel.

Woe unto you, scribes and Pharisees, hypocrites! for ye make clean the outside of the cup and of the platter, but within they are full of extortion and excess. Thou blind Pharisee, cleanse first that which is within the cup and platter, that the outside of them may be clean also.

Woe unto you, scribes and Pharisees, hypocrites! for ye are like unto whited sepulchres, which indeed appear beautiful outward, but are within full of dead men's bones, and of all uncleanness. Even so ye also outwardly appear righteous unto men, but within ye are full of hypocrisy and iniquity.

Woe unto you, scribes and Pharisees, hypocrites! because ye build the tombs of the prophets, and garnish the sepulchres of the righteous, and say, If we had been in the days of our fathers, we would not have been partakers with them in the blood of the prophets.

Joseph Lumpkin

Wherefore ye be witnesses unto yourselves, that ye are the children of them which killed the prophets. Fill ye up then the measure of your fathers. Ye serpents, ye generation of vipers, how can ye escape the damnation of hell?

Wherefore, behold, I send unto you prophets, and wise men, and scribes: and some of them ye shall kill and crucify; and some of them shall ye scourge in your synagogues, and persecute them from city to city: that upon you may come all the righteous blood shed upon the earth, from the blood of righteous Abel unto the blood of Zacharias son of Barachias, whom ye slew between the temple and the altar. Verily I say unto you, All these things shall come upon this generation.

[**]O Jerusalem, Jerusalem, thou that killest the prophets, and stonest them which are sent unto thee, how often would I have gathered thy children together, even as a hen gathereth her chickens under her wings, and ye would not!

Behold, your house is left unto you desolate. For I say unto you, Ye shall not see me henceforth, till ye shall say, Blessed is he that cometh in the name of the Lord.

Footnotes

^108:* Turn back and reread LIV in this book.

LXX

GREEKS DESIRE TO SEE JESUS--HE FORESEES HIS DEATH: "NOW IS MY SOUL TROUBLED"--FAITH EXALTED, PRAYER EXTOLLED--"I AM COME A LIGHT INTO THE WORLD. . . . TO SAVE THE WORLD"

A.D. 30. Age 33. Jerusalem, in the Temple.

John 12, 20-36; 42-50.

CERTAIN Greeks came up to worship at the feast: the same came to Philip, saying, Sir, we would see Jesus.

Philip and Andrew tell Jesus. Jesus answered them, saying, The hour is come, that the Son of man should be glorified.

Verily, verily, I say unto you, Except a corn of wheat fall into the ground and die, it abideth alone: but if it die, it bringeth forth much fruit. He that loveth his life shall lose it; and he that hateth his life in his world shall keep it unto life eternal.

If any man serve me, let him follow me; and where I am, there shall also my servant be: if any man serve me, him will my Father honor.

Now is my soul troubled; and what shall I say? Father, save me from this hour? but for this cause came I unto this hour.

Father, glorify thy name.

Then came there a voice from heaven, saying, I have both glorified it, and will glorify it again.

The people that stood by, and heard it, said that it thundered: others said, An angel spake.

Jesus said, This voice came not because of me, but for your sakes.

Now is the judgment of this world: now shall the prince of this world be cast out. And I, if I be lifted up from the earth, will draw all men unto me.

This he said, signifying what death he should die.

The people answered, We have heard out of the law that Christ abideth for ever; and how sayest thou, The Son of man must be lifted up? Who is this Son of man? Then Jesus said, Yet a little while is the light with you. Walk while ye have the light, lest darkness come upon you: for he that walketh in darkness knoweth not whither he goeth. While ye have light, believe in the light, that ye may be the children of light.

Among the chief rulers many believed on Jesus; but because of the Pharisees they did not confess him, lest they should be put out of the synagogue: for they loved the praise of men more than the praise of God.

Jesus cried and said, He that believeth on me believeth not on me, but on him that sent me. And he that seeth me seeth him that sent me.

I am come a light into the world, that whosoever believeth on me should not abide in darkness. And if any man hear my words, and believe not, I judge him not: for I came not to judge the world, but to save the world.

He that rejecteth me, and receiveth not my words, hath one that judgeth him: the word that I have spoken, the same shall judge him in the last day. For I have not spoken of myself; but the Father which sent me, he gave me a commandment, what I should say, and what I should speak. And I know that his commandment is life everlasting: whatsoever 1 speak therefore, even as the Father said unto me, so I speak.

LXXI

THE TEMPLE DOOMED--NATION TO RISE AGAINST NATION--
"I WILL GIVE YOU WISDOM"--"IN YOUR PATIENCE POSSESS
YE YOUR SOULS"--THE SON OF MAN COMING WITH POWER

A.D. 30. Age 33. Jerusalem. Mt. of Olives.

Matthew 24, 1-31: Mark 13, 1-27: Luke 21, 5-28.

AS Jesus went out from the temple, his disciples came for to show
him the buildings of the temple. One saith, Master, see what
buildings are here! Some spake of the temple how it was adorned
with goodly stones and gifts. Jesus answering said,

[**]Seest thou these great buildings? See ye not all these things?
Verily I say unto you, As for these things which ye behold, the days
will come, in the which there shall not be left here one stone upon
another, that shall not be thrown down.

As Jesus sat upon the mount of Olives, over against the temple,
Peter and James, John and Andrew asked him privately, What sign
will there be when these things shall come to pass? What shall be
the sign of thy coming, and of the end of the world? Jesus
answering them began to say, Take heed lest any man deceive you.
For many shall come in my name, saying, I am Christ; and shall

463

deceive many; and the time draweth near; go ye not therefore after them.

Take heed that ye be not deceived but when ye shall hear commotions, and wars, and rumors of wars, see that ye be not troubled; be not terrified. Such things must needs be: for all these things must first come to pass; but the end shall not be yet (is not by and by).

Nation shall rise against nation, and kingdom against kingdom; and there shall be famines, and troubles, and pestilences, and great earthquakes, in divers places; and fearful sights and great signs shall there be from heaven. All these things are the beginnings of sorrows.

But take heed to yourselves: for before all these, they shall lay their hands on you, and persecute you; delivering you up to councils, and into prisons, to be afflicted: and in the synagogues ye shall be beaten: and ye shall be brought before rulers and kings for my name's sake. And it shall turn to you for a testimony against them. Then shall they kill you, and ye shall be hated of all nations for my name's sake.

But the gospel must first be published among all nations.

And when they shall lead you, and deliver you up, take no thought beforehand what ye shall speak, neither do ye premeditate: but whatsoever shall be given you in that hour, that speak ye: for it is not ye that speak, but the Holy Ghost. Settle it therefore in your hearts, not to meditate before what ye shall answer; for I will give you a mouth and wisdom, which all your adversaries shall not be able to gainsay nor resist.

And then shall many be offended, [**] and shall betray one another. And ye shall be betrayed both by parents, and brethren, and kinsfolks, and friends. Now the brother shall betray the brother to death, and the father the son; and children shall rise up against their parents, and shall cause them to be put to death; and some of you shall they cause to be put to death. And ye shall be hated of all men for my name's sake.

But there shall not a hair of your head perish. In your patience possess ye your souls.

And many false prophets shall rise and shall deceive many. And because iniquity shall abound, the love of many shall wax cold. But he that shall endure unto the end, the same shall be saved. And this gospel of the kingdom shall be preached in all the world for a witness unto all nations; and then shall the end come.

When ye therefore shall see the abomination of desolation, spoken of by Daniel the prophet, standing in the holy place, where it ought not (let him that readeth understand): and when ye shall see Jerusalem compassed with armies, then know that the desolation thereof is nigh; then let them which are in Judea flee to the mountains: and let them which are in the midst of it depart out; and let not them that are in the countries enter thereinto. And let him that is on the housetop not come down into the house, neither enter therein, to take anything out of his house; and let him which is in the field not return back for to take his clothes.

For these be the days of vengeance, that all things which are written may be fulfilled.

And woe unto them that are with child, and to them that give suck, in those days! for there shall be great distress in the land, and wrath upon the people. And pray ye that your flight be not in winter, neither on the sabbath day: for in those days shall be great affliction, tribulation such as was not since the beginning of the creation which God created, unto this time; no, nor ever in the world shall be. And except that the Lord had shortened those days, there should no flesh be saved: but for the elect's sake, whom he hath chosen, those days shall be shortened.

And they shall fall by the edge of the sword, and shall be led away captive into all nations: and Jerusalem shall be trodden down of the Gentiles, until the times of the Gentiles be fulfilled.

And then if any man shall say to you, Lo, here is Christ; or, lo, he is there; believe it not: for there shall arise false Christs and false prophets, and shall show great signs and wonders, to seduce; insomuch that, if it were possible, they shall deceive even the very elect.

But take ye heed: behold, I have foretold you all things.

Wherefore if they shall say unto you, Behold, he is in the desert; go not forth: Behold, he is in the secret chambers; believe it not. For as the lightning cometh out of the east, and shineth even unto the west; so shall also the coming of the Son of man be. For wheresoever the carcass is, there will the eagles be gathered together.

But immediately, in those days after that tribulation, there shall be signs in the sun, and in the moon, and in the stars: the sun shall be darkened, and the moon shall not give her light, and the stars of heaven shall fall; and the powers that are in the heavens shall be shaken: and upon the earth [shall be] distress of nations, with perplexity; the sea and waves roaring: men's hearts failing them for fear, and for looking after those things which are coming on the earth: for the powers of heaven shall be shaken.

And then shall appear the sign of the Son of man in heaven: and then shall all the tribes of the earth mourn, and they shall see the

Son of man coming in the clouds of heaven with power and great glory.

And then shall he send his angels with a great sound of a trumpet, and they shall gather together his elect from the four winds, from the uttermost part of the earth to the uttermost part of heaven; from one end of heaven to another.

And when these things begin to come to pass, then look up, and lift up your heads; for your redemption draweth nigh.

Footnotes

^110:* The text here of the three narrators furnishes phrasings so varied that the interested reader will be repaid by an attentive perusal of all three (book, chapter, and verse designated above).

^111:* . . . be offended: stumble, fall away.

LXXII

PARABLES: THE FIG TREE IN LEAF, ABSENT HOUSEHOLDER AND THE HOUSE SERVANTS, VIRGINS WISE AND VIRGINS FOOLISH--"WATCH AND PRAY"

A.D. 30. Age 33. Mount of Olives.

Matthew 24, 32-51; 25, 1-13: Mark 13, 28-37: Luke 21, 29-36.

[**]NOW learn a parable of the fig tree: Behold the fig tree when her branch is yet tender, and putteth forth leaves; and behold the trees when they now shoot forth: ye see and know of your own selves that summer is nigh at hand.

So in like manner, when ye shall see all these things come to pass, know ye that the kingdom of God is nigh at hand, even at the doors. Verily I say unto you, This generation shall not pass, till all these things be done. Heaven and earth shall pass away, but my words shall not pass away.

And take heed to yourselves, lest at any time your hearts be overcharged with surfeiting and drunkenness, and cares of this life; and so that day come upon you unawares. For as a snare shall it come on all them that dwell on the face of the whole earth.

Watch ye therefore, and pray always, that ye may be accounted worthy to escape all these things that shall come to pass, and to stand before the Son of man.

But of that day and that hour knoweth no man, no, not the angels which are in heaven, neither the Son, but my Father only.

Take ye heed, watch and pray: for ye know not when the time is. [**]But as the days of Noe were, so shall also the coming of the Son of man be. For as in the days that were before the flood they were eating and drinking, marrying and giving in marriage, until the day that Noe entered into the ark, and knew not till the flood came, and took them all away: so shall also the coming of the Son of man be. Then shall two be in the field; the one shall be taken, and the other left. Two women shall be grinding at the mill; the one shall be taken, and the other left.

Watch therefore: for ye know not what hour your Lord doth come.

For the Son of man is as a man taking a far journey, who left his house, and gave authority to his servants, and to every man his work, and commanded the porter to watch.

Watch ye therefore: for ye know not when the master of the house cometh, at even, or at midnight, or at the cockcrowing, or in the morning: lest coming suddenly he find you sleeping.

And what I say unto you I say unto all, Watch.

[*+]But know this, that if the goodman of the house had known in what watch the thief would come, he would have watched, and would not have suffered his house to be broken up. Therefore be ye also ready: for in such an hour as ye think not the Son of man cometh. And what I say unto you I say unto all, Watch.

Who then is a faithful and wise servant, whom his lord hath made ruler over his household, to give them meat in due season?

Blessed is that servant, whom his lord when he cometh shall find so doing. Verily I say unto you, That he shall make him ruler over all his goods.

But and if that evil servant shall say in his heart, My lord delayeth his coming; and shall begin to smit his fellow servants, and to eat and drink with the drunken; the lord of that servant shall come in a day when he looketh not for him, and in an hour that he is not aware of, and shall cut him asunder, and appoint him his portion with the hypocrites: there shall be weeping and gnashing of teeth.

Then shall the kingdom of heaven be likened unto ten virgins, which took their lamps, and went forth to meet the bridegroom. And five of them were wise, and five were foolish. They that were foolish took their lamps, and took no oil with them. But the wise took oil in their vessels with their lamps.

While the bridegroom tarried, they all slumbered and slept. And at midnight there was a cry made, Behold, the bridegroom cometh; go ye out to meet him.

Then all those virgins arose, and trimmed their lamps. And the foolish said unto the wise, Give us of your oil; for our lamps are gone out.

But the wise answered, saying, Not so; lest there be not enough for us and you, but go ye rather to them that sell, and buy for yourselves.

And while they went to buy, the bridegroom came: and they that were ready went in with him to the marriage: and the door was shut.

Afterward came also the other virgins, saying, Lord, Lord, open to us. But he answered and said, Verily I say unto you, I know you not.

Watch, therefore, for ye know neither the day nor the hour wherein the Son of man cometh.

Footnotes

^112:* Here again the three texts exhibit the three narrators in their wonted likenesses and contrasts of phrase (book, chapter, and verse designated above).

^113:* Compare the text of this passage (Matthew 24, 36-41) with the text of the similar Passage in LIX of this hook (Luke 17, 26-36).

^113:+ Compare this paragraph and the following two paragraphs (Matthew 24, 43-51) with the similar passage in LI-LII of this book (Luke 12, 39-46).

LXXIII

PARABLE: THE MASTER, THE SERVANTS, THE MONEY (TALENTS)--ON THE LAST JUDGMENT: "WHEN THE SON OF MAN SHALL COME"

A.D. 30. Age 33. Mount of Olives.

Matthew 25, 14-46.

[**]FOR the kingdom of heaven is as a man travelling into a far country, who called his own servants, and delivered unto them his goods. And unto one he gave five talents, to another, two, and to

another, one; to every man according to his several ability; and straightway took his journey.

Then he that had received the five talents went and traded with the same, and made them other five talents. And likewise he that had received two, he also gained other two. But he that had received one went and digged in the earth, and hid his lord's money.

After a long time the lord of those servants cometh, and reckoned with them.

And so he that had received five talents came and brought other five talents, saying, Lord, thou deliveredst unto me five talents: behold, I have gained beside them five talents more. His lord said unto him, Well done, thou good and faithful servant: thou hast been faithful over a few things, I will make thee ruler over many things: enter thou into the joy of thy lord.

He also that had received two talents came and said, Lord, thou deliveredst unto me two talents: behold, I have gained two other talents beside them. His lord said unto him, Well done, good and faithful servant: thou hast been faithful over a few things, I will make thee ruler over many things: enter thou into the joy of thy lord.

Then he which had received the one talent came and said, Lord, I knew thee that thou art a hard man, reaping where thou hast not sown, and gathering where thou hast not strewed; and I was afraid, and went and hid thy talent in the earth: lo, there thou hast that is thine.

His lord answered and said unto him, Thou wicked and slothful servant, thou knewest that I reap where I sowed not, and gather where I have not strewed: Thou oughtest therefore to have put my money to the exchangers, and then at my coming I should have received mine own with usury.

Take therefore the talent from him, and give it unto him which hath ten talents.

For unto every one that hath shall be given, and he shall have abundance: but from him that hath not shall be taken away even that which he hath. And cast ye the unprofitable servant into outer darkness: there shall be weeping and gnashing of teeth.

When the Son of man shall come in his glory, and all the holy angels with him, then shall he sit upon the throne of his glory: and before him shall be gathered all nations: and he shall separate them one from another, as a shepherd divideth his sheep from the goats: and he shall set the sheep on his right hand, but the goats on the left.

Then shall the King say unto them on his right hand, Come, ye blessed of my Father, inherit the kingdom prepared for you from the foundation of the world: for I was a hungered, and ye gave me meat: I was thirsty, and ye gave me drink: I was a stranger, and ye took me in: naked, and ye clothed me: I was sick, and ye visited me: I was in prison, and ye came unto me.

Then shall the righteous answer him, saying, Lord, when saw we thee a hungered, and fed thee? or thirsty, and gave thee drink? When saw we thee a stranger, and took thee in? or naked, and clothed thee? Or when saw we thee sick, or in prison, and came unto thee?

And the King shall answer and say unto them, Verily I say unto you, Inasmuch as ye have done it unto one of the least of these my brethren, ye have done it unto me.

Then shall he say also unto them on the left hand, Depart from me, ye cursed, into everlasting fire, prepared for the devil and his angels: for I was a hungered, and ye gave me no meat: I was thirsty, and ye gave me no drink: I was a stranger, and ye took me not in: naked, and ye clothed me not; sick, and in prison, and ye visited me not.

Then shall they also answer him, saying, Lord, when saw we thee a hungered, or athirst, or a stranger, or naked, or sick, or in prison, and did not minister unto thee?

Then he shall answer them, saying, Verily I say unto you, Inasmuch as ye did it not to one of the least of these, ye did it not to me.

And these shall go away into everlasting punishment: but the righteous into life eternal.

Footnotes

^114:* Compare this passage (Matthew 25, 14-30) with the similar passage in LXIII of this book (Luke 19, 12-27).

LXXIV

JESUS SUPS IN BETHANY: MARTHA SERVES, MARY'S DEVOTION, JUDAS' DUPLICITY, JESUS LAUDS MARY'S HOMAGE--CHIEF PRIESTS ASTIR

A.D. 30. Age 33. Bethany.

John 12, 1-11: Matthew 26, 6-13: Mark 14, 3-9.

JESUS came, six days before the passover, to Bethany, where Lazarus was, whom he had raised from the dead. In the house of Simon the leper there, they made Jesus a supper; and Martha served. Lazarus was one of them at the table with Jesus.

Mary, having an alabaster box of ointment of spikenard very precious, brake the box, and poured it on Jesus' head as he sat at meat, and anointed his feet, and wiped his feet with her hair. [**]

Some disciples had indignation, saying, To what purpose is this waste? Judas Iscariot [which should betray Jesus] saith, Why was not this ointment sold for three hundred pence, and given to the poor? And they murmured against Mary.

When Jesus understood it, he said, Let her alone: why trouble ye the woman? Against the day of my burying hath she done this.

For ye have the poor with you always, and whensoever ye will ye may do them good: but me ye have not always. She hath wrought a good work upon me; for she hath done what she could: for in that she hath poured this ointment on my body, she is come aforehand to anoint my body to the burying (she did it for my burial). Why trouble ye her?

Verily I say unto you, Wheresoever this gospel shall be preached throughout the whole world, there shall also this that this woman hath done, be told for a memorial of her.

The Jews knew that Jesus was there: and they came, not for Jesus' sake only, but that they might see Lazarus, whom he had raised from the dead.

But the chief priests consulted that they might put Lazarus also to death; because that by reason of him many of the Jews believed on Jesus.

Footnotes

^116:* Turn back to LVIII in this book, and read again the story of Mary's brother Lazarus. And in XXV read of a like service done by the "woman which was a sinner."

LXXV

CONSPIRACY AT THE HIGH PRIEST'S PALACE--JUDAS HIRED--THE PASSOVER SUPPER--CHRIST'S HUMILITY: HE WASHES THE FEET OF THE TWELVE

A.D. 30. Age 33. Bethany. Jerusalem: Upper Room.

Luke 21, 37-38; 22, 1-18: Matthew 26, 1-5; 14-20: Mark 14, 1-2; 10-17: John 13, 2-17.

NOW the feast of unleavened bread drew nigh, which is called the passover. In the daytime Jesus was teaching in the temple. At night he abode in the mount of Olives; in the morning the people came early to the temple for to hear him.

Two days before the feast, the chief priests, the scribes, and the elders of the people, assembled unto the palace of the high priest Caiaphas, and consulted that they might take Jesus by craft. But they said, Not on the feast day, lest there be an uproar of people.

Then Judas surnamed Iscariot, one of the twelve, went and said unto the chief priests, What will ye give me, and I will deliver Jesus unto you? They were glad, and to give Judas thirty pieces of silver. Judas promised: and sought opportunity how he might conveniently betray Jesus unto them in the absence of the multitude.

Now before the feast of the passover, when Jesus knew that his hour was come that he should depart out of this world unto the Father, he said unto his disciples, Ye know that after two days is the feast of passover, and the Son of man is betrayed to be crucified.

Then came the first day of the feast of unleavened bread, when the passover must be killed; and Jesus sent Peter and John, saying, Go and prepare the passover, that we may eat.

And they said, Where wilt thou that we prepare? He said, When ye are entered into the city, behold, there shall meet you a man bearing a pitcher of water: go ye into the city to such a man, and follow him into the house where he entereth in. And wheresoever he shall go in, say ye to the goodman of the house, The Master saith unto thee, My time is at hand; I will keep the passover at thy house with my disciples. Where is the guestchamber, where I shall eat the passover with my disciples?

And he will shew you a large upper room furnished and prepared: there make ready for us.

They went, and found as he had said: and they made ready the passover. In the evening Jesus cometh with the twelve apostles, and when the hour was come, he sat down, the twelve with him.

And he said unto them, With desire I have desired to eat this passover with you before I suffer: for I say unto you, I will not any more eat thereof, until it be fulfilled in the kingdom of God.

And he took the cup and gave thanks, and said, Take this, and divide it among yourselves: for I say unto you, I will not drink of the fruit of the vine, until the kingdom of God shall come.

Supper being ended, Jesus riseth; and he laid aside his garments, and took a towel, and girded himself. After that he poureth water into a basin, and began to wash the disciples' feet, and to wipe them with the towel.

Then Simon Peter saith, Lord, dost thou wash my feet? Jesus answered, What I do thou knowest not now; but thou shalt know hereafter.

Peter saith unto him, Thou shalt never wash my feet. Jesus answered,

If I wash thee not, thou hast no part with me.

Peter saith, Lord, not my feet only, but also my hands and my head. Jesus saith unto him, He that is washed needeth not save to wash his feet, but is clean every whit: and ye are clean, but not all.

For he knew who should betray him; therefore said he, Ye are not all clean.

So after he had washed their feet, and had taken his garments, and was set down again, he said unto them, Know ye what I have done to you?

Ye call me Master and Lord: and ye say well; for so I am. If I then, your Lord and Master, have washed your feet: ye also ought to wash one another's feet. For I have given you an example, that ye should do as I have done to you.

Verily, verily, I say unto you, The servant is not greater than his lord: neither he that is sent greater than he that sent him. If ye know these things, happy are ye if ye do them.

LXXVI

CHRIST INSTITUTES HIS HOLY SUPPER--JUDAS THE BETRAYER--PETER'S THREE DENIALS PREDICTED--"YET A LITTLE WHILE I AM WITH YOU: LET NOT YOUR HEART BE TROUBLED"--MANY MANSIONS

A.D. 30 Age 33. Jerusalem: Upper Room.

Paul I. Corinthians 11, 24-25: Matthew 26, 21-29: Mark 14, 18-25: Luke 22, 19-38: John 13, 18-38; 14, 1-4.

THE same night in which he was betrayed, the Lord Jesus took bread, and gave thanks, and blessed it, and brake it, and gave it to his disciples, and said, Take, eat; this is my body, which is given [**] for you: this do in remembrance of me.

As they sat and did eat, Jesus said, Verily I say unto you, that one of you shall betray me.

But, behold, the hand of him that betrayeth me is with me on the table. And truly the Son of man goeth, as it was determined: but woe unto that man by whom he is betrayed!

I speak not of you all: I know whom I have chosen: but that the Scripture may be fulfilled, He that eateth bread with me hath lifted up his heel against me.

Now I tell you before it come, that, when it is come to pass, ye may believe that I am he.

Verily, verily, I say unto you, He that receiveth whomsoever I send receiveth me; and he that receiveth me receiveth him that sent me.

When Jesus had thus said, he was troubled in spirit; and testified, Verily, verily, I say unto you, that one of you which eateth with me shall betray me.

The disciples looked one on another, doubting of whom he spake. They were exceeding sorrowful, and began every one of them to say unto Jesus, one by one, Lord, is it I? and another, Is it I? He answered, It is one of the twelve: he that dippeth his hand with me in the dish, the same shall betray me.

The Son of man indeed goeth, as it is written of him; but woe to that man by whom the Son of man is betrayed! good were it for that man if he had never been born.

Now there was leaning on Jesus' bosom one whom Jesus loved. [*+] Simon Peter beckoned to him, that he should ask who it should be of whom Jesus spake. He then lying on Jesus' breast saith, Lord, who is it? Jesus answered, He it is, to whom I shall give a sop, when I have dipped it.

He dipped the sop: he gave it to Judas Iscariot: then said unto him, That thou doest, do quickly.

Judas said, Master, is it I? Jesus said unto him, Thou hast said.

Judas went immediately out: and it was night. When he was gone, Jesus said, Now is the Son of man glorified, and God is in him. If God be glorified in him, God shall also glorify him in himself, and shall straightway glorify him.

Little children, yet a little while I am with you. Ye shall seek me: and as I said unto the Jews, [**] so now I say to you, Whither I go, ye cannot come.

A new commandment I give unto you, That ye love one another; as I have loved you, that ye also love one another. By this shall all men know that ye are my disciples, if ye have love one to another.

Simon Peter said unto him, Lord, whither goest thou? Jesus answered, Whither I go, thou canst not follow me now: but thou shalt follow me afterwards.

Peter said, Lord, why cannot I follow thee now? I will lay down my life for thy sake. Jesus answered, Wilt thou lay down thy life for my sake? Verily, verily, I say unto thee, The cock shall not crow, till thou hast denied me thrice.

There was a strife among the disciples, which of them should be accounted the greatest. And Jesus said unto them, The kings of the Gentile exercise lordship over them; and they that exercise authority upon them are called benefactors. But ye shall not be so; but he that is greatest among you, let him be as the younger; and he that is chief, as he that doth serve.

For whether is greater, he that sitteth at meat, or he that serveth? is not he that sitteth at meat? but I am among you as he that serveth.

Ye are they which have continued with me in my temptations. And I appoint unto you a kingdom, as my father hath appointed unto me; that ye may eat and drink at my table in my kingdom, and sit on thrones judging the twelve tribes of Israel.

And the Lord said, Simon, Simon, behold, Satan hath desired to have you, that he may sift you as wheat: but I have prayed for thee, that thy faith fail not: and when thou art converted, strengthen thy brethren.

And Simon said, Lord, I am ready to go with thee, both into prison, and to death. And Jesus said, I tell thee, Peter, the cock shall not crow this day, before that thou shalt thrice deny that thou knowest me.

And he said unto them, When I sent you without purse, and scrip, and shoes, lacked ye anything?

They said, Nothing. Then said Jesus, But now, he that hath a purse, let him take it, and likewise his scrip: and he that hath no sword, let him sell his garment, and buy one.

For I say unto you, that this that is written must yet be accomplished in me, And he was reckoned among the transgressors.

For the things concerning me have an end.

And they said, Lord, behold, here are two swords. And he answered, It is enough.

When he had supped, Jesus after the same manner took the cup, and when he had given thanks, gave it to them, saying,
Drink ye all of it.

And they all drank of it. And he said unto them, This cup is the new testament in my blood, which is shed for you; for this is my blood of the new testament which is shed for many for the remission of sins: this do ye, as oft as ye drink it, in remembrance of me.

Verily I say unto you, I will drink henceforth no more of this fruit of the vine, until that day when I drink it new with you in the kingdom of God, my Father's kingdom.

Let not your heart be troubled: ye believe in God, believe also in me.

In my Father's house are many mansions: if it were not so, I would have told you. I go to prepare a place for you. And if I go and prepare a place for you, I will come again, and receive you unto myself; that where I am, there ye may be also. And whither I go ye know, and the way ye know.

Footnotes

^119:* Paul has it, "broken."

^119:+ Supposed to be John, the brother of James and son of Zebedee.

^120:* Told in XLVI of this book.

LXXVII

SAYING "I GO UNTO MY FATHER," CHRIST EXALTS PEACE, GOOD WILL, LOVE--"I AM THE WAY, THE TRUTH, THE LIFE"-- REASSURES THE APOSTLES--THE COMFORTER: "PEACE I LEAVE WITH YOU"

A.D. 30. Age 33. Jerusalem: Upper Room.

John 14, 5-31.

THOMAS saith unto Jesus, Lord, we know not whither thou goest; and how can we know the way. Jesus saith unto him, I am the way, the truth, and the life: no man cometh unto the Father, but by me. If ye had known me, ye should have known my Father also: and from henceforth ye know him, and have seen him.

Philip saith, Lord, shew us the Father, and it sufficeth us. Jesus answered, Have I been so long time with you, and yet hast thou not known me, Philip? he that hath seen me hath seen the Father; and how sayest thou then, Shew us the Father?

Believest thou not that I am in the Father, and the Father in me? The words I speak unto you, I speak not of myself: but the Father that dwelleth in me, he doeth the works. Believe me that I am in the

Father, and the Father in me: or else believe me for the very works' sake.

Verily, verily, I say unto you, He that believeth on me, the works that I do shall he do also; and greater works than these shall he do; because I go unto my Father.

And whatsoever ye shall ask in my name, that will I do, that the Father may be glorified in the Son. If ye shall ask anything in my name, I will do it.

If ye love me keep my commandments. And I will pray the Father, and he shall give you another Comforter, that he may abide with you for ever; even the Spirit of truth; whom the world cannot receive, because it seeth him not, neither knoweth him: but ye know him; for he dwelleth with you, and shall be in you. I will not leave you comfortless; I will come to you.

Yet a little while, and the world seeth me no more; but ye see me: because I live, ye shall live also. At that day ye shall know that I am in my Father, and ye in me, and I in you.

He that hath my commandments, and keepeth them, he it is that loveth me: and he that loveth me shall be loved of my Father, and I will love him, and will manifest myself to him.

Judas, not Iscariot, saith unto him, Lord, how is it that thou wilt manifest thyself unto us, and not unto the world? Jesus answered, If a man love me, he will keep my words: and my Father will love him, and we will come unto him, and make our abode with him. He that loveth me not keepth not my sayings: and the word which ye hear is not mine, but the Father's which sent me.

These things have I spoken unto you, being yet present with you.

But the Comforter, which is the Holy Ghost, whom the Father will send in my name, he shall teach you all things, and bring all things to your remembrance, whatsoever I have said unto you. Peace I leave with you, my peace I give unto you: not as the world giveth, give I unto you.

Let not your heart be troubled, neither let it be afraid. Ye have heard how I said unto you, I go away, and come again unto you. If ye loved me, ye would rejoice, because I said, I go unto the Father: for my Father is greater than I.

And now I have told you before it come to pass, that, when it is come to pass, ye might believe.

Hereafter I will not talk much with you: for the prince of this world cometh, and hath nothing in me. But that the world may know that I love the Father; and as the Father gave me commandment, even so I do.

LXXVIII

"I AM THE TRUE VINE"--RELATIONSHIP IN LOVE--"WHEN THE COMFORTER IS COME"--"GREATER LOVE HATH NO MAN THAN THIS. . ."

A.D. 30. Age 33. Jerusalem: Upper Room.

John 15, 1-27; 16, 1.

I AM the true vine, and my Father is the husbandman. Every branch in me that beareth not fruit he taketh away: and every branch that beareth fruit, he purgeth it, that it may bring forth more fruit. Now ye are clean through the word which I have spoken unto you.

Abide in me, and I in you. As the branch cannot bear fruit of itself, except it abide in the vine; no more can ye, except ye abide in me. I am the vine, ye are the branches; he that abideth in me, and I in him, the same bringeth forth much fruit; for without me ye can do nothing.

If a man abide not in me, he is cast forth as a branch, and is withered; and men gather them, and cast them into the fire, and they are burned. If ye abide in me, and my words abide in you, ye shall ask what ye will, and it shall be done unto you.

Herein is my Father glorified, that ye bear much fruit; so shall ye be my disciples.

As the Father hath loved me, so have I loved you: continue ye in my love. If ye keep my commandments, ye shall abide in my love; even as I have kept my Father's commandments and abide in his love.

These things have I spoken unto you, that my joy might remain in you, and that your joy might be full. This is my commandment, that ye love one another, as I have loved you.

Greater love hath no man than this, that a man lay down his life for his friends. Ye are my friends, if ye do whatsoever I command you. Henceforth I call you not servants; for the servant knoweth not what his lord doeth; but I have called you friends; for all things that I have heard of my Father I have made known unto you.

Ye have not chosen me, but I have chosen you, and ordained you, that ye should go and bring forth fruit, and that your fruit should remain: that whatsoever ye shall ask of the Father in my name, he may give it you. These things I command you, that ye love one another.

If the world hate you, ye know that it hated me before it hated you. If ye were of the world, the world would love his own: but because ye are not of the world but I have chosen you out of the world, therefore the world hateth you.

Remember the word that I said unto you, The servant is not greater than his lord.

If they have persecuted me, they will also persecute you; if they have kept my saying, they will keep yours also. But all these things will they do unto you for my name's sake, because they know not him that sent me.

If I had not come and spoken unto them, they had not had sin: but now they have no cloak for their sin. He that hateth me hateth my Father also.

If I had not done among them the works which none other man did, they had not had sin: but now have they both seen and hated both me and my Father.

But this cometh to pass, that the word might be fulfilled that is written in their law, They hated me without a cause.

But when the Comforter is come, whom I will send unto you from the Father, even the Spirit of truth, which proceedeth from the

Father, he shall testify of me: and ye also shall bear witness, because ye have been with me from the beginning.

These things have I spoken unto you, that ye should not be offended. [**]

Footnotes

^124:* . . . be offended: fall away, or falter.

LXXIX

THE COMFORTER, THE SPIRIT OF TRUTH: "BE OF GOOD CHEER, I HAVE OVERCOME THE WORLD"--"YOUR SORROW SHALL BE TURNED TO JOY"--CHRIST TO DEPART THIS LIFE

A.D. 30. Age 33. Jerusalem: Upper Room.

John 16, 2-33.

THEY shall put you out of the synagogues: yea, the time cometh, that whosoever killeth you, you will think that he doeth God service. And these things will they do unto you, because they have not known the Father, nor me.

But these things have I told you, that when the time shall come, ye may remember that I told you of them. And these things I said not unto you at the beginning, because I was with you.

But now I go my way to him that sent me; and none of you asketh me, Whither goest thou? But because I have said these things unto you, sorrow hath filled your heart. Nevertheless I tell you the truth; It is expedient for you that I go away: for if I go not away, the Comforter will not come unto you; but if I depart, I will send him unto you. And when he is come, he will reprove the world of sin, and of righteousness, and of judgment: of sin, because they believed not on me; of righteousness, because I go to my Father, and ye see me no more; of judgment, because the prince of this world is judged.

I have yet many things to say unto you, but ye cannot bear them now. Howbeit when he, the Spirit of truth, is come, he will guide you into all truth: for he shall not speak of himself; but whatsoever he shall hear, that shall he speak: and he will shew you things to come. He shall glorify me: for he shall receive of mine, and shall shew it unto you.

All things that the Father hath are mine: therefore said I, that he shall take of mine, and shall shew it unto you.

A little while, and ye shall not see me: and again, a little while, and ye shall see me, because I go to the Father.

Then said some of his disciples among themselves, What is this that he saith, A little while, and ye shall not see me: and again, A little while, and ye shall see me: and, Because I go to the Father?

Now Jesus knew that they were desirous to ask him, and he said, Do ye inquire among yourselves of that I said, A little while, and ye shall not see me: and again, a little while, and ye shall see me?

Verily, verily, I say unto you, That ye shall weep and lament, but the world shall rejoice; and ye shall be sorrowful, but your sorrow shall be turned into joy.

A woman when she is in travail hath sorrow, because her hour is come: but as soon as she is delivered of the child, she remembereth no more the anguish, for joy that a man is born into the world. And ye now therefore have sorrow: but I will see you again, and your heart shall rejoice, and your joy no man taketh from you.

And in that day ye shall ask me nothing. Verily, verily, I say unto you, Whatsoever ye shall ask the Father in my name, he will give it you. Hitherto have ye asked nothing in my name: ask, and ye shall receive, that your joy may be full.

These things have I spoken unto you in proverbs: but the time cometh, when I shall no more speak unto you in proverbs, but I shall shew you plainly of the Father. At that day ye shall ask in my name: and 1 say not unto you, that I will pray the Father for you: for the Father himself loveth you, because ye have loved me, and have believed that I came out from God.

I came forth from the Father, and am come into the world: again, I leave the world, and go to the Father.

His disciples said unto him, Lo, now speakest thou plainly, and speakest no proverb. Now are we sure that thou knowest all things: by this we believe that thou camest forth from God. Jesus answered, Do ye now believe? Behold, the hour cometh, yea, is now come, that ye shall be scattered, every man to his own, and shall leave me alone: and yet I am not alone, because the Father is with me.

These things I have spoken unto you, that in me ye might have peace. In the world ye shall have tribulation: but be of good cheer; I have overcome the world.

LXXX

CHRIST PRAYS FOR AID--"I HAVE FINISHED THE WORK"-- PRAYS FOR THE APOSTLES ALSO, AND THEIR WORK--PRAYS FOR ALL BELIEVERS

A.D. 30. Age 33. Jerusalem: Upper Room.

John 17, 1-26.

THESE words spake Jesus, and lifted up his eyes to heaven,

Father, the hour is come; glorify thy Son, that thy Son also may glorify thee: as thou hast given him power over all flesh, that he should give eternal life to as many as thou hast given him. And this is life eternal, that they might know thee the only true God, and Jesus Christ whom thou hast sent. I have glorified thee on the earth: I have finished the work which thou gavest me to do. And now, O Father, glorify thou me with thine own self with the glory which I had with thee before the world was.

I have manifested thy name unto the men which thou gavest me out of the world: thine they were, and thou gavest them me; and they have kept thy word. Now they have known that all things whatsoever thou hast given me are of thee. For I have given unto them the words which thou gavest me; and they have received them, and have known surely that I came out from thee, and they have believed that thou didst send me.

I pray for them: I pray not for the world, but for them which thou hast given me; for they are thine. And all mine are thine, and thine are mine; and I am glorified in them. And now I am no more in the world, but these are in the world, and I come to thee. Holy Father, keep through thine own name those whom thou hast given me, that they may be one, as we are. While I was with them in the world, I kept them in thy name: those that thou gavest me I have kept, and none of them is lost, but the son of perdition: that the Scripture might be fulfilled.

And now come I to thee; and these things I speak in the world, that they might have my joy fulfilled in themselves. I have given them thy word; and the world hath hated them, because they are not of the world, even as I am not of the world. I pray not that thou shouldest take them out of the world, but that thou shouldest keep them from the evil. They are not of the world, even as I am not of the world. Sanctify them through thy truth: thy word is truth. As thou hast sent me into the world, even so have I also sent them into the world. And for their sakes I sanctify myself, that they also might be sanctified through the truth.

Neither pray I for these alone, but for them also which shall believe on me through their word; that they all may be one; as thou, Father, art in me, and I in thee, that they also may be one in us: that the world may believe that thou hast sent me. And the glory which thou gavest me I have given them: that they may be one, even as we are one; I in them, and thou in me, that they may be made perfect in one; and that the world may know that thou hast sent me, and hast loved them, as thou hast loved me.

Father, I will that they also, whom thou hast given me, be with me where I am; that they may behold my glory, which thou hast given me: for thou lovedst me before the foundation of the world.

O righteous Father, the world hath not known thee: but I have known thee, and these have known that thou hast sent me. And I have declared unto them thy name, and will declare it: that the love wherewith thou hast loved me may be in them, and I in them.

Arise, let us go hence.

LXXXI

CHRIST AGAIN FORETELLS PETER'S THREE DENIALS--IN GETHSEMANE PRAYS WHILE APOSTLES SLEEP--THE SPIRIT WILLING, THE FLESH WEAK --JUDAS AND CROWD WITH WEAPONS FIND JESUS

A.D. 30. Age 33. Mount of Olives. Gethsemane.

Matthew 26, 30-47: Mark 14, 26-43: Luke 22, 39-47: John 18, 1-9.

[**]WHEN they had sung a hymn, Jesus came out; and he went as he was wont, to the mount of Olives; and his disciples followed him. Then saith Jesus unto them, All ye shall be offended [*+]

because of me this night: for it is written, I will smite the Shepherd, and the sheep of the flock shall be scattered abroad.

But after that I am risen again, I will go before you into Galilee.

Peter answered, Although all shall be offended because of thee, yet will not I. I will never be offended. Jesus saith unto him, Verily I say unto thee, That this day, even in this night, before the cock crow twice, thou shalt deny me thrice.

But Peter spake the more vehemently, Though I should die with thee, yet will I not deny thee in any wise. Likewise said they all.

They came to a place named Gethsemane, over the brook Cedron, where was a garden, into the which Jesus entered and his disciples. And he said unto them, Sit ye here, while I go and pray yonder. Pray that ye enter not into temptation.

He was withdrawn from them about a stone's cast; with him Peter, James, and John. Then saith he unto them, My soul is exceeding sorrowful, even unto death: tarry ye here, and watch with me.

He went forward a little, and kneeled, and prayed, Abba, Father, all things are possible unto thee: Father, if it be possible, if thou be willing, remove this cup from me: nevertheless not my will, but thine, be done. [*++]

Being in an agony he prayed more earnestly: and his sweat was as it were great drops of blood.

And he cometh unto the disciples, and findeth them sleeping. He saith unto Peter, Simon, sleepest thou? What, couldest not thou watch with me one hour? Watch ye and pray, lest ye enter into temptation. The spirit truly is willing, but the flesh is weak.

Jesus went away the second time, and prayed, O my Father, if it be possible, let this cup pass from me: if this cup may not pass away from me, except I drink it, thy will be done.

When he rose up, and was come to the disciples, he found them sleeping for sorrow, and he said unto them, Why sleep ye? rise and pray, lest ye enter into temptation.

He went away again, and prayed the third time, saying the same words, Father, take away this cup from me: nevertheless not what I will, but what thou wilt.

And he cometh the third time, and again he found the disciples asleep; and he saith, Sleep on now, and take your rest: it is enough: behold, the hour is come; behold, the hour is at hand, and the Son of man is betrayed into the hands of sinners. Rise up, let us be going: lo, he is at hand that doth betray me.

Judas knew the place: for Jesus ofttimes resorted thither with his disciples.

Immediately, while Jesus yet spake, cometh Judas, and with him a multitude: a band of men from the chief priests and Pharisees; and the scribes and elders of the people, with lanterns and torches, and weapons: swords and staves.

Jesus knowing all things that should come upon him, went forth, and said unto them, Whom seek ye?
They answered, Jesus of Nazareth. Jesus saith, I am he.

They went backward, and fell to the ground. Then asked he them again, Whom seek ye?
They said, Jesus of Nazareth. Jesus answered, I have told you that I am he: if therefore ye seek me, let these go their way.

That the saying might be fulfilled, which he spake, Of them which thou gavest me have I lost none.

Footnotes

^128:* Much of interest can be gleaned from a comparison, paragraph by paragraph, of the texts of the several narrators, from this point to the end (Matthew 26, 30 . .. Mark 14, 26 . . .: Luke 22, 39 . . .: John 18, 1 . . .; and so on).

^128:+ . . . be offended: fall away, desert.

^128:++ Mark has it, ". . . nevertheless not what I will, but what thou wilt."

LXXXII

THE BETRAYAL: JUDAS' KISS--PETER MILITANT--CHRIST HAILED TO COURT--AN OFFICER STRIKES JESUS THOUGH BOUND--"ALL THE DISCIPLES FORSOOK HIM"

A.D. 30. Age 33. Gethsemane. Jerusalem.

Matthew 26, 48-58: Mark 14, 44-50; 53-54: Luke 22, 47-55: John 18, 10-16; 19-23.

NOW Judas had given them a token (sign), saying, Whomsoever I shall kiss, that same is he: hold him fast.

[**]Judas went before, and drew near unto Jesus, to kiss him: and saith, Hail, Master; and kissed him.

Jesus said unto Judas, Friend, wherefore art thou come? [*+] Judas, betrayest thou the Son of man with a kiss?

Then they laid hands on Jesus.

They which were about him said, Lord, shall we smite them with the sword?

And Simon Peter having a sword smote the high priest's servant, Malchas, and cut off his right ear. Jesus said, Suffer thus far.
and he touched his ear and healed him. Then said Jesus unto Peter, Put up again thy sword into his place in the sheath: for all they that take the sword shall perish with the sword: the cup which my Father hath given me, shall I not drink it? Thinkest thou that I cannot now pray to my , and he shall presently give me more than twelve legions of angels? But how then shall the Scriptures be fulfilled, that thus it must be?

In that same hour said Jesus unto the multitude, Be ye come out, as against a thief, with swords and staves for to take me?

When I sat daily with you, teaching in the temple, ye stretched forth no hands against me: ye laid no hold on me: ye took me not: but this is your hour, and the power of darkness. But all this was done that the Scriptures of the prophets might be fulfilled. The Scriptures must be fulfilled.

Then all the disciples forsook him, and fled.

The officers of the Jews bound Jesus and led him away. They brought him into the palace of the high priest, Caiaphas that year.

Simon Peter followed, to see the end. And so did another disciple: that disciple was known to Caiaphas, and went with Jesus into the palace. But Peter stood at the door without. Then went out that disciple and spake unto her that kept the door, and brought in Peter.

When they had kindled a fire in the midst of the hall, Peter sat amongst the servants, and warmed himself at the fire.

With Caiaphas the high priest were assembled the chief priests and the elders and the scribes.

Caiaphas asked Jesus of his disciples, and of his doctrine, Jesus answered, I spake openly to the world: I ever taught in the synagogues, and in the temple, whither the Jews always resort: and in secret have I said nothing. Ask them which heard me, what I have said unto them: behold, they know what I said. Why askest thou me?

When Jesus had thus spoken, one of the officers struck him with the palm of his hand, saying, Answerest thou the high priest so? Jesus answered, If I have spoken evil, bear witness to the evil: but if well, why smitest thou me?

Footnotes

^130:* See footnote at the beginning of LXXXI. The several narrators exhibit their wonted likenesses and contrasts in the phrasing.

^130:+ Thus the King James Version (Matthew 26, 50). The Revised Version: Friend, do that for which thou art come. The Goodspeed Translation (1923): My friend, do your errand. The Moffat Translation (1922): My man, do your errand.

LXXXIII

CHRIST'S TRIAL CONTINUED--FALSE WITNESS--PETER THRICE DENIES CHRIST--MORNING: FURTHER QUESTIONING--JUDAS A SUICIDE

A.D. 30. Age 33. Jerusalem.

Matthew 26, 59-75; 27, 1-7: Mark 14, 55-72: Luke 22, 56-71: John 18, 17-27.

THE chief priests and all the council sought witness against Jesus, to put him to death. Many bare false witness against him, but their witness agreed not together. At the last came two, saying, We heard this fellow say, I am able to destroy the temple of God, that is made with hands, and within three days I will build another made without hands.

The high priest arose, and asked Jesus, Answerest thou nothing? But Jesus held his peace, and answered nothing.

The high priest said, Tell us whether thou be the Christ, the Son of God. And Jesus said, Thou hast said. I am. Nevertheless I say unto you, Hereafter shall ye see the Son of man sitting on the right hand of power, and coming in the clouds of heaven.

Then saith the high priest, Now ye have heard his blasphemy: what need ye any further witnesses? What think ye?

They answered, He is guilty of death.

When they had blindfolded Jesus, they struck him on the face, and say unto him, Prophesy, who is it that smote thee?

Now Peter was beneath in the palace: and the damsel that kept the door came and looked upon him as he sat by the fire, and said, Thou also wart with Jesus of Galilee.

But he denied before them all, saying, I know him not: I know not, neither understand I what thou sayest.

And he went into the porch; and the cock crew.

After a little while another saw Peter, and said, Thou art also of them, for thou art a Galilean: thy speech agreeth thereto: thy speech betrayeth thee.

And Peter denied again, Man, I am not.

About the space of an hour after, another confidently affirmed, Of a truth this fellow was with Jesus.

But Peter began to swear, saying, I know not this man of whom ye speak.

And the second time the cock crew. Then Peter called to mind the word that Jesus said unto him, Before the cock crow twice, thou shalt deny me thrice.

And when Peter thought thereon, he wept. [**]

As soon as it was day, the elders of the people, and the chief priests and the scribes led Jesus into their council, saying, Art thou the Christ? And he said, If I tell you, ye will not believe: and if I also ask you, ye will not answer me, nor let me go. Hereafter shall the Son of man sit on the right hand of the power of God.

Then said they, Art thou then the Son of God? And Jesus said, Ye say that I am.

They said, We ourselves have heard of his own mouth.

And the whole council held a consultation, to put Jesus to death.

Judas, when he saw that Jesus was condemned, repented, and brought the thirty pieces of silver to the chief priests, saying, I have sinned in that I have betrayed the innocent blood.

They said, What is that to us? see thou to that.

Then Judas cast down the pieces of silver in the temple, and went and hanged himself.

The chief priests said, It is the price of blood: it is not lawful to put them into the treasury. They took counsel, and bought with them the potter's field, to bury strangers in.

Footnotes

^132:* The interested reader should compare, in the text, the four accounts of Peter's denials: Matthew 26, 69-75: Mark 14, 66-72: Luke 22, 56-62: John 18, 17-27.

LXXXIV

CHRIST HALED BEFORE PILATE: PILATE'S DILEMMA--
"CRUCIFY HIM"--PILATE VACILLATES: SENDS JESUS TO
HEROD, WHO SENDS HIM BACK--JESUS SCOURGED--PILATE
DELIVERS JESUS TO BE CRUCIFIED

A.D. 30. Age 33. Jerusalem.

John 18, 28-40; 19, 1-16: Luke 23, 1-11; 13-25: Mark 15, 1-15: Matthew
27, 11-26.

THE whole council arose and led Jesus away from the high priest,
Caiaphas, and delivered him to Pontius Pilate the governor, in the
hall of judgment.

Pilate went out unto them, and said, Take ye him, and judge him
according to your law.

The Jews answered, It is not lawful for us to put any man to death.

Then Pilate entered into the judgment hall again, and called Jesus,
and said unto him, Art thou the King of Jews? Jesus answered,
Sayest thou this thing of thyself, or did others tell it thee of me?

Pilate answered, Am I a Jew? Thine own nation have delivered thee unto me: what hast thou done? Jesus answered, My kingdom is not of this world: if my kingdom were of this world, then would my servants fight, that I should not be delivered to the Jews: but now is my kingdom not from hence.

Pilate therefore said, Art thou a king then? Jesus answered, Thou sayest that I am a king. To this end was I born, and for this cause came I into the world, that I should bear witness unto the truth. very one that is of the truth heareth my voice.

Pilate answered, What is truth? And when he had said this, he went out again unto the Jews, and saith unto them, I find in him no fault at all. But ye have a custom that I should release unto you one at the passover: will ye that I release the King of the Jews?

Then cried they all, Not this man, but Barabbas.

Now Barabbas was a robber.

The chief priests and the officers cried out, Crucify him, crucify him.

Pilate saith, Take ye him, and crucify him: for I find no fault in him.

The Jews answered, By our law he ought to die, because he made himself the Son of God.

When Pilate heard that saying, he saith unto Jesus, Whence art thou? But Jesus gave no answer.

Then saith Pilate, Speakest thou not unto me? knowest thou not that I have power to crucify thee, and have power to release thee? Jesus answered, Thou couldest have no power at all against me, except it were given thee from above: therefore he that delivered me unto thee hath the greater sin.

Thenceforth Pilate sought to release Jesus: but the Jews cried out, We found this fellow forbidding to give tribute to Cesar, saying that he himself is Christ a king. If thou let this man go, thou art not Cesar's friend: whosoever maketh himself a king speaketh against Cesar.

Pilate asked him, Art thou the King of the Jews? And Jesus saith, Thou sayest it.

The chief priests accused him of many things: but he answered nothing.

And Pilate asked him again, Answerest thou nothing? hearest thou not how many things they witness against thee?

Jesus answered him to never a word; so that Pilate marvelled: and he said to the people, I find no fault in this man.

They were the more fierce, saying, He stirreth up the people throughout Jewry, from Galilee to this place.

When Pilate heard of Galilee, he asked whether the man were a Galilean. And as soon as he knew that Jesus belonged unto Herod's jurisdiction, he sent him to Herod, who was at Jerusalem at that time.

Herod was exceeding glad: for he had heard many things of Jesus; and had hoped to see some miracle done by him. He questioned with Jesus in many words; but Jesus answered him nothing. And Herod sent him back to Pilate.

Pilate called together the chief priests and the rulers of the people; and he said unto them, Ye have brought this man unto me, as one that perverteth the people; and, behold, I, having examined him before you, have found no fault in him touching those things whereof ye accuse him: no, nor yet Herod.

Now at that feast the governor must of necessity release unto the people a prisoner, whom they would.

Pilate therefore said, Will ye that I release unto you Barabbas? or Jesus which is called the Christ?

They cried out all at once, Release Barabbas.

Pilate saith, What shall I do then with Jesus?

They cried out again, Let him be crucified.

Pilate saith, Shall I crucify your King?

The chief priests answered, We have no king but Cesar.

When Pilate saw that he could prevail nothing, he took water, and washed his hands before the multitude, saying, I am innocent of the blood of this just person: see ye to it.

Then answered the people, His blood be on us, and on our children.

And so Pilate, willing to content the people, gave sentence that it should be as they required. He released him that for sedition and murder was cast into prison: but he delivered Jesus, when he had scourged him, to their will, to be crucified.

LXXXV

CHRIST CROWNED WITH THORNS, ROBED IN SCARLET-- MOCKED--"IN A GREEN TREE, IN THE DRY?"--THE

CRUCIFIXION--"FATHER, FORGIVE THEM"--PILATE WRITES THE TITLE

A.D. 30. Age 33. Jerusalem. Golgotha: Calvary.

Matthew 27, 27-38: Mark 15, 16-27: Luke 23, 26-34: John 19, 17-20.

THE soldiers of the governor led Jesus into the common hall, called Pretorium. They stripped him, and clothed him with purple (put on him a scarlet robe): they platted a crown of thorns, and put it about his head.

Then came Jesus forth wearing the crown of thorns, and the purple robe. They mocked him, saying, Hail, King of the Jews!

After they had mocked him, they took off the purple from him, put his own raiment on him, smote him with their hands, and led him away to crucify him.

There followed a great company of people, and of women, which bewailed him. But Jesus turning said, Daughters of Jerusalem, weep not for me, but weep for yourselves, and for your children. For, behold, the days are coming, in the which they shall say, Blessed are the barren, and the wombs that never bare, and the paps which never gave suck.

Then shall they begin to say to the mountains, Fall on us: and to the hills, Cover us.

For if they do these things in a green tree, what shall be done in the dry?

And Jesus bearing his cross went forth.

As they came out, one Simon, a man of Cyrene, passed by, coming out of the country: him they compelled, and on him they laid the cross, that he might bear it after Jesus.

When they were come to a place called the place of a skull, which is in the Hebrew, Golgotha: to the place called Calvary, they gave to Jesus wine mingled with myrrh (vinegar mingled with gall): when he had tasted thereof, he would not drink. It was the third hour.

And there they crucified Jesus: him and the two malefactors: one on the right hand, and the other on the left, and Jesus in the midst. Then said Jesus, Father, forgive them; for they know not what they do.

Pilate wrote a title, and put it on the cross. It was written in Hebrew, and Greek, and Latin: JESUS OF NAZARETH THE KING OF THE JEWS.

LXXXVI

CASTING LOTS FOR THE SAVIOR'S CLOTHES--THE PENITENT THIEF REWARDED--CHRIST'S FILIAL FAREWELL TO HIS MOTHER--"IT IS FINISHED"

A.D. 30. Age 33. Jerusalem. Golgotha: Calvary.

Matthew 27, 39-56: Mark 15, 29-41: Luke 23, 35-49: John 19, 23-30.

THE soldiers, when they had crucified Jesus, took his garments, and made four parts, to every soldier a part: casting lots upon them.

The people that passed by derided him, wagging their heads, and saying, Ah, thou that destroyest the temple, and buildest it in three days, save thyself!

The soldiers also mocked him, saying, If thou be the King of the Jews, save thyself!

Likewise the chief priests mocking said among themselves with the scribes, He saved others; himself he cannot save!

One of the two thieves which were crucified with him cast the same in his teeth; but the other rebuked him, saying, Dost thou not fear

God? We receive the due reward of our deeds: but this man hath done nothing amiss.

And he said unto Jesus, Lord, remember me when thou comest into thy kingdom.

Jesus said unto him, Verily I say unto thee, To day shalt thou be with me in paradise.

Now there stood by the cross Jesus' mother, and his mother's sister; Mary the wife of Cleophas, and Mary Magdalene. Jesus saw his mother, and the disciple standing by, whom he loved: [**] and he saith unto his mother, Woman, behold thy son!

Then saith he to the disciple, Behold thy mother!
And from that hour that disciple took her unto his own home.

Now from the sixth hour there was darkness over all the land until the ninth hour. At the ninth hour Jesus cried with a loud voice, saying, My God, my God, why hast thou forsaken me?

After this, Jesus knowing that all things were now accomplished, saith, I thirst. Straightway one of them ran, and filled a sponge with vinegar, put it upon hysop (on a reed), and put it to Jesus' mouth. When he had received the vinegar, he said, It is finished.

And when he had cried again with a loud voice, he said, Father, into thy hands I commend my spirit!

Having said thus, Jesus bowed his head, and yielded up the ghost.

All his acquaintance stood afar off, beholding these things. There were also women looking on: among which was Mary Magdalene; and Mary the mother of James the less and of Joses; and Salome the mother of Zebedee's children; and many other women which came up with Jesus into Jerusalem.

Footnotes

^136:* Supposed to be John the brother of James and son of Zebedee.

LXXXVII

PILATE GIVES CHRIST'S BODY TO THE ARIMATHEAN--LAID IN JOSEPH'S NEW TOMB--THE GALILEAN WOMEN WATCHING--THE PRIESTS SET A WATCH

A.D. 30. Age 33. Jerusalem: The Sepulchre.

Mark 15, 42-47: Luke 23, 50-56: John 19, 38-42: Matthew 27, 57-66.

AND now when the even was come, because it was the preparation, that is, the day before the sabbath, Joseph of Arimathea went in unto Pilate, and craved the body of Jesus.

A rich man of Arimathea, a city of the Jews, Joseph was an honorable counsellor, a good man, and a just (he had not consented to the counsel and deed of them). He also waited for the kingdom of God, being a disciple of Jesus, but secretly for fear of the Jews.

This man went boldly in unto Pilate, and begged that he might take away the body of Jesus. Pilate gave him leave.

Joseph came therefore, and took the body of Jesus. And there came also Nicodemus (which at the first came by night [**]), and brought a mixture of myrrh and aloes.

Then took they the body, and wound it in a clean cloth of fine linen, with the spices, as the manner of the Jews is to bury.

Now in the place where Jesus was crucified there was a garden; and in the garden a new sepulchre, wherein was never man yet laid.

When Joseph had laid the body in his own new tomb which he had hewn out in the rock, he rolled a great stone, nigh at hand, to the door of the sepulchre, and departed.

The women which came with Jesus from Galilee beheld the sepulchre, and how the body was laid. And there was Mary Magdalene, and the other Mary, the mother of Joses, sitting over against the sepulchre. That day was the preparation. They returned (home) and prepared spices and ointments: and rested the sabbath day. Now the next day, that followed the day of preparation, the chief priests and Pharisees came unto Pilate, saying, Sir, that deceiver said, while he was yet alive, After three days I will rise again.

Command therefore that the sepulchre be made sure until the third day, lest his disciples come by night, and steal him away, and say unto the people, He is risen from the dead: so the last error shall be worse than the first.

Pilate said, Ye have a watch: make it as sure as you can. So they went, and made the sepulchre sure, sealing the stone, and setting a watch.

Footnotes

^137:* Told in VIII in this book.

LXXXVIII

AFTER THE RESURRECTION: THE DEVOTED MARYS--CHRIST IN PERSON: "ALL HAIL"--TALKS WITH MARY MAGDALENE

A.D. 30. Age 33. Jerusalem: The Sepulchre.

Matthew 28, 1, and 8-10: Mark 16, 1-11: Luke 24, 1-9: John 20, 11-18.

IN the end of the sabbath, as it began to dawn toward the first day of the week, came Mary Magdalene and the other Mary, to see the sepulchre at the rising of the sun. They came bringing the sweet spices which they, and Salome, had prepared, that they might anoint him.

They said among themselves, Who shall roll away the stone from the door? and they found the stone rolled away.

They entered in, and found not the body of the Lord Jesus. And it came to pass, as they were perplexed, behold, two men stood by them in shining garments: they said, Why seek ye the living among the dead? he is not here: he is risen: remember how he spake when yet in Galilee, saying, The Son of man must be delivered into the hands of sinful men, and be crucified, and the third day rise again.

They remembered: they trembled, and went out quickly, with great joy; and did run to bring his disciples word. And, behold, Jesus met them, saying, All hail!

And they worshipped him. Then said Jesus unto them, Be not afraid: go tell my brethren that they go into Galilee, and there shall they see me.

Mary (Magdalene) stood without at the sepulchre weeping: and she looked into the sepulchre, and seeth two angels in white, sitting. They say, Why weepest thou?

She saith, They have taken away my Lord.

When she had thus said, she turned, and saw Jesus standing, and knew not that it was Jesus. He saith, Woman, why weepest thou? whom seekest thou?

She, supposing him to be the gardener, saith, Sir, if thou have borne him hence, tell me where thou hast laid him, and I will take him away. Jesus saith, Mary.
She turned, and saith unto him, Master. Jesus saith unto her, Touch me not; for I am not yet ascended to my Father: but go to my brethren, and say unto them, I ascend unto my Father, and your Father; and to my God, and your God.

Mary Magdalene came and told the disciples that she had seen the Lord, that he was alive, and that he had spoken these things unto her.

And they believed her not.

LXXXIX

AFTER THE RESURRECTION (CONTINUED): CHRIST IN PERSON: WITH THE TWO MEN; WITH THE ELEVEN-- DOUBTING THOMAS

A.D. 30. Age 33. Emmaus. Jerusalem.

Mark 16, 12-13: Luke 24, 13-31; 33-43: John 20, 19-29.

AFTER that, Jesus appeared in another form unto two of them, that same day, as they walked to Emmaus, a village which was from Jerusalem about three-score furlongs.

While they talked together of all these things which had happened, Jesus himself drew near. But their eyes were holden that they should not know him. And he said unto them, What manner of communications are these that ye have one to another, as ye walk, and are sad?

One of them (Cleopas) answering said, Art thou a stranger in Jerusalem, and hast not known the things which are come to pass there in these days? Jesus said, What things?

They answered, Concerning Jesus of Nazareth: and how our rulers have crucified him. But we trusted that it had been he which should have redeemed Israel.

Jesus said unto them, O fools [**], and slow of heart to believe all that the prophets have spoken: ought not Christ to have suffered these things, and to enter into his glory?

And beginning at Moses, he expounded the things in all the Scriptures concerning himself.

They drew nigh unto the village whither they went: and Jesus made as though he would have gone further. But they constrained him, saying, Abide with us: for it is toward evening. And he went in to tarry with them.

As he sat at meat with them, he took bread, and blessed it, and brake, and gave to them. And their eyes were opened, and they knew him; and he vanished out of their sight.

The same hour, they returned to Jerusalem, and found the eleven gathered together, saying, The Lord is risen indeed, and hath appeared to Simon. They (the two) told what things were done in the way, and how Jesus was known of them in breaking of bread.

As they spake, the same day at evening, being the first day of the week, when the doors were shut where the disciples were assembled for fear of the Jews, Jesus himself stood in the midst of them, and saith, Peace be unto you.

But they supposed they had seen a spirit, and were affrighted. And he said, Why are ye troubled? and why do thoughts arise in your hearts? Behold my hands and my feet, that it is myself: handle me, and see; for a spirit hath not flesh and bones, as ye see me have.

While they wondered, he said, Have ye here any meat?

They gave him of a fish, and of a honeycomb; and he did eat before them. Then said he to them again, Peace be unto you; as my Father hath sent me, even so I send you.

Receive ye the Holy Ghost. Whosesoever sins ye remit, they are remitted unto them: and whosesoever sins ye retain, they are retained.

But Thomas was not with them. When the other disciples said unto him, We have seen the Lord, he said, Except I shall see in his hands the print of the nails, and put my finger into the print of the nails, and thrust my hand into his side, I will not believe.

After eight days, again the disciples were within, and Thomas with them: then came Jesus, as they sat at meat, the doors being shut, and stood in the midst, and said, Peace be unto you.

Then saith he to Thomas, Reach hither thy finger, and behold my hands; and reach hither thy hand, and thrust it into my side: and be not faithless, but believing.

Thomas answered, My Lord and my God. Jesus said unto him, Thomas, because thou hast seen me, thou hast believed: blessed are they that have not seen, and yet have believed.

Footnotes

^140:* O fools: Moffat's Translation (1922) has it, "O foolish men . . ."

XC

AFTER THE RESURRECTION (CONTINUED): JESUS IN PERSON: ON THE SHORE--THE GREAT CATCH OF FISH--PETER--THAT OTHER LOVED ONE

A.D. 30. Age 33. Sea of Galilee.

John 21, 1-25.

JESUS shewed himself again to the disciples at the sea of Tiberias; [**] and on this wise: there were together Simon Peter and Thomas called Didymus, and Nathanael of Cana in Galilee, and the sons of Zebedee, and two others of his disciples.

Simon Peter saith unto them, I go a fishing. They say, We go with thee. They entered into a ship immediately; and that night they caught nothing.

But when the morning was come, Jesus stood on the shore: but the disciples knew not that it was Jesus. Then saith he unto them,

Children, have ye any meat? They answered, No. And he said, Cast the net on the right side of the ship, and ye shall find.

They cast; and as soon as they were come to land, they saw a fire of coals there, and fish laid thereon, and bread. Jesus saith, Bring of the fish which ye have now caught.

Peter drew the net to land full of great fishes, and for all there were so many; yet was not the net broken.

Jesus saith unto them, Come and dine.

Jesus then taketh bread, and giveth them, and fish likewise.

So when they had dined, Jesus saith, Simon, son of Jonas, lovest thou me more than these?

He saith, Yea, Lord; thou knowest that I love thee. Jesus saith, Feed my lambs.

He saith the second time, Simon, son of Jonas, lovest thou me?

He saith, Yea, Lord; thou knowest that I love thee. Jesus saith, Feed my sheep.

He saith the third time, Simon, son of Jonas, lovest thou me?

Peter was grieved because he said the third time, Lovest thou me? And he said, Lord, thou knowest all things; thou knowest that I love thee. Jesus saith unto him, Feed my sheep.

Verily, verily, I say unto thee, When thou wast young, thou girdedst thyself, and walkedst whither thou wouldest: but when thou shall be old, thou shalt stretch forth thy hands, and another shall gird thee, and carry thee whither thou wouldest not.

This spake he, signifying by what death he should glorify God. And he saith unto Peter, Follow me.

Peter, turning about, seeth the disciple following, whom Jesus loved. [**] Seeing him, Peter saith, Lord, and what shall this man do? Jesus answered, If I will that he tarry till I come, what is that to thee? follow thou me.

This is the disciple [**] which testifieth of these things: and wrote these things. And there are also many other things which Jesus did, the which, if they should be written every one, I suppose that even the world itself could not contain the books that should be written.

Footnotes

^141:* Sea of Tiberias: Another name of the sea of Galilee (John 6, 1). Still another name was lake of Gennesaret (Luke 5, 1).

^142:* John (John 21, 20-24).

XCI

AFTER THE RESURRECTION (CONTINUED): CHRIST IN PERSON: HIS LAST TALK WITH THE ELEVEN--"GO YE AND PREACH THE GOSPEL TO EVERY CREATURE"--THE ASCENSION

A.D. 30. Age 33. Galilee. Mt. Olivet. Bethany.

Matthew 28, 16-20: Mark 16, 12-18: Luke 24, 44-53; and Luke's Acts of The Apostles 1, 12.

THE eleven disciples went into a mountain in Galilee, where Jesus had appointed them. And he came, saying, Go ye into all the world, and preach the gospel to every creature.

He that believeth and is baptized shall be saved; but he that believeth not shall be damned.

And these signs shall follow them that believe: In my name shall they cast out devils; they shall speak with new tongues; they shall take up serpents; and if they drink any deadly thing, it shall not hurt them; they shall lay hands on the sick, and they shall recover.

All power is given unto me in heaven and in earth.

Go ye therefore, and teach all nations, baptizing them in the name of the Father, and of the Son, and of the Holy Ghost: teaching them to observe all things whatsoever I have commanded you: and, lo, I am with you alway, even unto the end of the world.

And Jesus said unto them (the eleven), These are the words which I spake unto you, while I was with you, That all things must be fulfilled, which were written in the law of Moses, and in the prophets, and in the psalms, concerning me.

Then opened he their understanding, that they might understand the Scriptures; and said unto them, Thus it is written, and thus it behooved Christ to suffer, and to rise from the dead the third day: and that repentance and remission of sins should be preached in his name among all nations, beginning at Jerusalem.

And ye are witnesses of these things.

And, behold, I send the promise of my Father upon you: but tarry ye in the city of Jerusalem, until ye be endued with power from on high.

And he led them out as far as to Bethany; and he lifted up his hands, and blessed them.

And it came to pass, while he blessed them, he was parted from them, and carried up into heaven; and a cloud received him out of their sight.

Then returned they with great joy unto Jerusalem, from the mount called Olivet, which is from Jerusalem a sabbath day's journey.

They were continually in the temple praising and blessing God.

XCII

AFTER THE RESURRECTION (CONTINUED): CHRIST IN PERSON: APOSTLES' QUESTION ANSWERED

A.D. 35. Mount of Olives.

Luke: Acts 1, 2-9.

UNTO the apostles whom he had chosen Jesus shewed himself alive after his passion: and, being assembled with them, [**] commanded them that they should not depart from Jerusalem: saith he, Wait (tarry in Jerusalem) for the promise of the Father, which ye have heard of me. For John truly baptized with water; but ye shall be baptized with the Holy Ghost not many days hence.

They asked him, Lord, wilt thou at this time restore again the kingdom to Israel? He said, It is not for you to know the times or the seasons, which the Father hath put in his own power. But ye shall receive power, after that the Holy Ghost is come upon you: and ye shall be witnesses unto me both in Jerusalem, and in all Judea, and in Samaria, and unto the uttermost parts of the earth.

When he had spoken, while they beheld, he was taken up.

SAUL'S VISION--ANANIAS' VISION--SAUL'S CONVERSION, BAPTISM

Luke: Acts 8, 3; 9, 1-20. Damascus. A.D. 34-35.

SAUL [*+] made havoc of the church, entering into every house, and haling men and women to prison.

Breathing out threatenings against the of the Lord, he went unto the high priest, and desired of him letters to the synagogues, that if he found any of this way, whether men or women, he might bring them bound to Jerusalem.

As he journeyed, he came near Damascus: and suddenly there shined about him a light from heaven: and he fell to the earth, and heard a voice saying, Saul, Saul, why persecutest thou me?
Saul said, Who art thou? And the Lord said,

I am Jesus whom thou persecutest: it is hard for thee to kick against the pricks.

Saul astonished said, Lord, what wilt thou have me to do? The Lord answered, Arise, and go into the city, and it shall be told thee what thou must do.

The men which journeyed with Saul stood speechless, hearing a voice, but seeing no man. Saul arose from the earth; and when his eyes were opened, he saw no man.

They led him by the hand into Damascus. And he was three days without sight, and neither did eat nor drink.

There was a certain disciple at Damascus, named Ananias; and to him said the Lord in a vision, Ananias! Arise, and go into the street which is called Straight, and inquire in the house of Judas for one called Saul of Tarsus: for, behold, he prayeth, and hath seen in a vision a man named Ananias coming in, and putting his hand on him, that he might receive his sight.

Ananias answered, Lord, much evil he hath done to thy saints at Jerusalem.

But the Lord said, Go thy way: for he is a chosen vessel unto me, to bear my name before the Gentiles, and kings, and the children of Israel: for I will show him how great things he must suffer for my name's sake.

Ananias entered into the house; and putting his hands on him said, Brother Saul, the Lord, even Jesus, hath sent me, that thou mightest receive thy sight, and be filled with the Holy Ghost.

Immediately there fell from Saul's eyes as it had been scales; and he received sight forthwith, and arose, and was baptized.

Straightway Saul preached Christ in the synagogues, that he is the Son of God.

SIMON PETER REMEMBERS

A.D. 41 Cesarea.

Luke: Acts 10, 44-45; and 11, 16.

WHILE Peter spake, the Holy Ghost fell on all them which heard, They of the circumcision which believed were astonished, because that on the Gentiles also was poured out the gift of the Holy Ghost.

Then remembered Peter how that the Lord said, John indeed baptized with water; but ye shall be baptized with the Holy Ghost.

And he commanded them to be baptized.

Footnotes

^144:* On the mount of Olives.

^144:+ Saul, a young Hebrew of Cilicia, of the sect of the Pharisees, was so passionately devoted to the religion and traditions of the Jews, that he undertook to seek out and persecute converts to the new religion, the gospel and faith of Christ. After his own conversion, Saul as the missionary and writer is more familiarly known as Paul (supposedly his baptismal Gentile name).

XCIII

THE LORD TO PAUL IN A VISION

A.D. 54. Corinth.

Luke: Acts 18, 7-11.

PAUL entered into a certain man's house, named Justus one that worshipped God, whose house joined hard to the synagogue.

Then spake the Lord to Paul in the night by a vision, Be not afraid, but speak, and hold not thy peace; for I am with thee, and no man shall set on thee to hurt thee; for I have much people in this city.

And Paul continued there for a year and six months, teaching the word of God.

PAUL'S FAREWELL TO THE EPHESIANS

A.D. 66. Miletus.

Luke: Acts 20, 17-19, 22, 25, 32-38.

FROM Miletus he (Paul) sent to Ephesus, and called the elders of the church.

When they were come, he said unto them, Ye know, from the first day that I came into Asia, after what manner I have been with you at all times, serving the Lord with humility, with temptations which befell me by the lying in wait of the Jews.

Now I go bound in the spirit unto Jerusalem. not knowing the things that shall befall me there. I know that ye all, among whom I have gone, preaching the kingdom of God, shall see my face no more.

Brethren, I commend you to God.

I have coveted no man's silver, or gold, or apparel. Yea, ye know, that these hands [**] have ministered unto my necessities. I have shewed you how that so laboring ye ought to support the weak, and to remember the words of the Lord Jesus, how he said,

It is more blessed to give than to receive.

When Paul had thus spoken, he prayed with them all. They all wept, sorrowing for the words which he spake, that they should see his face no more. And they accompanied him unto the ship.

Footnotes

^146:* By tent-making. The custom of the Jewish rabbis was to acquire a mechanical trade. Paul's was tent-making.

APPENDIX
PAUL'S WITNESS
HEARD BY PAUL IN VISIONS

OTHER POSTHUMOUS SAYINGS OF JESUS WITH ENOUGH OF THE CONTEXT TO ENABLE A READY GRASP OF THE CONNECTION

XCIV

PAUL AT CESAREA AND JERUSALEM

A.D. 60.

Luke: Acts (parts of) Chapters 21, 22, 23, 24, 25, 26, 27.

WE [**] that were of Paul's company came unto Cesarea, into the house of Philip the evangelist. As we tarried there many days, there came down to us from Judea a certain prophet, named Agabus.

And Agabus took Paul's girdle, and bound his own hands and feet, and said, Thus saith the Holy Ghost, So shall the Jews at Jerusalem bind the man that owneth this girdle, and shall deliver him into the hands of the Gentiles.

We besought Paul not to go up to Jerusalem. He would not be persuaded; and we went up to Jerusalem. The brethren received him gladly.

Paul entered into the temple. When the Jews which were of Asia saw him in the temple, they stirred up the people, and laid hands on him, and drew him out of the temple. But when they went about to kill him, the chief captain and the soldiers took him, demanded who he was, and what he had done.

Some cried one thing, some another, crying out, Men of Israel, help: This is the man that teacheth all men every where against the people, and the law: and further brought Greeks also into the temple, and hath polluted this holy place.

Paul said, I am verily a man which am a Jew, born in Tarsus, a city in Cilicia, yet brought up in this city, and taught according to the perfect manner of the law of the fathers, and was zealous toward God. I persecuted this way unto the death, binding and delivering into prisons both men and women.

The high priest doth bear me witness: from whom I received letters unto the brethren, and went to Damascus, to bring them which were there bound unto Jerusalem, for to be punished.

As I made my journey, and was come nigh unto Damascus about noon, suddenly there shone from heaven a great light round about me. I fell unto the ground, and heard a voice saying, Saul, Saul, why persecutest thou me?

I answered, Who art thou, Lord? And he said unto me, I am Jesus of Nazareth, whom thou persecutest.
I said, What shall I do, Lord? And the Lord said unto me, Arise, and go into Damascus; and there it shall be told thee of all things which are appointed for thee to do.

I could not see for the glory of that light. Led by the hand of them that were with me, I came into Damascus.

One Ananias, a devout man according to the law, came and said, Brother Saul, receive thy sight.

And I looked up upon him. And he said, The God of our fathers hath chosen thee, that thou shouldest know his will, and see that Just One, and hear the voice of his mouth. For thou shalt be his witness unto all men of what thou hast seen and heard.

When I was come again to Jerusalem, even while I prayed in the temple, I was in a trance; and saw him saying unto me, Make haste, and get thee quickly out of Jerusalem: for they will not receive thy testimony concerning me.

I said, Lord, they know that I imprisoned and beat in every synagogue them that believed on thee: and when the blood of thy martyr Stephen was shed, I also was standing by, and consented unto his death.

He said unto me, Depart: for I will send thee far hence unto the Gentiles.

The Jews gave Paul audience unto this word, and then lifted up their voices, and said, Away with such a fellow from the earth: for it is not fit that he should live.

The chief captain, fearing lest Paul should have been pulled in pieces of them, commanded the soldiers to take him by force from among them, and to bring him into the castle.

The night following the Lord stood by Paul, and said, Be of good cheer, Paul: for as thou hast testified of me in , so must thou bear witness also at Rome.

When it was day, certain of the Jews banded together, under a curse, neither to eat nor drink till they had killed Paul.

Paul's sister's son heard of their lying in wait. One of the centurions brought the young man to the chief captain. He told him.

So the chief captain called two centurions, saying, Make ready two hundred soldiers to go to Cesarea, and horsement three score and ten, and spearmen two hundred, at the third hour of the night. Provide them beasts, that they may set Paul on, and bring him safe unto Felix the governor.

And he wrote a letter unto the governor after this manner: This man was taken of the Jews, and should have been killed of them: then came I with an army, and rescued him, having understood that he was a Roman.

The horsemen, when they came to Cesarea and delivered the epistle to the governor, presented Paul also before him. He commanded Paul to be kept in Herod's judgment-hall.

After certain days Felix (the governor) sent for Paul, and heard him. And as Paul reasoned of righteousness, temperance, and judgment to come, Felix trembled, and answered, Go thy way for this time; when I have a convenient season, I will call for thee.

But after two years Porcius Festus came into Felix' room: and Felix, willing to shew the Jews a pleasure, left Paul bound.

Festus, willing to do the Jews a pleasure, said to Paul, Wilt thou go up to Jerusalem, and there be judged of these things before me?

Then said Paul, I stand at Cesar's judgment seat, where I ought to be judged: to the Jews have I done no wrong, as thou very well knowest. For if I be an offender, or have committed any thing worthy of death, I refuse not to die: but if there be none of these things these accuse me, no man may deliver me unto them. I appeal unto Cesar.

After certain days king Agrippa came unto Cesarea to salute Festus.

Festus declared Paul's cause unto the king, saying, There is a certain man left in bonds by Felix: about whom, when I was at Jerusalem, the chief priests and the elders of the Jews informed me, desiring to have judgment against him. To whom I answered, It is not the manner of the Romans to deliver any man to die, before that he which is accused have the accusers face to face, to answer for himself.

But Paul appealed to be reserved unto the hearing of Augustus.

Then Agrippa said unto Festus, I would also hear the man myself.

And on the morrow, when Agrippa was come with great pomp into the place of hearing, with the chief captains, and principal men of the city, Paul was brought forth.

Festus said, King Agrippa, the Jews have dealt with me, crying that he ought not to live. But when I found that he had committed nothing worthy of death, and that he himself hath appealed to Augustus, I have determined to send him. Of whom I have no certain thing to write unto my lord. Wherefore I have brought him forth before you, O king Agrippa, that, after examination had, I might have somewhat to write.

PAUL'S DEFENCE BEFORE AGRIPPA

A.D. 62. Cesarea.

Luke: Acts 26, 1-32.

AGRIPPA said unto Paul, Thou art permitted to speak. Then Paul answered: I think myself happy, king Agrippa, because I shall answer for myself this day before thee: especially, because I know thee to be expert in all customs and questions which are among the Jews: wherefore I beseech thee to hear me patiently.

My manner of life from my youth, which was at the first among mine own nation at Jerusalem, know all the Jews; which knew me from the beginning (if they would testify), that after the most straitest sect of our religion, I lived a Pharisee.

And now I stand, and am judged for the hope of the promise made of God unto our fathers: unto which promise our twelve tribes, instantly serving God day and night, hope to come. For which hope's sake, king Agrippa, I am accused of the Jews.

Why should it be thought a thing incredible with you, that God should raise the dead?

I verily thought with myself, that I ought to do many things contrary to the name of Jesus of Nazareth: and many of the saints did I shut up in prison; and when they were put to death, I gave my voice against them. And I punished them oft in every synagogue, and compelled them to blaspheme; and being exceedingly mad against them, I persecuted them even unto strange cities.

Whereupon, as I went to Damascus, with authority and commission from the chief priests, at midday, O king, I saw in the way a light from heaven, above the brightness of the sun, shining round about me. And when we were all fallen to the earth, I heard a voice saying in the Hebrew tongue,

Saul, Saul, why persecutest thou me? it is hard for thee to kick against the pricks.

I said, Who art thou, Lord? And he said, I am Jesus whom thou persecutest.

But rise, and stand upon thy feet: for I have appeared unto thee for this purpose, to make thee a minister and a witness both of these things which thou hast seen, and of those things in the which I will appear unto thee; delivering thee from the people, and from the Gentiles, unto whom now I send thee, to open their eyes, and to turn them from darkness to light, and from the power of Satan unto God, that they may receive forgiveness of sins, and inheritance among them which are sanctioned by faith that is in me.

Whereupon, O king Agrippa, I was not disobedient unto the heavenly vision: but shewed first unto them of Damascus, and at Jerusalem, and throughout all the coast of Judea, and then to the Gentiles, that they should repent and turn to God, and do works meet for repentance.

For these causes the Jews caught me in the temple, and went about to kill me.

Having therefore obtained help of God, I continue unto this day, witnessing both to small and great, saying none other things than those which the prophets and Moses did say should come: That

Christ should suffer, and that he should be the first that should rise from the dead, and should shew light unto the people, and to the Gentiles.

As Paul thus spake for himself, Festus said with a loud voice, Paul, thou art beside thyself; much learning doth make thee mad.

Paul said, I am not mad, most noble Festus, but speak forth the words of truth and soberness. For the king knoweth of these things, before whom also I speak freely: for I am persuaded that none of these things are hidden from him; for this thing was not done in a corner.

King Agrippa, believest thou the prophets? I know that thou believest. Then Agrippa said unto Paul, Almost thou persuadest me to be a Christian.

Paul said, I would to God, that not only thou, but also all that hear me this day, were both almost, and altogether such as I am, except these bonds.

Then said Agrippa unto Festus, This man might have been set at liberty, if he had not appealed unto Cesar.

A.D. 62. En route to Rome.

Luke: Acts 27, 1-6.

WHEN it was determined that we [**] should sail into Italy, they delivered Paul and certain other prisoners unto one named Julius, a centurion of Augustus' band.

Entering into a ship of Adramyttium, we launched, meaning to sail by the coasts of Asia. The next day we touched at Sidon.

When we had launched from thence, we sailed under Cyprus, because the winds were contrary. We came to Myra, a city of Lycia. There the centurion found a ship of Alexandria sailing into Italy; and he put us therein.

Paul: II. Corinthians 12, 7-9.

THERE was given to me a thorn in the flesh, the messenger of Satan to buffet me, lest I should be exalted above measure.

For this thing I besought the Lord thrice, that it might depart from me. And he said unto me, My grace is sufficient for thee: for my strength is made perfect in weakness.

Footnotes

^147:* Luke, the narrator, was one of "Paul's company."

^151:* Luke, Paul, and his party.

THE REVELATION

ST. JOHN THE DIVINE

HEARD BY JOHN IN VISIONS

XCV

JESUS CHRIST AS ALPHA AND OMEGA DIRECTS JOHN TO WRITE TO THE SEVEN CHURCHES IN ASIA

A.D. 96.

Revelation 1, 1-3; 9-20.

THE Revelation of Jesus Christ, which God gave unto him: sent unto his servant John: who bare record of the word of God, and of the testimony of Jesus Christ, and of all things that he saw. Blessed is he that readeth, and they that hear the words of this prophecy, and keep those things which are written therein: for the time is at hand.

I, John, was in the Spirit on the Lord's day, and heard behind me a great voice as of a trumpet, saying, [*+]

I am Alpha and Omega, the first and the last, the beginning and the ending: What thou seest, write in a book, and send it unto the seven churches which are in Asia; unto Ephesus, and unto Smyrna, and unto Pergamos, and unto Thyatira, and unto Sardis, and unto Philadelphia, and unto Laodicea.

And I turned to see the voice that spake:
I saw seven golden candlesticks; and in the midst of the seven candlesticks one like unto the Son of man, clothed with a garment down to the foot, and girt about the paps with a golden girdle. His head and his hairs were white like wool, as white as snow; and his eyes were as a flame of fire; and his feet like unto fine brass, as if they burned in a furnace; and his voice as the sound of many waters. And he had in his right hand seven stars: and out of his mouth went a sharp twoedged sword: and his countenance was as the sun shineth in his strength. And when I saw him, I fell at his feet as dead.

He laid his right hand upon me, saying unto me, Fear not; I am the first and the last: I am he that liveth, and was dead; and, behold, I am alive forever more, Amen; and have the keys of hell and of death.

Write the things which thou hast seen, and the things which are, and the things which shall be hereafter; the mystery of the seven stars which thou sawest in my right hand, and the seven golden candlesticks. The seven stars are the angels of the seven churches: and the seven candlesticks which thou sawest are the seven churches.

Footnotes

^151:+ Here (following) are set down those sayings only which John has ascribed to Christ, along with so much of John's context as barely to establish the sequences. The Revelation contains a series of prophetic visions--it is the only prophetic book in the New Testament. Its date is supposed to be A.D. 96.

XCVI

TO THE CHURCH OF EPHESUS--"I WILL GIVE TO EAT OF THE TREE OF LIFE"

A.D. 96.

Revelation 2, 1-7.

UNTO the angel of the church of Ephesus write;

These things saith he that holdeth the seven stars in his right hand, who walketh in the midst of the seven golden candlesticks;

I know thy works, and thy labor, and thy patience, and how thou canst not bear them which are evil: and thou hast tried them which say they are apostles, and are not, and hast found them liars: and hast borne, and hast patience, and for my name's sake hast labored, and hast not fainted.

Nevertheless I have somewhat against thee, because thou hast left thy first love.

Remember therefore from whence thou art fallen, and repent, and do the first works; or else I will come unto thee quickly, and will remove thy candlestick out of his place, except thou repent.

But this thou hast, that thou hatest the deeds of the Nicolaitans, which I also hate.

He that hath an ear, let him hear what the Spirit saith unto the churches;

To him that overcometh will I give to eat of the tree of life, which is in the midst of the paradise of God.

XCVII

TO THE CHURCH IN SMYRNA--"BE THOU FAITHFUL UNTO DEATH"

A.D. 96

Revelation 2, 8-11.

AND unto the angel of the church in Smyrna write;

These things saith the first and the last, which was dead, and is alive; I know thy works, and tribulation, and poverty (but thou art rich); and I know the blasphemy of them which say they are Jews, and are not, but are the synagogue of Satan.

Fear none of those things which thou shalt suffer: behold, the devil shall cast some of you into prison, that ye may be tried; and ye shall have tribulation ten days: be thou faithful unto death, and I will give thee a crown of life.

He that hath an ear, let him hear what the Spirit saith unto the churches;

He that overcometh shall not be hurt of the second death.

XCVIII

TO THE CHURCH IN PERGAMOS--"REPENT, OR ELSE I WILL COME QUICKLY"

A.D. 96

Revelation 2, 12-17.

AND to the angel of the church in Pergamos write;
These things saith he which hath the sharp sword with two edges;

I know thy works, and where thou dwellest, even where Satan's seat is; and thou holdest fast my name, and hast not denied my faith, even in those days wherein Antipas was my faithful martyr, who was slain among you, where Satan dwelleth.

But I have a few things against thee, because thou hast there them that hold the doctrine of Balaam, who taught Balak to cast a stumbling-block before the children of Israel, to eat things sacrificed unto idols, and to commit fornication.

So hast thou also them that hold the doctrine of the Nicolaitans, which thing I hate.

Repent; or else I will come unto thee quickly, and will fight against them with the sword of my mouth.

He that hath an ear, let him hear what the Spirit saith unto the churches; To him that overcometh will I give to eat of the hidden manna, and will give him a white stone, and in the stone a new name written, which no man knoweth saving he that receiveth it.

XCIX

TO THE CHURCH IN THYATIRA--"I WILL GIVE UNTO EVERY ONE OF YOU ACCORDING TO HIS WORKS"

A.D. 96.

Revelation 2, 18-29.

AND unto the angel of the church in Thyatira write;

These things saith the Son of God, who hath his eyes like unto a flame of fire, and his feet are like fine brass; I know thy works, and charity, and service, and faith, and thy patience, and thy works; and the last to be more than the first.

Notwithstanding I have a few things against thee, because thou sufferest that woman Jezebel, which calleth herself a prophetess, to teach and to seduce my servants to commit fornication, and to eat things sacrificed unto idols. And I gave her space to repent of her fornication; and she repented not. Behold, I will cast her into a bed, and them that commit adultery with her into great tribulation, except they repent of their deeds. And I will kill her children with death; and all the churches shall know that I am he which searcheth the reins and hearts: and I will give unto every one of you according to your works.

But unto you I say, and unto the rest in Thyatira, as many as have not this doctrine, and which have not known the depths of Satan, as they speak; I will put upon you none other burden. But that which ye have already, hold fast till I come.

And he that overcometh, and keepeth my works unto the end, to him will I give power over the nations: and he shall rule them with a rod of iron; as the vessels of a potter shall they be broken to shivers: even as I received of my Father. And I will give him the morning star.

He that hath an ear, let him hear what the Spirit saith unto the churches.

C

TO THE CHURCH IN SARDIS--"BE WATCHFUL: I WILL COME AS A THIEF"

A.D. 96.

Revelation 3, 1-6.

AND unto the angel of the church in Sardis write; These things saith he that hath the seven Spirits of God, and the seven stars;

I know thy works, that thou hast a name that thou livest, and art dead. Be watchful, and strengthen the things which remain, that are ready to die: for I have not found thy works perfect before God.

Remember therefore how thou hast received and heard, and hold fast, and repent. If therefore thou shalt not watch, I will come on thee as a thief, and thou shalt not know what hour I will come upon thee.

Thou hast a few names even in Sardis which have not defiled their garments; and they shall walk with me in white; for they are worthy. He that overcometh, the same shall be clothed in white raiment; and I will not blot out his name out of the book of life, but I will confess his name before my Father, and before his angels.

He that hath an ear, let him hear what the Spirit saith unto the churches.

CI

TO THE CHURCH IN PHILADELPHIA--"I HAVE SET BEFORE THEE AN OPEN DOOR"

A.D. 96.

Revelation 3, 7-13.

AND to the angel of the church in Philadelphia write;
These things saith he that is holy, he that is true, he that hath the key of David, he that openeth, and no man shutteth; and shutteth, and no man openeth;

I know thy works: behold, I have set before thee an open door, and no man can shut it: for thou hast a little strength, and hast kept my word, and hast not denied my name.

Behold, I will make them of the synagogue of Satan, which say they are Jews, and are not, but do lie; behold, I will make them to come and worship before thy feet, and to know that I have loved thee.

Because thou hast kept the word of my patience, I also will keep thee from the hour of temptation, which shall come upon all the world, to try them that dwell upon the earth.

Behold, I come quickly; hold that fast which thou hast, that no man take thy crown.

Him that overcometh will I make a pillar in the temple of my God, and he shall go no more out: and I will write upon him the name of my God, and the name of the city of my God, which is new Jerusalem, which cometh down out of heaven from my God; and I will write upon him my new name.

Him that hath an ear, let him hear what the Spirit saith unto the churches.

CII

TO THE CHURCH OF THE LAODICEANS--I STAND AT THE DOOR, AND KNOCK

A.D. 96.

Revelation 3, 14-22.

AND unto the angel of the church of the Laodiceans write; These things saith the Amen, the faithful and true witness, the beginning of the creation of God; I know thy works, that thou art neither cold nor hot: I would thou wert cold or hot. So then because thou art lukewarm, and neither cold nor hot, I will spew thee out of my mouth. Because thou sayest, I am rich, and increased with goods, and have need of nothing; and knowest not that thou art wretched, and miserable, and poor, and blind, and naked: I counsel thee to buy of me gold tried in the fire, that thou mayest be rich; and white raiment, that thou mayest be clothed, and that the shame of thy nakedness do not appear; and anoint thine eyes with eyesalve, that thou mayest see.

As many as I love, I rebuke and chasten; be zealous, therefore, and repent.

Behold, I stand at the door, and knock: if any man hear my voice, and open the door, I will come in to him, and will sup with him, and he with me.

To him that overcometh will I grant to sit with me in my throne, even as I also overcame, and am set down with my Father in his throne.

He that hath an ear, let him hear what the Spirit saith unto the churches.

CIII

"JOHN SEETH THE THRONE OF GOD IN HEAVEN"

A.D. 96.

Revelation 4, 1-2; 14, 13; 16, 15; 19, 9-10; 21, 5-8; 22, 6-21.

AFTER this I looked, and, behold, a door was opened in heaven: and the first voice which I heard was as it were of a trumpet talking with me; which said, Come up hither, and I will shew thee things which must be hereafter. And immediately I was in the Spirit: and, behold, a throne was set in heaven, and one sat on the throne.

And I heard a voice from heaven saying unto me, Write, Blessed are the dead which die in the Lord from henceforth: Yea, Saith the Spirit, That they may rest from their labors: and their works do follow them.

And I heard a great voice saying, Behold, I come as a thief.

Blessed is he that watcheth, and keepeth his garments, lest he walk naked, and they see his shame.

And he saith unto me, Write, Blessed are they which are called unto the marriage supper of the Lamb.

And he saith unto me, These are the true sayings of God.

And I, John, fell at his feet to worship him. And he said unto me, See thou do it not: I am thy fellow servant, and of thy brethren that have the testimony of Jesus: worship God: for the testimony of Jesus is the spirit of prophecy.

And he that sat upon the throne said, Behold, I make all things new.

And he said unto me, Write: for these words are true and faithful.

And he said unto me, It is done. I am Alpha and Omega, the beginning and the end. I will give unto him that is athirst of the fountain of the water of life freely.

He that overcometh shall inherit all things; and I will be his God, and he shall be my son. But the fearful, and unbelieving, and the abominable, and murderers, and whoremongers, and sorcerers, and idolaters, and all liars, shall have their part in the lake which burneth with fire and brimstone: which is the second death.

And he said unto me, These sayings are faithful and true: and the Lord God of the holy prophets sent his angel to shew unto his servants the things which must shortly be done.

Behold, I come quickly: blessed is he that keepeth the sayings of the prophecy of this book.

And I, John, saw these things, and heard them. And when I had heard and seen, I fell down to worship before the feet of the angel which shewed me these things.

Then saith he unto me, See thou do it not: for I am thy fellow servant, and of thy brethren the prophets, and of them which keep the sayings of this book: worship God.

And he saith unto me, Seal not the sayings of the prophecy of this book: for the time is at hand.

He that is unjust, let him be unjust still: and he which is filthy, let him be filthy still: and he that is righteous, let him be righteous still: and he that is holy, let him be holy still.

And, behold, I come quickly; and my reward is with me, to give every man according as his work shall be.

I am Alpha and Omega, the beginning and the end, the first and the last.

Blessed are they that do his commandments, that they may have right to the tree of life, and may enter in through the gates into the city. For without are dogs, and sorcerers, and whoremongers, and murderers, and idolaters, and whosoever loveth and maketh a lie.

I Jesus have sent mine angel to testify unto you these things in the churches. I am the root and the offspring of David, and the bright and morning star.

And the Spirit and the bride say, Come. And let him that heareth say, Come. And let him that is athirst come. And whosoever will, let him take the water of life freely.

For I testify unto every man that heareth the words of the prophecy of this book, If any man shall add unto these things, God shall add unto him the plagues that are written in this book. And if any man shall take away from the words of the book of this prophecy, God shall take away his part out of the book of life, and out of the holy city, and from the things which are written in this book.

He which testifieth these things saith, Surely I come quickly. Amen.

Even so, come, Lord Jesus.
 The grace of our Lord Jesus Christ be with you all. Amen.

Made in the USA
Las Vegas, NV
25 October 2021